W9-CPA-332

The *Constitution of the Presbyterian Church (U.S.A.),* as defined in G-1.0500, consists of *The Book of Confessions* (Part I) and the *Book of Order* (Part II).

The Book of Confessions contains the Nicene Creed, the Apostles' Creed, the Scots Confession, the Heidelberg Catechism, the Second Helvetic Confession, the Westminster Confession of Faith, the Larger Catechism, the Shorter Catechism, the Theological Declaration of Barmen, the Confession of 1967, and A Brief Statement of Faith—Presbyterian Church (U.S.A.).

The *Book of Order* contains the Form of Government, Directory for Worship, and Rules of Discipline.

In this *Book of Order*

(1) SHALL and IS TO BE/ARE TO BE signify practice that is mandated,

(2) SHOULD signifies practice that is strongly recommended,

(3) IS APPROPRIATE signifies practice that is commended as suitable,

(4) MAY signifies practice that is permissible but not required.

The amendments to the Form of Government, Directory for Worship, and Rules of Discipline, proposed to the presbyteries by the 210th General Assembly (1998) and declared made by the 211th General Assembly (1999), are included in this volume. The new wording appears in boldface within the appropriate paragraphs. Amendments have been made in the following places:

Book of Order	Minutes, 1998
G-9.0406	163
G-9.0503	89
G-11.0404	59
G-11.0414a	60
G-14.0202	67
G-14.0513a	67, 661
G-14.0513f	401
G-14.0801a	89
W-3.3616e	86, 666
D-6.0202	164–65

June 1999

Clifton Kirkpatrick
Stated Clerk of the General Assembly,
Presbyterian Church (U.S.A.)

The

CONSTITUTION

of the

PRESBYTERIAN CHURCH (U.S.A.)

PART II

BOOK OF ORDER

THE CONSTITUTION

OF THE

PRESBYTERIAN CHURCH (U.S.A.)

PART II
BOOK OF ORDER
1999–2000

PUBLISHED BY
THE OFFICE OF THE GENERAL ASSEMBLY

100 Witherspoon Street
Louisville, KY 40202-1396

Printed in the United States of America
ISBN 0-664-50115-X

Additional copies available at $7.50 from Presbyterian Distribution Service (PDS), 100 Witherspoon Street, Louisville, KY 40202-1396, by calling 1-800-524-2612 (PDS) or OGA Sales 1-888-219-6700.

Please specify PDS order #OGA-99-001—Standard Version
#OGA-99-010—Large Print

EXPLANATION OF THE REFERENCE NUMBER SYSTEM
OF THE
BOOK OF ORDER

The three parts of the *Book of Order* are abbreviated by the use of capital letters:

G - Form of Government

W - Directory for Worship

D - Rules of Discipline

Each reference in the text begins with the appropriate letter. The numeral appearing after the letter, and to the left of the decimal, indicates the chapter number. There are four numerals to the right of the decimal. The first two indicate the number of a section. The second two indicate the number of a titled subsection.

Each page is noted in numerals preceded by the proper letter to identify the material that appears on it. For example, in the Form of Government, the first page of Chapter VI bears the notation:

G-6.0000-.0106

This indicates that Chapter VI of the Form of Government begins here and the page includes Section 1 with six titled subsections: 6.0101, 6.0102, 6.0103, 6.0104, 6.0105, and 6.0106.

The chapters and sections of the *Book of Order* are so notated that it is possible for chapters and sections to be added by amendment without changing any of the present notations.

By avoiding page numbers, this notation makes it possible for citations to the *Book of Order* in minutes, reports, and correspondence to remain the same from year to year in English, Korean, Spanish, and Braille editions.

The words "[This section was stricken by. . . .]" have been used in a few places to avoid renumbering, which would confuse citations to the *Book of Order.*

CONTENTS

FORM OF GOVERNMENT

DIRECTORY FOR WORSHIP

Preface

RULES OF DISCIPLINE

The
FORM OF GOVERNMENT
[TEXT]

FORM OF GOVERNMENT[1]

G-1.0000   CHAPTER I. PRELIMINARY PRINCIPLES

G-1.0100

Christ Is Head
of the Church

1. The Head of the Church

a. All power in heaven and earth is given to Jesus Christ by Almighty God, who raised Christ from the dead and set him above all rule and authority, all power and dominion, and every name that is named, not only in this age but also in that which is to come. God has put all things under the Lordship of Jesus Christ and has made Christ Head of the Church, which is his body.

Christ Calls the
Church Into
Being

b. Christ calls the Church into being, giving it all that is necessary for its mission to the world, for its building up, and for its service to God. Christ is present with the Church in both Spirit and Word. It belongs to Christ alone to rule, to teach, to call, and to use the Church as he wills, exercising his authority by the ministry of women and men for the establishment and extension of his Kingdom.

Christ Gives the
Church Its Faith
and Life

c. Christ gives to his Church its faith and life, its unity and mission, its officers and ordinances. Insofar as Christ's will for the Church is set forth in Scripture, it is to be obeyed. In the worship and service of God and the government of the church, matters are to be ordered according to the Word by reason and sound judgment, under the guidance of the Holy Spirit.

Christ Is the
Church's
Authority

d. In affirming with the earliest Christians that Jesus is Lord, the Church confesses that he is its hope and that the Church, as Christ's body, is bound to his authority and thus free to live in the lively, joyous reality of the grace of God.

G-1.0200

The Great Ends
of the Church

2. The Great Ends of the Church

The great ends of the church are the proclamation of the gospel for the salvation of humankind; the shelter, nurture, and spiritual fellowship of the children of God; the maintenance of divine worship; the preservation of the truth; the promotion of social

---

[1]The following abbreviations are used throughout:

G - Form of Government

W - Directory for Worship

D - Rules of Discipline.

righteousness; and the exhibition of the Kingdom of Heaven to the world.[2]

G-1.0300

Historic
Principles of
Church Order

3.   The Historic Principles of Church Order[3]

In setting forth the following form of government, worship, and discipline, the Presbyterian Church (U.S.A.) reaffirms the historic principles of Church order which have been a part of our common heritage in this nation and which are basic to our Presbyterian concept and system of church government, namely:

G-1.0301
Right of
Judgment

(1) (a)   That "God alone is Lord of the conscience, and hath left it free from the doctrines and commandments of men[4] which are in anything contrary to his Word, or beside it, in matters of faith or worship."[5]

(b)   Therefore we consider the rights of private judgment, in all matters that respect religion, as universal and unalienable: We do not even wish to see any religious constitution aided by the civil power, further than may be necessary for protection and security, and at the same time, be equal and common to all others.

G-1.0302
Corporate
Judgment

(2)   That, in perfect consistency with the above principle of common right, every Christian Church, or union or association of particular churches, is entitled to declare the terms of admission into its communion, and the qualifications of its ministers and members, as well as the whole system of its internal government which Christ hath appointed; that in the exercise of this right they

---

[2]This statement of the great ends of the Church, slightly edited here, came from the United Presbyterian Church of North America, which united with the Presbyterian Church in the United States of America in 1958. The statement was then made a part of the Constitution of The United Presbyterian Church in the United States of America, as the united body was called. This now classic statement was adopted by the United Presbyterian Church of North America in 1910, following various actions between 1904 and 1910 looking forward to the revision of the church's Constitution.

[3]This section, with the exception of the first paragraph, was first drawn up by the Synod of New York and Philadelphia, and prefixed to the Form of Government as published by that body in 1788. In that year, the synod was divided into four synods and gave place to the General Assembly of the Presbyterian Church in the United States of America, which held its first meeting the following year. The four synods formed were the Synod of New York and New Jersey, the Synod of Philadelphia, the Synod of Virginia, and the Synod of the Carolinas. The presbyteries of these four synods were represented in the first General Assembly, which met in Philadelphia on May 21, 1789. The general plan drawn up in 1788 became that by which the Presbyterian Church in the United States and The United Presbyterian Church in the United States of America were subsequently governed.

[4]The words "men" and "man's" throughout this quotation from the eighteenth century should be understood as applying to all persons.

[5]This quotation may be found in The Westminster Confession of Faith, 6.109, in *The Book of Confessions*.

may, notwithstanding, err, in making the terms of communion either too lax or too narrow; yet, even in this case, they do not infringe upon the liberty or the rights of others, but only make an improper use of their own.

G-1.0303
Officers

(3) That our blessed Savior, for the edification of the visible Church, which is his body, hath appointed officers, not only to preach the gospel and administer the Sacraments, but also to exercise discipline, for the preservation of both truth and duty; and that it is incumbent upon these officers, and upon the whole Church, in whose name they act, to censure or cast out the erroneous and scandalous, observing, in all cases, the rules contained in the Word of God.

G-1.0304
Truth and
Goodness

(4) That truth is in order to goodness; and the great touchstone of truth, its tendency to promote holiness, according to our Savior's rule, "By their fruits ye shall know them." And that no opinion can be either more pernicious or more absurd than that which brings truth and falsehood upon a level, and represents it as of no consequence what a man's opinions are. On the contrary, we are persuaded that there is an inseparable connection between faith and practice, truth and duty. Otherwise, it would be of no consequence either to discover truth or to embrace it.

G-1.0305
Differences of
Views

(5) That, while under the conviction of the above principle we think it necessary to make effectual provision that all who are admitted as teachers be sound in the faith, we also believe that there are truths and forms with respect to which men of good characters and principles may differ. And in all these we think it the duty both of private Christians and societies to exercise mutual forbearance toward each other.

G-1.0306
Election by the
People

(6) That though the character, qualifications, and authority of Church officers are laid down in the Holy Scriptures, as well as the proper method of their investiture and institution, yet the election of the persons to the exercise of this authority, in any particular society, is in that society.

G-1.0307
Church Power

(7) That all Church power, whether exercised by the body in general or in the way of representation by delegated authority, is only ministerial and declarative; that is to say, that the Holy Scriptures are the only rule of faith and manners; that no Church governing body ought to pretend to make laws to bind the conscience in virtue of their own authority; and that all their decisions should be founded upon the revealed will of God. Now though it will easily be admitted that all synods and councils may err, through the frailty inseparable from humanity, yet there is much greater danger from the usurped claim of making laws than from the right of judging upon laws already made, and common to all who profess the gospel, although this right, as necessity requires in the present state, be lodged with fallible men.

G-1.0308
Church Discipline

(8) Lastly, that if the preceding scriptural and rational principles be steadfastly adhered to, the vigor and strictness of its discipline will contribute to the glory and happiness of any church. Since ecclesiastical discipline must be purely moral or spiritual in its object, and not attended with any civil effects, it can derive no force whatever but from its own justice, the approbation of an impartial public, and the countenance and blessing of the great Head of the Church universal.

G-1.0400

Historic
Principles of
Church
Government

4. The Historic Principles of Church Government

The radical[6] principles of Presbyterian church government and discipline are:

That the several different congregations of believers, taken collectively, constitute one Church of Christ, called emphatically the Church; that a larger part of the Church, or a representation of it, should govern a smaller, or determine matters of controversy which arise therein; that, in like manner, a representation of the whole should govern and determine in regard to every part, and to all the parts united: that is, that a majority shall govern; and consequently that appeals may be carried from lower to higher governing bodies, till they be finally decided by the collected wisdom and united voice of the whole Church. For these principles and this procedure, the example of the apostles and the practice of the primitive Church are considered as authority.

G-1.0500

Definition of the
Constitution

G-1.0501

5. The Constitution Defined

The *Constitution of the Presbyterian Church (U.S.A.)* consists of *The Book of Confessions* and the *Book of Order.*

The Book of Confessions includes:
The Nicene Creed
The Apostles' Creed
The Scots Confession
The Heidelberg Catechism
The Second Helvetic Confession
The Westminster Confession of Faith
The Larger Catechism
The Shorter Catechism

---

[6]The text of this section was adopted in 1797 by the General Assembly of the Presbyterian Church in the United States of America. In this quotation, the word "radical" is used in its primary meaning of "fundamental and basic," and the word "appeals" is used in a general sense rather than with reference to a case involved in judicial process.

The Theological Declaration of Barmen
The Confession of 1967
A Brief Statement of Faith—Presbyterian Church (U.S.A.).

G-1.0502   The *Book of Order* includes:
Form of Government
Directory for Worship
Rules of Discipline.

G-2.0000

CHAPTER II. THE CHURCH AND ITS CONFESSIONS

G-2.0100
Purpose of
Confessional
Statements

a.   The Presbyterian Church (U.S.A.) states its faith and bears witness to God's grace in Jesus Christ in the creeds and confessions in *The Book of Confessions*. In these confessional statements the church declares to its members and to the world

who and what it is,

what it believes,

what it resolves to do.

Church as
Community

b.   These statements identify the church as a community of people known by its convictions as well as by its actions. They guide the church in its study and interpretation of the Scriptures; they summarize the essence of Christian tradition; they direct the church in maintaining sound doctrines; they equip the church for its work of proclamation.

G-2.0200
Confessional
Statements as
Subordinate
Standards

These confessional statements are subordinate standards in the church, subject to the authority of Jesus Christ, the Word of God, as the Scriptures bear witness to him. While confessional standards are subordinate to the Scriptures, they are, nonetheless, standards. They are not lightly drawn up or subscribed to, nor may they be ignored or dismissed. The church is prepared to counsel with or even to discipline one ordained who seriously rejects the faith expressed in the confessions. Moreover, a more exacting amendment process is required to change the confessions of the church than is required to change the Constitution in matters of government, worship, or discipline. Yet the church, in obedience to Jesus Christ, is open to the reform of its standards of doctrine as well as of governance. The church affirms "Ecclesia reformata, semper reformanda," that is, "The church reformed, always reforming," according to the Word of God and the call of the Spirit.

G-2.0300
Faith of the
Church Catholic

In its confessions, the Presbyterian Church (U.S.A.) gives witness to the faith of the Church catholic. The confessions express the faith of the one, holy, catholic, and apostolic Church in the recognition of canonical Scriptures and the formulation and adoption of the ecumenical creeds, notably the Nicene and Apostles' Creeds with their definitions of the mystery of the triune God and of the incarnation of the eternal Word of God in Jesus Christ.

G-2.0400
Faith of the
Protestant
Reformation

In its confessions, the Presbyterian Church (U.S.A.) identifies with the affirmations of the Protestant Reformation. The focus of these affirmations is the rediscovery of God's grace in Jesus Christ as revealed in the Scriptures. The Protestant watchwords—grace alone, faith alone, Scripture alone—embody principles of understanding which continue to guide and motivate the people of God in the life of faith.

G-2.0500
Faith of the
Reformed
Tradition

a.   In its confessions, the Presbyterian Church (U.S.A.) expresses the faith of the Reformed tradition. Central to this tradition is the affirmation of the majesty, holiness, and providence of God who creates, sustains, rules, and redeems the world in the freedom of sovereign righteousness and love. Related to this central affirmation of God's sovereignty are other great themes of the Reformed tradition:

(1) The election of the people of God for service as well as for salvation;

(2) Covenant life marked by a disciplined concern for order in the church according to the Word of God;

(3) A faithful stewardship that shuns ostentation and seeks proper use of the gifts of God's creation;

(4) The recognition of the human tendency to idolatry and tyranny, which calls the people of God to work for the transformation of society by seeking justice and living in obedience to the Word of God.

Reflect a
Particular Stance

b.   Thus, the creeds and confessions of this church reflect a particular stance within the history of God's people. They are the result of prayer, thought, and experience within a living tradition. They serve to strengthen personal commitment and the life and witness of the community of believers.

G-3.0000

CHAPTER III. THE CHURCH AND ITS MISSION

G-3.0100
Form

The mission of the Church is given form by God's activity in the world as told in the Bible and understood by faith.

G-3.0101
God's Activity

a.　God created the heavens and the earth and made human beings in God's image, charging them to care for all that lives; God made men and women to live in community, responding to their Creator with grateful obedience. Even when the human race broke community with its Maker and with one another, God did not forsake it, but out of grace chose one family for the sake of all, to be pilgrims of promise, God's own Israel.

God's Covenant

b.　God liberated the people of Israel from oppression; God covenanted with Israel to be their God and they to be God's people, that they might do justice, love mercy, and walk humbly with the Lord; God confronted Israel with the responsibilities of this covenant, judging the people for their unfaithfulness while sustaining them by divine grace.

G-3.0102
God in Christ

God was incarnate in Jesus Christ, who announced good news to the poor, proclaimed release for prisoners and recovery of sight for the blind, let the broken victims go free, and proclaimed the year of the Lord's favor. Jesus came to seek and to save the lost; in his life and death for others God's redeeming love for all people was made visible; and in the resurrection of Jesus Christ there is the assurance of God's victory over sin and death and the promise of God's continuing presence in the world.

G-3.0103
The Holy Spirit

God's redeeming and reconciling activity in the world continues through the presence and power of the Holy Spirit, who confronts individuals and societies with Christ's Lordship of life and calls them to repentance and to obedience to the will of God.

G-3.0200
The Church as the Body of Christ

The Church of Jesus Christ is the provisional demonstration of what God intends for all of humanity.

a.　The Church is called to be a sign in and for the world of the new reality which God has made available to people in Jesus Christ.

b.　The new reality revealed in Jesus Christ is the new humanity, a new creation, a new beginning for human life in the world:

(1)　Sin is forgiven.

(2)　Reconciliation is accomplished.

(3)　The dividing walls of hostility are torn down.

c.　The Church is the body of Christ, both in its corporate life and in the lives of its individual members, and is called to give shape and substance to this truth.

G-3.0300
The Church's
Calling

a.   The Church is called to tell the good news of salvation by the grace of God through faith in Jesus Christ as the only Savior and Lord, proclaiming in Word and Sacrament that

(1) the new age has dawned.

(2) God who creates life, frees those in bondage, forgives sin, reconciles brokenness, makes all things new, is still at work in the world.

Present Claims of
Christ

b.   The Church is called to present the claims of Jesus Christ, leading persons to repentance, acceptance of him as Savior and Lord, and new life as his disciples.

Christ's Faithful
Evangelist

c.   The Church is called to be Christ's faithful evangelist

(1) going into the world, making disciples of all nations, baptizing them in the name of the Father and of the Son and of the Holy Spirit, teaching them to observe all he has commanded;

(2) demonstrating by the love of its members for one another and by the quality of its common life the new reality in Christ; sharing in worship, fellowship, and nurture, practicing a deepened life of prayer and service under the guidance of the Holy Spirit;

(3) participating in God's activity in the world through its life for others by

(a) healing and reconciling and binding up wounds,

(b) ministering to the needs of the poor, the sick, the lonely, and the powerless,

(c) engaging in the struggle to free people from sin, fear, oppression, hunger, and injustice,

(d) giving itself and its substance to the service of those who suffer,

(e) sharing with Christ in the establishing of his just, peaceable, and loving rule in the world.

G-3.0400
Called to Risk
and Trust

The Church is called to undertake this mission even at the risk of losing its life, trusting in God alone as the author and giver of life, sharing the gospel, and doing those deeds in the world that point beyond themselves to the new reality in Christ.

G-3.0401
Called to
Openness

The Church is called

a.   to a new openness to the presence of God in the Church and in the world, to more fundamental obedience, and to a more joyous celebration in worship and work;

b.   to a new openness to its own membership, by affirming itself as a community of diversity, becoming in fact as well as in faith a community of women and men of all ages, races, and conditions, and by providing for inclusiveness as a visible sign of the new humanity;

    c.   to a new openness to the possibilities and perils of its institutional forms in order to ensure the faithfulness and usefulness of these forms to God's activity in the world;

    d.   to a new openness to God's continuing reformation of the Church ecumenical, that it might be a more effective instrument of mission in the world.

G-4.0000 | # CHAPTER IV. THE CHURCH AND ITS UNITY

G-4.0100 | ## 1. The Church—Universal and Particular

G-4.0101
Universal Church

The Church universal consists of all persons in every nation, together with their children, who profess faith in Jesus Christ as Lord and Savior and commit themselves to live in a fellowship under his rule.

G-4.0102
Universal and
Particular

Since this whole company cannot meet together in one place to worship and to serve, it is reasonable that it should be divided into particular congregations. The particular church is, therefore, understood as a local expression of the universal Church.

G-4.0103
Particular Church

A particular church consists of those persons in a particular place, along with their children, who profess faith in Jesus Christ as Lord and Savior and who have been gathered for the service of God as set forth in Scripture, subject to a particular form of church government.

G-4.0104
A Particular
Presbyterian
Church

Each particular church of the Presbyterian Church (U.S.A.) shall be governed by this Constitution. Its officers are ministers of the Word and Sacrament, elders, and deacons. Its government and guidance are the responsibility of the session. It shall fulfill its responsibilities as the local unit of mission for the service of all people, for the upbuilding of the whole church, and for the glory of God.

G-4.0200 | ## 2. The Unity of the Church

G-4.0201
Unity in Mission

The unity of the Church is a gift of its Lord and finds expression in its faithfulness to the mission to which Christ calls it. The Church is a fellowship of believers which seeks the enlargement of the circle of faith to include all people and is never content to enjoy the benefits of Christian community for itself alone.

G-4.0202
Oneness

There is one Church. As the Bible speaks of the one body which is the Church living under the one Spirit of God known through Christ, it reminds us that we have "one Lord, one faith, one baptism, one God and Father of us all." (Ephesians 4:5-6)

G-4.0203
Visible Oneness

Visible oneness, by which a diversity of persons, gifts, and understandings is brought together, is an important sign of the unity of God's people. It is also a means by which that unity is achieved. Further, while divisions into different denominations do not destroy this unity, they do obscure it for both the Church and the world. The Presbyterian Church (U.S.A.), affirming its historical continuity with the whole Church of Jesus Christ, is committed to the reduction of that obscurity and is willing to seek and to maintain communion and community with all other branches of the one, catholic Church. (G-15.0000)

G-4.0300

G-4.0301
Presbyterian
Polity

3. Principles of Presbyterian Government

The Presbyterian Church (U.S.A.) reaffirms, within the context of its commitment to the Church universal, a special commitment to basic principles of Presbyterian polity:

a. The particular churches of the Presbyterian Church (U.S.A.) wherever they are, taken collectively, constitute one church;

b. This church shall be governed by presbyters (elders and ministers of the Word and Sacrament, traditionally called ruling and teaching elders);

c. These presbyters shall come together in governing bodies (traditionally called judicatories or courts) in regular gradation;

d. Presbyters are not simply to reflect the will of the people, but rather to seek together to find and represent the will of Christ;

e. Decisions shall be reached in governing bodies by vote, following opportunity for discussion, and a majority shall govern;

f. A higher governing body shall have the right of review and control over a lower one and shall have power to determine matters of controversy upon reference, complaint, or appeal;

g. Presbyters are ordained only by the authority of a governing body;

h. Ecclesiastical jurisdiction is a shared power, to be exercised jointly by presbyters gathered in governing bodies;

i. Governing bodies possess whatever administrative authority is necessary to give effect to duties and powers assigned by the Constitution of the church.

G-4.0302
Presbyterian
Unity

The nature of Presbyterian order is such that it shares power and responsibility. The system of governing bodies, whether they have authority over one or many churches, sustains such mutual relationships within the structures as to express the unity of the church.

G-4.0303
Historical
Awareness

The Presbyterian system of government calls for continuity with and faithfulness to the heritage which lies behind the contemporary church. It calls equally for openness and faithfulness to the renewing activity of the God of history.

G-4.0304
Ecumenical
Awareness

This form of government is established in the light of Scripture to give order to this church but is not regarded as essential to the existence of the Church of Jesus Christ nor to be required of all Christians.

G-4.0400

4. Diversity and Inclusiveness

G-4.0401
Variety of Forms

The church in its witness to the uniqueness of the Christian faith is called to mission and must be responsive to diversity in both the church and the world. Thus the fellowship of Christians as it gathers for worship and orders its corporate life will display a rich variety of form, practice, language, program, nurture, and service to suit culture and need.

G-4.0402
Openness to
Others

Our unity in Christ enables and requires the church to be open to all persons and to the varieties of talents and gifts of God's people, including those who are in the communities of the arts and sciences.

G-4.0403
Full Participation

The Presbyterian Church (U.S.A.) shall give full expression to the rich diversity within its membership and shall provide means which will assure a greater inclusiveness leading to wholeness in its emerging life. Persons of all racial ethnic groups, different ages, both sexes, various disabilities, diverse geographical areas, different theological positions consistent with the Reformed tradition, as well as different marital conditions (married, single, widowed, or divorced) shall be guaranteed full participation and access to representation in the decision making of the church. (G-9.0104ff)

G-5.0000

CHAPTER V. THE CHURCH AND ITS MEMBERS

G-5.0100

1. The Meaning of Membership

G-5.0101
Membership
Through Faith

a.   The incarnation of God in the life, death, and resurrection of Jesus Christ gives to the church not only its mission but also its understanding of membership. One becomes an active member of the church through faith in Jesus Christ as Savior and acceptance of his Lordship in all of life. Baptism and a public profession of faith in Jesus as Lord are the visible signs of entrance into the active membership of the church.

Into Active
Membership

b.   Persons may enter into active church membership in the following ways: by profession of faith, reaffirmation of faith in Jesus Christ, or transfer of certificate from some other church.

Baptized
Previously

c.   When persons baptized as infants reach an age when they are ready to make public their profession of faith and accept their responsibility in the life of the church, the session should invite, encourage, and help them prepare for their responsibility as active church members. The age at which young persons should make such public profession is not precisely fixed. It is left to the prudence of the session to judge, after careful examination, the readiness of those who apply for active membership.

Not Baptized
Previously

d.   When persons who have not been baptized desire to profess their faith in Christ and be incorporated in the life of the church as believers, they shall do so by making public their profession of faith and receiving baptism after appropriate instruction and examination by the session.

Certificate of
Transfer

e.   Persons who have made a profession of faith and have been received into membership in a particular church may be received by the session upon receipt of a certificate of transfer from the church in which they have been most recently a member.

Reaffirmation of
Faith

f.   It is sometimes the case that persons who previously made a profession of faith and became active members in a particular church are unable to secure a certificate of transfer or other evidence of church membership. After instruction and examination by the session, these persons shall reaffirm publicly their profession of faith and their acceptance of responsibility in the life of the church.

G-5.0102
Membership as
Ministry

A faithful member accepts Christ's call to be involved responsibly in the ministry of his Church. Such involvement includes

a.   proclaiming the good news,

b.   taking part in the common life and worship of a particular church,

c.   praying and studying Scripture and the faith of the Christian Church,

d.   supporting the work of the church through the giving of money, time, and talents,

e.   participating in the governing responsibilities of the church,

f.   demonstrating a new quality of life within and through the church,

g.   responding to God's activity in the world through service to others,

h.   living responsibly in the personal, family, vocational, political, cultural, and social relationships of life,

i.   working in the world for peace, justice, freedom, and human fulfillment.

G-5.0103
Inclusiveness

The congregation shall welcome all persons who respond in trust and obedience to God's grace in Jesus Christ and desire to become part of the membership and ministry of his Church. No persons shall be denied membership because of race, ethnic origin, worldly condition, or any other reason not related to profession of faith. Each member must seek the grace of openness in extending the fellowship of Christ to all persons. (G-9.0104) Failure to do so constitutes a rejection of Christ himself and causes a scandal to the gospel.

G-5.0200

2.   Categories of Membership

The membership of a particular church of the Presbyterian Church (U.S.A.) includes baptized members, active members, inactive members, and affiliate members.

G-5.0201
Baptized Member

A baptized member of a particular church is a person who has received the Sacrament of Baptism and who has been enrolled as a baptized member by the session but who has not made a profession of faith in Jesus Christ as Lord and Savior. Such baptized members are entitled to the pastoral care and instruction of the church, and to participation in the Sacrament of the Lord's Supper.

G-5.0202
Active Member

An active member of a particular church is a person who has made a profession of faith in Christ, has been baptized, has been received into membership of the church, has voluntarily submitted to the government of this church, and participates in the church's work and worship. An active member is entitled to all the rights and privileges of the church, including the right to participate in the Sacrament of the Lord's Supper, to present children for baptism, to take part in meetings of the congregation, and to vote and hold office. Other conditions of active membership that meet the needs of the particular church and are consistent with the order and confessions of the Presbyterian Church (U.S.A.) may be adopted by the session after careful study and discussion with the congregation.

G-5.0203
Inactive Member

An inactive member of a particular church is one who does not participate in the church's work and worship. An inactive member is entitled to all the rights and privileges of an active member except the right to speak in the meetings of the congregation and to vote and hold office.

G-5.0204
Affiliate Member

An affiliate member of a particular church is an active member of another church of this denomination or of another denomination or Christian body, who has temporarily moved from the community where the church of active membership is situated, has presented a certificate of good standing from the appropriate governing body of that church, and has been received by the session as an affiliate member. An affiliate member is entitled to all the rights and privileges of an active member except the right to vote and hold office.

G-5.0300

G-5.0301
Nonmember
Privileges

3. Nonmember Privileges

Persons not members of the Presbyterian Church (U.S.A.) are entitled to the following privileges:

a. All persons are welcome to participate in the life and worship of this church.

b. All baptized persons, whether children or adults, even though they have made no profession of their faith in Christ, are entitled to participation in the Lord's Supper, to pastoral care and instruction of the church.

c. Confessing members of other Christian churches may participate in the Sacrament of the Lord's Supper and may present children for baptism.

G-5.0400

G-5.0401
Session's Duty

4. Preparation for Membership

The session shall have responsibility for preparing those who would become members of the congregation.

G-5.0402
Profession by
Children

a. While the preparation is a part of the continuing nurture of the congregation, particular care shall be taken to prepare children of members for public profession of faith in Jesus Christ. Instruction shall be given in the meaning of this profession, the responsibilities of membership, and the faith and order of the Presbyterian Church (U.S.A.).

Profession by
Adults

b. Similar instruction shall be given to others who make a profession of faith. The session shall determine whether this instruction shall be given before or after the public profession.

G-5.0403
Reaffirmation,
Transfer

Appropriate instruction shall be offered to those who unite with a particular congregation by reaffirmation of faith or by transfer of certificate of church membership.

G-5.0500   ## 5. Review of Membership

G-5.0501   Accepting the privilege and responsibility of membership in
By the Member   the church is a commitment to Jesus Christ that binds the individ-
                  ual to fulfillment of the obligations of membership. Members shall,
                  when encouraged by the session, regularly review and evaluate the
                  integrity with which they are involved in the ministry of the church
                  and consider ways in which their participation in the worship and
                  service of the church may be increased and made more meaningful.

G-5.0502   The session shall review the roll of members at least annually,
By the Session   and shall counsel with those who have neglected the responsibili-
                  ties of membership.

G-6.0000   **CHAPTER VI. THE CHURCH AND ITS OFFICERS**

G-6.0100   **1. Offices of Ministry**

G-6.0101
Christ's Ministry

All ministry in the Church is a gift from Jesus Christ. Members and officers alike serve mutually under the mandate of Christ who is the chief minister of all. His ministry is the basis of all ministries; the standard for all offices is the pattern of the one who came "not to be served but to serve." (Matt. 20:28)

G-6.0102
Offices of
Ministry

One responsibility of membership in the church is the election of officers who are ordained to fulfill particular functions. The existence of these offices in no way diminishes the importance of the commitment of all members to the total ministry of the church. These ordained officers differ from other members in function only.

G-6.0103
Offices Named

The Church offices mentioned in the New Testament which this church has maintained include those of presbyters (ministers of the Word and Sacrament and elders) and deacons.

G-6.0104
Variety of Forms

While the ministry is one, specific forms of ministry may emphasize special tasks and skills and the ordering of the offices of ministry shall reflect this variety. There may be forms of ministry in which primary emphasis is given to proclamation of the Word and the celebration of the Sacraments, forms that stress deeds of love and mercy, forms that are primarily educational, administrative, legislative, or judicial, and forms that are primarily prophetic.

G-6.0105
Called to Ministry

Both men and women shall be eligible to hold church offices. When women and men, by God's providence and gracious gifts, are called by the church to undertake particular forms of ministry, the church shall help them to interpret their call and to be sensitive to the judgments and needs of others. As persons discover the forms of ministry to which they are called, and as they are called to new forms, they and the church shall pray for the presence and guidance of the Holy Spirit upon them and upon the mission of the Church.

G-6.0106
Gifts and
Requirements

a. To those called to exercise special functions in the church —deacons, elders, and ministers of the Word and Sacrament—God gives suitable gifts for their various duties. In addition to possessing the necessary gifts and abilities, natural and acquired, those who undertake particular ministries should be persons of strong faith, dedicated discipleship, and love of Jesus Christ as Savior and Lord. Their manner of life should be a demonstration of the Christian gospel in the church and in the world. They must have the approval of God's people and the concurring judgment of a governing body of the church.

b. Those who are called to office in the church are to lead a life in obedience to Scripture and in conformity to the historic confessional standards of the church. Among these standards is the requirement to live either in fidelity within the covenant of marriage between a man and a woman (W-4.9001), or chastity in singleness. Persons refusing to repent of any self-acknowledged practice which the confessions call sin shall not be ordained and/or installed as deacons, elders, or ministers of the Word and Sacrament.

G-6.0107
Election by the
People

The government of this church is representative, and the right of God's people to elect their officers is inalienable. Therefore, no person can be placed in any permanent office in a congregation or governing body of the church except by election of that body.

G-6.0108
Freedom of
Conscience—
Individual and
Corporate

a.   It is necessary to the integrity and health of the church that the persons who serve in it as officers shall adhere to the essentials of the Reformed faith and polity as expressed in *The Book of Confessions* and the Form of Government. So far as may be possible without serious departure from these standards, without infringing on the rights and views of others, and without obstructing the constitutional governance of the church, freedom of conscience with respect to the interpretation of Scripture is to be maintained.

Within Certain
Bounds

b.   It is to be recognized, however, that in becoming a candidate or officer of the Presbyterian Church (U.S.A.) one chooses to exercise freedom of conscience within certain bounds. His or her conscience is captive to the Word of God as interpreted in the standards of the church so long as he or she continues to seek or hold office in that body. The decision as to whether a person has departed from essentials of Reformed faith and polity is made initially by the individual concerned but ultimately becomes the responsibility of the governing body in which he or she serves. (G-1.0301; G-1.0302) [1]

Candidates for
Ministry

c.   Persons seeking to be received as candidates for ministry in the Presbyterian Church (U.S.A.) shall have their attention drawn to the constitutional documents of the church including its statement on freedom of conscience. (G-14.0304)

---

[1]Very early in the history of the Presbyterian Church in the United States of America, even before the General Assembly was established, the plan of reunion of the Synod of New York and Philadelphia contained the following sentences: "That when any matter is determined by a major vote, every member shall either actively concur with or passively submit to such determination; or if his conscience permit him to do neither, he shall, after sufficient liberty modestly to reason and remonstrate, peaceably withdraw from our communion without attempting to make any schism. Provided always that this shall be understood to extend only to such determination as the body shall judge indispensable in doctrine or Presbyterian government." (Hist. Dig. (P) p. 1310.) (Plan of Union of 1758, par. II.)

G-6.0200

2. Ministers of the Word and Sacrament

G-6.0201
Ministers and Presbytery

As the Lord has set aside through calling and training certain members to perform a special ministry of the Word and Sacrament and has committed to them a variety of work to do, the church through the presbytery calls them to the responsibility and office of ministers of the Word and Sacrament. Such ministers shall be members of presbytery which shall designate them to such work as may be helpful to the church in mission, in the performance of which they shall be accountable to the presbytery. They shall be responsible for participation in the larger ministry of the church in addition to the duties to which they are called and designated by the presbytery. Ministers of the Word and Sacrament have membership in presbytery by action of the presbytery itself, and maintain their membership in accordance with G-11.0000.

G-6.0202
Pastors, Associate Pastors

a. The permanent pastoral offices of ministers of the Word and Sacrament are pastors and associate pastors. When a minister of the Word and Sacrament is called as pastor or associate pastor of a particular church or churches, she or he is to be responsible for a quality of life and relationships that commend the gospel to all persons and that communicate its joy and its justice. The pastor is responsible for studying, teaching, and preaching the Word, for administering Baptism and the Lord's Supper, for praying with and for the congregation. With the elders, the pastor is to encourage the people in the worship and service of God; to equip and enable them for their tasks within the church and their mission in the world; to exercise pastoral care, devoting special attention to the poor, the sick, the troubled, and the dying; to participate in governing responsibilities, including leadership of the congregation in implementing the principles of participation and inclusiveness in the decision making of the church, and its task of reaching out in concern and service to the life of the human community as a whole. With the deacons the pastor is to share in the ministries of sympathy, witness, and service. In addition to these pastoral duties, he or she is responsible for sharing in the ministry of the church in the governing bodies above the session and in ecumenical relationships.

Co-Pastors

b. A particular church, with the consent of presbytery, may elect pastors to serve as co-pastors in exercising the responsibility of minister of the Word and Sacrament for the congregation.

Assistant Pastors

c. Those persons serving as assistant pastors on December 31, 1985, may continue in that pastoral relation so long as the individual holding such relationship continues that relationship to the same particular church.

G-6.0203
Teachers, Chaplains, and Others

When ministers are designated as educators, chaplains, pastoral counselors, campus ministers, missionaries, partners in mission, evangelists, administrators, social workers, consultants, or in other specific tasks appropriate to the ministry of the church, they shall evidence a quality of life which helps to share the ministry of the good news. They shall exercise pastoral care of those for whom they are responsible and shall seek to fulfill their ministry by serving Christ and their fellow men and women, strengthening the church and equipping it for concern and service to the life of the human community. In addition to fulfilling the particular responsibilities to which they are called, they shall participate in a congregation, in their presbytery, and in ecumenical relationships, and shall be eligible for election to the higher governing bodies of the church and to the boards and agencies of those governing bodies.

G-6.0300

G-6.0301
Scriptural
Practice

G-6.0302
Governmental
Responsibilities

G-6.0303
Gifts and
Requirements

G-6.0304
Specific
Responsibilities

3. Elders

As there were in Old Testament times elders for the government of the people, so the New Testament Church provided persons with particular gifts to share in governing and ministry.

Elders are chosen by the people. Together with ministers of the Word and Sacrament, they exercise leadership, government, and discipline and have responsibilities for the life of a particular church as well as the church at large, including ecumenical relationships. They shall serve faithfully as members of the session. (G-10.0102) When elected commissioners to higher governing bodies, elders participate and vote with the same authority as ministers of the Word and Sacrament, and they are eligible for any office.

Elders should be persons of faith, dedication, and good judgment. Their manner of life should be a demonstration of the Christian gospel, both within the church and in the world. (G-6.0106)

It is the duty of elders, individually and jointly, to strengthen and nurture the faith and life of the congregation committed to their charge. Together with the pastor, they should encourage the people in the worship and service of God, equip and renew them for their tasks within the church and for their mission in the world, visit and comfort and care for the people, with special attention to the poor, the sick, the lonely, and those who are oppressed. They should inform the pastor and session of those persons and structures which may need special attention. They should assist in worship. (See W-1.4003, W-2.3011–.3012, W-3.1003, W-3.3616, and W-4.4003.) They should cultivate their ability to teach the Bible and may be authorized to supply places which are without the regular ministry of the Word and Sacrament. In specific circumstances and with proper instruction, specific elders may be authorized by the presbytery to administer the Lord's Supper in accord with G-11.0103z. Those duties which all Christians are bound to perform by the law of love are especially incumbent upon elders because of their calling to office and are to be fulfilled by them as official responsibilities.

G-6.0400

G-6.0401
The Ministry and
Gifts of Deacons

G-6.0402
Responsibilities

G-6.0403
Organization

G-6.0404
Supervised by
Session

G-6.0405
Meetings

G-6.0406
Related Service

4. Deacons

The office of deacon as set forth in Scripture is one of sympathy, witness, and service after the example of Jesus Christ. Persons of spiritual character, honest repute, of exemplary lives, brotherly and sisterly love, warm sympathies, and sound judgment should be chosen for this office.

It is the duty of deacons, first of all, to minister to those who are in need, to the sick, to the friendless, and to any who may be in distress both within and beyond the community of faith. They shall assume such other duties as may be delegated to them from time to time by the session, such as leading the people in worship through prayers of intercession, reading the Scriptures, presenting the gifts of the people, and assisting with the Lord's Supper. (See W-3.3616.)

The deacons of a particular church shall be organized in one or both of the following ways.

a. They may be organized as a board, of which the pastor, co-pastors, associate pastors, and assistant pastors shall be advisory members. (See G-6.0202c) The board of deacons shall elect a moderator and a secretary from among its members. The secretary shall keep a record of the board's proceedings.

b. They may be individually commissioned by the session to particular tasks consistent with the responsibility of their office. (See G-6.0402.) The session shall ordinarily conduct an annual review of their service, at which time their commission may be renewed, altered, or terminated.

As the whole church is under the jurisdiction of the session, the board of deacons shall be under its supervision and authority. The records of the board of deacons shall be submitted to the session at least annually and at other times upon the request of the session. The session may void or amend any action of the board of deacons, or direct the board to reconsider such action.

The board shall meet regularly, or upon the call of its moderator, or when directed to meet by the session, but it shall meet at least quarterly. The board shall determine its own quorum. A joint meeting of the session and board of deacons shall be held at least annually to confer on matters of common interest, with the moderator of the session presiding. No binding decision may be reached in such joint meeting, but the session and the board may act separately on matters committed to their care.

Deacons may be appointed by governing bodies to serve on committees or as trustees. The session may select and appoint other members of the congregation to assist the deacons in their ministry of compassion.

G-6.0407
Decision Not to
Use Deacons

A congregation by a majority vote may elect not to use the office of deacon. In such a case, or in the case where deacons cannot be secured, the function of the office shall always be preserved and shall devolve upon the elders and the session.

G-6.0500

5. Renunciation of Jurisdiction

G-6.0501
Renunciation of
Jurisdiction

When a church officer, whether a minister of the Word and Sacrament, elder, or deacon, renounces the jurisdiction of this church in writing to the clerk or stated clerk of the governing body of jurisdiction, the renunciation shall be effective upon receipt. Renunciation of jurisdiction shall remove the officer from membership and ordained office and shall terminate the exercise of office.

G-6.0502
Persistence in
Disapproved
Work

When a church officer, after consultation and notice, persists in a work disapproved by the governing body having jurisdiction, the governing body may presume that the officer has renounced the jurisdiction of this church.

G-6.0503
Effect of
Renunciation

The renunciation shall be reported by the clerk or stated clerk at the next meeting of the governing body, which shall record the renunciation, delete the officer's name from the appropriate roll, and take such other actions of an administrative character as may be required by the Constitution.

CHAPTER VII. THE PARTICULAR CHURCH

G-7.0000

G-7.0100

G-7.0101
Organized by
Presbytery as Part
of the Whole

G-7.0102
Ministry

G-7.0103
Government

1. Organization, Mission, and Government

The church is both catholic and particular. Both characteristics are to be found in a particular church. A particular church in the Presbyterian Church (U.S.A.) can be organized only by the authority of a presbytery and shall function under the provisions of this Constitution.

The particular church carries a vital responsibility in the mission of the church. There God's people perform especially the ministries of worship, proclamation, sharing the Sacraments, evangelism, nurture, counseling, personal and social healing, and service. Without this basic ministry to persons, neighborhoods, and communities, and the support given at the congregational level through prayer, personnel, and money, any other significant ministry of the church becomes impossible. Congregations serve as essential mission arms of the presbytery and of the larger church.

The members of a particular church voluntarily put themselves under the leadership of their officers, whom they elect. The session, which consists of the pastor or co-pastors, the associate pastors, and the elders in active service, is the governing body in a particular church. The law and government of the Presbyterian Church (U.S.A.) presuppose the fellowship of women and men with their children in voluntary covenanted relationship with one another and with God through Jesus Christ. The organization rests upon the fellowship and is not designed to work without trust and love.

G-7.0200

G-7.0201
Constituting
Covenant

2. Organizing a Particular Church

In organizing a particular church, presbytery, proceeding directly or through a commission, shall receive applications for membership in the church—whether by profession of faith, reaffirmation, or transfer of membership—from persons wishing to unite in forming a new congregation. These persons shall covenant together as follows:

We, the undersigned, in response to the grace of God, desire to be constituted and organized as a church to be known as _____ _____.We promise and covenant to live together in unity and to work together in ministry as disciples of Jesus Christ, bound to him and to one another as a part of the body of Christ in this place according to the principles of faith, mission, and order of the Presbyterian Church (U.S.A.).

(Signatures)

G-7.0202
Presbytery
Relationship

a.   They shall be declared a constituted congregation of the presbytery and shall proceed to the election of elders and deacons, making provision in cooperation with the presbytery for their preparation, examination, ordination, and installation.

b.   Presbytery shall continue to work closely with the congregation in securing pastoral leadership, in plans for the service and witness of the particular church, in coordinating its work with other churches, in counseling concerning bylaws for the congregation conforming to the *Constitution of the Presbyterian Church (U.S.A.)*, and in giving other forms of support and encouragement that will strengthen the mission of the congregation in the larger life of the denomination.

G-7.0300

G-7.0301
Congregation

3.   Meetings of the Congregation

The congregation is made up of all members on the active roll of a particular church. All such members who are present at a congregational meeting are entitled to vote.

G-7.0302
Annual Meetings

a.   The congregation shall hold an annual meeting and may hold other meetings as necessary. The annual meeting may consider such business as electing officers, hearing reports of the session along with plans for the coming year, hearing reports from the board of deacons and other organizations of the church, and transacting other business as is appropriate. It shall review the adequacy of the compensation of the pastor or pastors upon report of the prior review by the session. (G-10.0102n) Public notice of the meeting shall be given on two successive Sundays.

Special Meetings

b.   Special meetings may be called for any or all of the purposes appropriate to an annual meeting or to conduct such other business as may be proper for congregational consideration. (G-7.0304) The business to be transacted shall be limited to items specifically listed in the call for the meeting.

G-7.0303
How Meetings
Are Called

a.   Meetings of the congregation shall be called

(1) by the session whenever it determines such a meeting is necessary,

(2) by the presbytery whenever it determines such a meeting is necessary,

(3) by the session when requested in writing by one fourth of the members on the active roll of the particular church.

Notice

b.   Public notice of the meeting shall be given on two successive Sundays. The meeting may be convened following the notice given on the second Sunday. (See G-14.0502a for notice of meetings to consider calling a pastor.)

G-7.0304
Business

a.   Business to be transacted at meetings of the congregation shall include the following:

(1) matters related to the electing of elders, deacons, and trustees;

(2) matters related to the calling of a pastor or pastors;

(3) matters related to the pastoral relationship, such as changing the call, or requesting or consenting or declining to consent to dissolution;

(4) matters related to buying, mortgaging, or selling real property (G-8.0500);

(5) matters related to the permissive powers of a congregation, such as the desire to lodge all administrative responsibility in the session, or the request to presbytery for exemption from one or more requirements because of limited size.

Limitations

b.   Business at congregational meetings shall be limited to the foregoing matters (1) through (5). Whenever permitted by civil law, both ecclesiastical and corporate business may be conducted at the same congregational meeting.

G-7.0305
Quorum

The quorum of a meeting of the congregation shall be not less than one tenth of the members unless the particular church upon application to the presbytery shall obtain the consent of the presbytery to a provision for a smaller quorum. A congregation by its own vote may fix a higher quorum. No meeting of fewer than three members shall be considered a congregational meeting.

G-7.0306
Moderator

The pastor shall be the moderator of all meetings of the congregation. In congregations where there are co-pastors, they shall, when present, alternately preside at meetings. When the church is without a pastor, the moderator of the session appointed by the presbytery shall preside at all congregational meetings. If it is impractical for the pastor or the moderator of session appointed by presbytery to preside, he or she shall invite, with the concurrence of the session, another minister of the presbytery to preside. In addition, the moderator of the session of a church with a vacant pulpit may request an elder who is a member of the presbytery's committee on ministry, the stated clerk, executive presbyter, or associate executive presbyter, to preside; such elder may not moderate the meeting of a congregation of which that elder is a member. When this is not expedient, and when both the pastor or the moderator of the session and the session concur, a member of the session may be invited to preside.

G-7.0307
Secretary

The clerk of the session shall be secretary of meetings of the congregation. If the congregation does not approve the minutes of a congregational meeting before adjournment, the session shall read, correct, and approve the minutes of that congregational meeting at its next scheduled meeting and shall enter them into the permanent record. At the next meeting of the congregation, the clerk shall have the minutes available and shall report the session's action. The congregation may ask to have them read and may make additions or corrections by vote. If the clerk is unable to serve, the congregation shall elect a secretary. The minutes of each meeting of the congregation shall be attested by the moderator and the secretary and shall be entered in the minute book of the session.

G-7.0308
In Case of a Tie

Since a minister is not a member of the congregation, she or he may not vote in the meeting of the congregation. When there is a tie vote, a minister presiding shall put the question a second time. If there is a tie vote again, the motion is lost.

G-7.0400

4. Incorporation and Trustees

G-7.0401
Incorporation and Trustees

Whenever permitted by civil law, each particular church shall cause a corporation to be formed and maintained. Only members on the active roll of the particular church shall be members of the corporation and eligible for election as trustees. The elders in active service in a church who are eligible under the civil law shall, by reason of their office, be the trustees of such corporation, unless the corporation shall determine another method for electing its trustees. Any such alternate method shall provide for a nominating committee elected by the corporation, and for terms for trustees the same as are provided for elders. Any particular church which is not incorporated may select trustees from the members on the active roll of the church. The power and duties of such trustees shall not infringe upon the powers and duties of the session or of the board of deacons. (G-10.0102, G-6.0402)

G-7.0402
Powers

The corporation so formed, or the individual trustees, shall have the following powers: to receive, hold, encumber, manage, and transfer property, real or personal, for the church; to accept and execute deeds of title to such property; to hold and defend title to such property; to manage any permanent special funds for the furtherance of the purposes of the church, all subject to the authority of the session and under the provisions of the *Constitution of the Presbyterian Church (U.S.A.),* provided further that in buying, selling, and mortgaging real property, the trustees shall act only after the approval of the congregation granted in a duly constituted meeting. (G-8.0500)

G-7.0403
Separate
Corporate
Meetings

Where civil law requires that corporate business be conducted in a separate corporate meeting of the congregation, the provisions of G-7.0300 shall apply, except:

a.   Such a meeting shall be called by the trustees at their discretion, or when directed by the session or by the presbytery.

b.   Unless the civil law provides otherwise, the trustees shall designate from among members on the active roll of the particular church a presiding officer and a secretary for such meeting.

c.   The minutes of each such meeting shall be attested by the presiding officer and the secretary and shall be entered in the minute book of the trustees.

G-7.0404
Vote by Proxy

Voting by proxy shall be permitted with respect to a corporate matter only where civil law specifically requires that voting by proxy shall be permitted as to that particular corporate matter.

CHAPTER VIII. THE CHURCH AND ITS PROPERTY

G-8.0000

G-8.0100

G-8.0101
Decisions
Regarding
Property

1. Decisions Pertaining to Property

The provisions of G-1.0400 and other provisions of this Constitution prescribing the manner in which decisions are made, reviewed, and corrected within this church are applicable to all matters pertaining to property.

G-8.0200

G-8.0201
Property Is Held
in Trust

2. All Property Held in Trust

All property held by or for a particular church, a presbytery, a synod, the General Assembly, or the Presbyterian Church (U.S.A.), whether legal title is lodged in a corporation, a trustee or trustees, or an unincorporated association, and whether the property is used in programs of a particular church or of a more inclusive governing body or retained for the production of income, is held in trust nevertheless for the use and benefit of the Presbyterian Church (U.S.A.).

G-8.0202
Incorporation and
Trustees

Whenever permitted by civil law, each presbytery, synod, and the General Assembly shall cause a corporation to be formed and maintained. The council of the governing body shall constitute the Board of Trustees of the corporation unless the governing body shall determine an alternative method to constitute the Board of Trustees.

G-8.0300

G-8.0301
Property Used
Contrary to
Constitution

3. Property Used Contrary to Constitution

Whenever property of, or held for, a particular church of the Presbyterian Church (U.S.A.) ceases to be used by that church as a particular church of the Presbyterian Church (U.S.A.) in accordance with this Constitution, such property shall be held, used, applied, transferred, or sold as provided by the presbytery.

G-8.0400

G-8.0401
Property of
Church Dissolved
or Extinct

4. Property of Church Dissolved or Extinct

Whenever a particular church is formally dissolved by the presbytery, or has become extinct by reason of the dispersal of its members, the abandonment of its work, or other cause, such property as it may have shall be held, used, and applied for such uses, purposes, and trusts as the presbytery may direct, limit, and appoint, or such property may be sold or disposed of as the presbytery may direct, in conformity with the *Constitution of the Presbyterian Church (U.S.A.)*.

G-8.0500

G-8.0501
Selling or
Encumbering
Church Property

G-8.0502
Leasing Church
Property

5. Selling, Encumbering, or Leasing Church Property

A particular church shall not sell, mortgage, or otherwise encumber any of its real property and it shall not acquire real property subject to an encumbrance or condition without the written permission of the presbytery transmitted through the session of the particular church.

A particular church shall not lease its real property used for purposes of worship, or lease for more than five years any of its other real property, without the written permission of the presbytery transmitted through the session of the particular church.

G-8.0600

G-8.0601
Property of
Church in Schism

6. Property of Church in Schism

The relationship to the Presbyterian Church (U.S.A.) of a particular church can be severed only by constitutional action on the part of the presbytery. (G-11.0103i) If there is a schism within the membership of a particular church and the presbytery is unable to effect a reconciliation or a division into separate churches within the Presbyterian Church (U.S.A.), the presbytery shall determine if one of the factions is entitled to the property because it is identified by the presbytery as the true church within the Presbyterian Church (U.S.A.). This determination does not depend upon which faction received the majority vote within the particular church at the time of the schism.

G-8.0700

G-8.0701
Exceptions

7. Exceptions

The provisions of this chapter shall apply to all particular churches of the Presbyterian Church (U.S.A.) except that any church which was not subject to a similar provision of the Constitution of the church of which it was a part, prior to the reunion of the Presbyterian Church in the United States and The United Presbyterian Church in the United States of America to form the Presbyterian Church (U.S.A.), shall be excused from that provision of this chapter if the congregation shall, within a period of eight years following the establishment of the Presbyterian Church (U.S.A.), vote to be exempt from such provision in a regularly called meeting and shall thereafter notify the presbytery of which it is a constituent church of such vote. The particular church voting to be so exempt shall hold title to its property and exercise its privileges of incorporation and property ownership under the provisions of the Constitution to which it was subject immediately prior to the establishment of the Presbyterian Church (U.S.A.). This paragraph may not be amended.

G-9.0000   **CHAPTER IX. GOVERNING BODIES**

G-9.0100

1. General

G-9.0101
Definition

The Presbyterian Church (U.S.A.) shall be governed by representative bodies composed of presbyters, both elders and ministers of the Word and Sacrament. These governing bodies shall be called

> session
> presbytery
> synod
> General Assembly.

G-9.0102
Distinct from
Government of
the State

a. Governing bodies of the church are distinct from the government of the state and have no civil jurisdiction or power to impose civil penalties. They have only ecclesiastical jurisdiction for the purpose of serving Jesus Christ and declaring and obeying his will in relation to truth and service, order and discipline.

Ecclesiastical
Jurisdiction

b. They may frame symbols of faith, bear testimony against error in doctrine and immorality in life, resolve questions of doctrine and of discipline, give counsel in matters of conscience, and decide issues properly brought before them under the provisions of the *Book of Order*. They may authorize the serving of the Lord's Supper in accordance with the principles of the Directory for Worship. (W-2.4012, W-3.6204). They have power to establish plans and rules for the worship, mission, government, and discipline of the church and to do those things necessary to the peace, purity, unity, and progress of the church under the will of Christ. They have responsibility for the leadership, guidance, and government of that portion of the church which is under their jurisdiction.

G-9.0103
Unity of
Governing Bodies

All governing bodies of the church are united by the nature of the church and share with one another responsibilities, rights, and powers as provided in this Constitution. The governing bodies are separate and independent, but have such mutual relations that the act of one of them is the act of the whole church performed by it through the appropriate governing body. The jurisdiction of each governing body is limited by the express provisions of the Constitution, with powers not mentioned being reserved to the presbyteries, and with the acts of each subject to review by the next higher governing body.

G-9.0104
Participation and
Representation

a. Governing bodies of the church shall be responsible for implementing the church's commitment to inclusiveness and participation as stated in G-4.0403. All governing bodies shall work to become more open and inclusive and shall pursue affirmative action hiring procedures aiming at correcting patterns of discrimination on the basis of the categories listed in G-4.0403.

Implementation
       b.   In implementing this commitment, consideration should be given to the gifts and requirements for ministry (G-6.0106) in persons elected or appointed to particular offices or tasks, and to the right of the people to elect their officers. (G-6.0107)

G-9.0105
Committee on
Representation
       a.   Each governing body above the session shall elect a committee on representation, whose membership shall consist of equal numbers of men and women. A majority of the members shall be selected from the racial ethnic groups (such as Presbyterians of African, Hispanic, and Asian descent and Native Americans) within the governing body, and the total membership shall include persons from each of the following categories:

      (1) majority male membership

      (2) majority female membership

      (3) racial ethnic male membership

      (4) racial ethnic female membership

      (5) youth male and female membership

      (6) persons with disabilities.

Advise Regarding
Membership
       b.   Its main function shall be to advise the governing bodies with respect to their membership and to that of their committees, boards, agencies, and other units in implementing the principles of participation and inclusiveness to ensure fair and effective representation in the decision making of the church.

Advocate and
Resource
       c.   The committee on representation shall serve both as an advocate for the representation of racial ethnic members, women, different age groups, and persons with disabilities, and as a continuing resource to the particular governing body in these areas. The committee on representation shall review the performance of its own governing body in these matters and shall report annually to it and to the next higher governing body with recommendations for any needed corrective action. The committee on representation shall consult with the nominating committee of its own governing body.

Consult with
Racial Ethnic
Membership
       d.   Prior to nomination or appointment of racial ethnic members to committees, boards, agencies, or other units, the committee on representation shall consult with the appropriate racial ethnic membership through a person or persons designated by that racial ethnic membership. In situations where racial ethnic membership is low, the committee on representation of each governing body shall consult with racial ethnic members, sessions, nominating committees, and persons designated by national racial ethnic membership to discover potential racial ethnic members of such body and to determine achievable representation. Prior to nomination or appointment of women to the above agencies, the committee on representation shall consult with the appropriate constituencies of women through a person or persons designated by those constituencies.

Employment of
Personnel

e.   The committee on representation shall advise the governing body on the employment of personnel, in accordance with the principles of participation and representation (G-4.0403), and in conformity with a churchwide plan for equal employment opportunity. (G-13.0201b)

f.   The committee on representation shall not, in any governing body, be merged with any other committee or designated as a subcommittee of any other committee.

G-9.0106
Exceptions

a.   Exceptions to the provisions of G-9.0105a requiring a majority of the members to be selected from racial ethnic groups shall be allowed by a governing or electing body only if it is unable to secure the participation or representation of the necessary persons, and this fact shall be made a part of the official record of the governing, electing, or appointing body. No exception is permitted to the requirement that each governing body above the session elect a committee on representation.

b.   An exception under G-9.0106a may be allowed for up to one year by governing body action at a meeting. The approval of such exception shall be promptly reported by the stated clerk to the next higher governing body through its stated clerk and committee on representation, which committee shall monitor the lower governing body and its committee on representation during the period of the exception.

G-9.0200

G-9.0201
Officers

2.   Officers

Officers of each of the governing bodies shall be a moderator and a clerk. Governing bodies may provide additional officers as required.

G-9.0202
Moderator and
Meeting

a.   The moderator possesses the authority necessary for preserving order and for conducting efficiently the business of the governing body. He or she shall convene and adjourn the governing body in accordance with its own action. The moderator may, in an emergency, convene the governing body by written notice at a time and place different from that previously designated by the body.

Moderator of
Congregation and
Governing Bodies

b.   The pastor of a particular church shall be the moderator of the session of that church. In congregations where there are co-pastors, they shall, when present, alternately preside in the session. The moderator of a presbytery shall be elected for such term as the presbytery may determine, not exceeding one year. The moderator of a synod shall be elected for such term as the synod may determine, not less than one year and not exceeding two years. The Moderator of the General Assembly shall be elected at each stated meeting. At the time of election, the moderator of a presbytery, a synod, or the General Assembly must be a continuing member of, or a commissioner to, the governing body over which he or she is elected to preside.

G-9.0203
Clerk and
Meeting

a.   The clerk shall record the transactions of the governing body, keep its rolls of membership and attendance, preserve its records carefully, and furnish extracts from them when required by another governing body of the church. Such extracts, verified by the clerk, shall be evidence in any governing body of the church.

Clerk and Stated
Clerk of
Congregations
and Governing
Bodies

b.   The clerk of the session shall be an elder elected by the session for such term as it may determine. The clerk of a presbytery, a synod, and the General Assembly shall be called stated clerk, shall be elected by the governing body for a definite term as it may determine, and must be eligible for membership in the governing body.

G-9.0300

3.   **Meetings**

G-9.0301
Opening of
Meetings

a.   The moderator of a governing body beyond the session shall open all stated meetings during his or her term of office and shall preside until a new moderator is elected. If the moderator is absent at the opening of the next meeting, the next previous moderator shall perform these duties.

Opened and
Closed with
Prayer

b.   All meetings of governing bodies shall be opened and closed with prayer. Presbyteries and synods that meet more often than annually shall designate one stated meeting each year, which shall include preaching the Word and sharing the Lord's Supper. Stated meetings of synods that meet annually or biennially and the General Assembly shall include a time for the preaching of the Word and the celebration of the Lord's Supper.

G-9.0302
Parliamentary
Procedure

Meetings of governing bodies, commissions, and committees shall be conducted in accordance with the most recent edition of *Robert's Rules of Order,* except in those cases where this Constitution provides otherwise.

G-9.0303
Dissent

A dissent is a declaration expressing disagreement with the action or decision of a governing body. A dissent shall be made at the particular session of the governing body during which the action or decision dissented from is taken. The name or names of the members dissenting shall be recorded.

G-9.0304
Protest

A protest is a written declaration, supported by reasons, expressing disagreement with what is believed by one or more members of a governing body to be an irregularity or a delinquency.

Notice

a.   Written notice of the protest shall be given at the particular session of the governing body during which it arose. The protest shall be filed with the clerk or stated clerk before adjournment.

Minutes

b.   If a protest is expressed in decorous and respectful language, the governing body shall enter it in its minutes in recognition of the person's right of conscience. That entry does not justify disobedience.

GOVERNING BODIES

G-9.0305-.0404

Response

c. A governing body against which a protest is taken may prepare an answer that shall be entered in its minutes. This shall terminate the protest.

G-9.0305
Who May Dissent
or Protest

Only a person who voted against the decision, except the moderator if unable to vote, shall be allowed to dissent or protest.

G-9.0306
Judicial Decision

When a case has been decided by a permanent judicial commission, any member of the governing body to which the decision is reported may enter a dissent or protest.

G-9.0307
Effect

A dissent or a protest does not initiate or prevent judicial process.

G-9.0308
Expenses

The expenses of elders and ministers of the Word and Sacrament attending governing bodies ordinarily shall be defrayed either by the governing body which elects them or by that which they are attending, to the extent of the expenses incurred within the bounds of that governing body. The General Assembly shall pay the expenses of commissioners who are elected by the presbyteries to attend the meetings of the General Assembly. Per capita funds may be used by each governing body to pay such expenses.

G-9.0400

4. Principles of Administration

G-9.0401
Definition of
Administration

Administration is the process by which a governing body implements decisions. It involves working with and through persons to accomplish goals and includes developing leadership, planning, communicating, organizing, budgeting, supervising, and evaluating.

G-9.0402
Structure of
Administration

a. Mission determines the form of structure and administration. All structures should enable the church to give effective witness to the Lordship of Christ in the contemporary world.

Governing Body
Nearest the
Congregation

b. The administration of mission should be performed by the governing body that can most effectively and efficiently accomplish it at the level of jurisdiction nearest the congregation.

Change

c. All structures shall be open to the possibility of change and new forms of ecumenical cooperation.

G-9.0403
Accountability to
Governing Body

A governing body may delegate particular aspects of its task to councils, boards, agencies, commissions, and committees, but always on the basis of accountability to the governing body.

G-9.0404
Nature of
Presbyterian
Polity

In order to give meaning to the interdependent nature of Presbyterian polity:

a. Each governing body shall participate through its representatives in the planning and administration of the next higher body.

b. Each governing body shall consult through appropriate representatives with governing bodies below and above it concerning mission priorities, program, budgeting, the establishment of administrative staff positions, equitable compensation, personnel policies, and fair employment practices.

c. Each governing body shall recruit, train, and employ its staff in accordance with the principles of inclusiveness and affirmative action found in G-9.0104.

d. Each governing body above the session shall prepare a budget annually for its operating expenses, including administrative personnel, and may fund it with a per capita apportionment among the particular churches within its bounds. The presbyteries shall be responsible for raising their own per capita funds, and for raising and timely transmission of per capita funds to their respective synods and to the General Assembly. The presbyteries may direct per capita apportionments to the sessions of the churches within their bounds.

G-9.0405
Manual of
Operations

Each governing body above the session shall, in consultation with the governing body above and below it, develop a manual of administrative operations.

G-9.0406
Ownership of
Records

Minutes and all other official records of church sessions, presbyteries, synods, and General Assemblies are the property in perpetuity of said governing bodies or their legal successors. When congregations, synods, or presbyteries are dissolved, their records are held for them by the next higher governing body within whose bounds they were before dissolution. All minutes and other official records of existing and dissolved sessions, minutes and other official records of existing and dissolved presbyteries and synods that are no longer required for frequent reference, are to be deposited for preserving and servicing **with the Department of History or in a temperature and humidity controlled environment of a seminary of the Presbyterian Church (U.S.A.).** It is the responsibility of the clerk of each governing body to make recommendation to that governing body for the permanent safekeeping of the governing body's records. **All governing bodies are strongly encouraged to microfilm their official records.**

G-9.0407
General
Administrative
Review

a. The congregation of a particular church and the committees, bodies, and organizations of that church shall report annually all proceedings and actions to the session, which shall review and summarize them and incorporate the summary in its minutes.

Annual Reporting

b. The moderator, the stated clerk, the councils, commissions, committees, boards, agencies, and organizations of every governing body above a session shall report annually all proceedings and actions to that governing body, which shall review them.

Review of
Records

c. At least once a year every governing body above a session shall review the records of the proceedings of the next lower governing body. If any lower governing body shall fail to send up its records for this purpose, the higher governing body shall order them to be produced at a specified time.

G-9.0408
Special
Administrative
Review

If a higher governing body learns at any time of any irregularity or delinquency by a lower governing body, it may require the governing body to produce any records and take appropriate action. (G-12.0102n, G-12.0304, G-13.0103k,n)

G-9.0409
Manner of
Review

a.   In reviewing the proceedings of a lower governing body, the higher governing body shall determine, either from the records of those proceedings or from any other information as may come to its attention, whether:

(1) The proceedings have been correctly recorded;

(2) The proceedings have been regular and in accordance with the *Constitution*;

(3) The proceedings have been prudent and equitable;

(4) The proceedings have been faithful to the mission of the whole church;

(5) The lawful injunctions of a higher governing body have been obeyed.

Who May Not
Vote

b.   When the proceedings of a lower governing body are being reviewed by a higher governing body, the members of the higher governing body who are also members of the lower governing body may participate in discussion but shall not vote.

G-9.0410
Action of Higher
Governing Body

It is ordinarily sufficient for the higher governing body to record in its own proceedings, and in those under review, its approval, disapproval, or correction. If necessary, the higher governing body may direct the lower governing body to reconsider and correct an irregularity or cure a delinquency.

G-9.0411
Review and
Correction by
Judicial Process

In addition to administrative review, review and correction of a lower governing body and of a council or an agency of the General Assembly may be obtained by judicial process by one or more persons or governing bodies filing a complaint in accordance with the provisions of D-6.0000.

G-9.0500

5.   **Committees and Commissions**

G-9.0501
Committee

a.   A committee is appointed either to study and recommend appropriate action or to carry out directions or decisions already made by a governing body. It shall make a full report to the governing body that created it, and its recommendations shall require action by the governing body.

Membership

b.   Committees of governing bodies above the session shall consist of laypersons and ministers of the Word and Sacrament with at least one half the members being laypersons.

G-9.0502
Commission

A commission is empowered to consider and conclude matters referred to it by a governing body. The appointing body shall state specifically the scope of power given to a commission. A commission shall keep a full record of its proceedings, which shall be submitted to its governing body to be incorporated in its minutes and to be regarded as the actions of the governing body itself.

**G-9.0503
Administrative
and Judicial**

a.   Commissions appointed by sessions, presbyteries, synods, or the General Assembly may be either administrative or judicial, except in the case of sessions, which may appoint only administrative commissions. The functions ordinarily entrusted to an administrative commission are:

(1) to ordain ministers of the Word and Sacrament and to install them in permanent pastoral relations;

(2) to organize churches. When such commissions are appointed by a presbytery to organize new congregations (G-11.0103h), the presbytery may authorize that commission to assume any or all powers and responsibilities of a session (G-10.0102) for the benefit and ministry of the new congregation. The presbytery may authorize the commission to delegate such powers and responsibilities to a committee of the new congregation.

(3) to merge churches

(4) to visit particular churches, governing bodies, or other organizations of the church reported to be affected with disorder, and to inquire into and settle the difficulties therein, except that no commission shall have the power to dissolve a pastoral relationship unless such power has been specifically delegated to it by the appointing body;

(5) to receive candidates under the care of presbytery (G-14.0301);

(6) in the case of administrative commissions appointed by sessions, to ordain and install elders and deacons, and to visit organizations within a particular church and settle differences therein.

Judicial

b.   The functions of a judicial commission are to consider and decide a case of process for the governing body according to the Rules of Discipline. (See D-5.0000 on Permanent Judicial Commissions.)

Additional Duties

c.   A commission may be assigned additional duties as a committee, the reporting of which shall be handled as is a committee's report.

**G-9.0504
Membership**

a.   An administrative commission of a session shall consist of at least two elders and the moderator of the session or other minister of the Word and Sacrament installed in a permanent relationship within the particular church governed by the session.

**Equal Number of
Ministers and
Elders**

b.   Administrative and judicial commissions of presbytery, synod, and the General Assembly shall be composed of ministers of the Word and Sacrament and elders in numbers as nearly equal as possible. When the commission consists of an odd number of members, the additional member may be either an elder or a minister of the Word and Sacrament. The minimum number and distribution of members shall be:

General
Assembly

(1) for the General Assembly, not fewer than fifteen members with at least one member from each of its constituent synods;

Synod

(2) for a synod, not fewer than eleven members with, insofar as practicable, not more than one member from any one of its constituent presbyteries;

Presbytery

(3) for a presbytery, not fewer than seven members, with not more than one of its elder members from any one of its constituent churches. For the performance of functions set forth in G-9.0503a(1), a presbytery may reduce the number to five members with not more than one of the elders from any one church.

Quorum

c. The quorum of an administrative commission shall be a majority of the members, unless the appointing governing body fixes the quorum at a higher number. The quorum of a judicial commission shall be a majority of the members. (D-5.0204)

G-9.0505
Decisions

a. The decision of an administrative commission shall be the action of the appointing governing body from the time of its completion by the commission and the announcement, where relevant, of the action to parties affected by it. Such decision shall be transmitted in writing to the stated clerk of the governing body, who shall report it to the governing body at its next meeting.

Hearings and Fair
Procedures

b. When an administrative commission has been appointed to settle differences within a church, a governing body, or an organization of the church, it shall, before making its final decision, afford to all persons to be affected by the decision fair notice and an opportunity to be heard on the matters at issue. (See G-9.0503a(3), a(5), G-9.0505b-d) Fair notice shall consist of a short and plain statement of the matters at issue as identified by the commission and of the time and place for a hearing upon the matters at issue. The hearing shall include at least an opportunity for all persons in interest to have their positions on the matters at issue stated orally. In its absolute discretion, a commission may give the required notice only to responsible representatives of persons aligned in interest and may require the oral statements of position to be made at the hearing by the same or other responsible representatives.

Additional
Procedural
Process

c. In its absolute discretion, a commission may, in particular proceedings, afford additional procedural process such as that afforded in cases of judicial process, either upon motion of persons in interest or on its own motion.

Right to Face
Accusers

    d.   Notwithstanding, that in any case where allegations or assertions concerning individuals are determined to be of such seriousness that their consequence, if proven true, could be the removal from office or position, discipline, or other serious result for the individual, those concerned shall be given the right to face their accusers, and to hear from them the allegations or assertions against them, and be given sufficient time to prepare and make a reasoned defense, including the cross-examination of witnesses. This paragraph shall apply whether or not formal charges under the Rules of Discipline have been filed or anticipated.

G-9.0600

G-9.0601
Mediation or
Conciliation

6.   Mediation Provisions

    Governing bodies may establish a system of mediation or conciliation for remedial matters that may be used prior to or during judicial process. In such a system, care must be taken to observe the provisions of the Rules of Discipline.

G-9.0602
Participation

    Participation in this process of mediation or conciliation may not be required of any party.

    [Historical Note: The original text of G-9.0600-.0601 was stricken by action of the 203rd General Assembly (1991). The original text of G-9.0602 was stricken by action of the 201st General Assembly (1989).]

G-9.0700

G-9.0701
Executives

7.   Administrative Staff

    a.   The executives of the presbyteries and synods shall be the administrators of those governing bodies, accountable to the governing bodies, through their councils, for the implementation of decisions and matters of strategy, program, and resources. They shall also provide staff services for the agencies and committees of the governing bodies. Additional responsibilities, along with the process of calling, the method of annual review of work, and the matter of reelection or termination of employment, shall be set forth clearly in the manuals called for in G-9.0405, above.

Election of
Executives

    b.   Each presbytery may elect an executive presbyter in consultation with synod council, or other unit designated by the synod when there is no council, and may do so jointly with other presbyteries if program and resources make that necessary. Each synod may elect an executive in consultation with the General Assembly Council.

G-9.0702
Other
Administrative
Staff

    Other administrative staff positions in presbyteries may be authorized by the presbytery in consultation with the synod council or other unit designated by the synod when there is no council. Other administrative staff positions in synod may be authorized by the synod in consultation with the General Assembly Council.

G-9.0703
General
Assembly Agency
Staff

General Assembly agencies shall elect, with the concurrence of the General Assembly Council, an executive or executives, subject, however, to confirmation by the General Assembly. Other administrative staff positions for General Assembly agencies may be authorized by those agencies with concurrence of the General Assembly Council.

G-9.0704
Participation and
Representation

All executive and administrative staff positions in all governing bodies above the session shall be filled in accordance with the principles of participation and representation found in G-9.0104 and with the requirement that a representative search committee for these positions be set forth clearly in the manuals called for in G-9.0405.

G-9.0705
Termination of
Synod and
Presbytery Staff

The relationship between executives or other administrative staff of presbyteries and synods and their respective governing bodies may be dissolved by majority vote of the electing governing body on request of the staff member or on recommendation of the council or a special committee or commission of the electing governing body. When the council, committee, or commission has decided to prepare a recommendation to terminate, it shall notify the person in writing, stating the reasons for proposing to terminate, and offering the staff member an opportunity to resign or to request a hearing before the recommendations are adopted and reported by the council, committee, or commission to the governing body for action. The hearing shall be one in which the staff person may appear personally with counsel (D-7.0301, D-11.0301) to respond to the findings of the committee or commission and present reasons and evidence why the relationship should not be terminated. The hearing shall afford safeguards as in cases of process, following the rules of evidence in the Rules of Discipline, Chapter XIV (D-14.0000). A record shall be made of the hearing, which shall become a part of the record filed under D-6.0304 in the event of a judicial complaint following the final action of the governing body.

G-9.0706
Temporary
Administrative
Staff

When a presbytery, synod, or General Assembly executive or administrative staff position is vacant, or when the incumbent is unable to perform her or his duties, the presbytery, synod, or General Assembly agency may secure the services of a temporary executive or administrative staff person. Temporary administrative positions include acting or interim presbytery, synod, or General Assembly agency executives and administrative staff persons. No one serving in a temporary position may be hired to fulfill that same position on a permanent basis as the next permanent executive or administrative staff person.

G-9.0707
Emeritus/ Emerita

When any executive or associate executive of a presbytery or synod retires, and that governing body is moved by affection and gratitude to continue an association in an honorary relationship, it may, at a regularly called meeting of the governing body, elect him or her as executive emeritus or emerita, with or without honorarium, but with no authority or duty. This action may take effect after the formal dissolution of the executive relationship or anytime thereafter.

G-9.0800

G-9.0801
Nominating
Committee

8. Nominating Committee

a.   Each presbytery and synod shall elect a nominating committee broadly representative of the member churches of the presbytery or presbyteries, with a membership of one third ministers of the Word and Sacrament, one third laywomen, and one third laymen. The nominating committee shall consist of three classes, each serving for a three-year term except where initial classes of one- and two-year terms are necessary to establish regular rotation.

Responsibility

b.   The nominating committee shall nominate persons to fill all vacancies on continuing committees (except the nominating committee), councils, boards, and other bodies that require election by the presbytery or synod. Consideration shall be given to the nomination of equal numbers of ministers of the Word and Sacrament, laymen, and laywomen (i.e., one third each), except that women elders and men elders shall be nominated to the committee on ministry to which presbytery functions may be delegated. (G-11.0501, G-12.0102d, G-13.0111, G-13.0202)

c.   The nominating committee shall consult, at least annually, with the committee on representation of its own governing body. If the committee on representation of that governing body has been granted an exception under the provisions of G-9.0106, the committee on representation of the next higher governing body shall be invited to participate in that consultation.

Relevant
Provisions

d.   In nominating persons to particular responsibilities the nominating committee shall observe the relevant provisions of G-6.0106, G-9.0104, G-11.0103d, G-11.0302, G-12.0102d, G-13.0108, and G-13.0202.

G-9.0900

G-9.0901
Councils,
Commissions,
Committees

9. Summary of Structures

Within this Constitution, it has been assumed that the governing bodies beyond the session will delegate particular aspects of their task to councils, commissions, and committees. The references made to such agencies are for clarification of organizing for mission, of establishing offices, and of administering the program of the church. Reference to these is given without formally entitling them wherever possible so that governing bodies may have freedom in structuring themselves and in naming their agencies. In several instances—such as the committees on representation, the General Assembly Council, and the presbytery's committee on ministry—definite titles are given in order to regularize the procedures that shall enable the governing bodies to work together in joint mission. Reference to such agencies, designated by functions or by formal titles, is not intended to limit the governing bodies to these structures but to describe those which will expedite the mutual work of the whole church.

G-9.0902
Structures Listed

Structures specified within this Constitution are:

Presbytery

a. In the Presbytery

A council for the coordination of mission and program (G-11.0103v)

Committee on Representation (G-9.0105, G-11.0302)

Committee on Ministry (G-11.0500, G-14.0502)

Committee on Preparation for Ministry (G-14.0300)

Nominating Committee (G-9.0800, G-11.0103w)

Permanent Judicial Commission (D-5.0000)

Synod

b. In the Synod

A council for the coordination of mission and program. (G-12.0102r) (The only exception to this requirement shall be when a synod chooses to retain the coordinating function for itself.)

Committee on Representation (G-9.0105, G-12.0301)

Nominating Committee (G-9.0800, G-12.0102s)

Permanent Judicial Commission (D-5.0000)

General
Assembly

c. In the General Assembly

General Assembly Council (G-13.0200)

Committee on Representation (G-9.0105, G-13.0108)

Nominating Committee (G-13.0111)

Advisory Committee on the Constitution (G-13.0112)

Board responsible for pensions (G-14.0506, G-16.0201t, G-17.0201j)

Permanent Judicial Commission (D-5.0000)

CHAPTER X. THE SESSION

G-10.0100

1. General

G-10.0101
Membership

The session of a particular church consists of the pastor or co-pastors, the associate pastors, and the elders in active service. All members of the session, including the pastor, co-pastors, and associate pastors, are entitled to vote.

G-10.0102
Responsibilities

The session is responsible for the mission and government of the particular church. It therefore has the responsibility and power

a. to provide opportunities for evangelism to be learned and practiced in and by the church, that members may be better equipped to articulate their faith, to witness in word and deed to the saving grace of Jesus Christ, and to invite persons into a new life in Christ, in accordance with G-3.0300;

b. to receive members into the church upon profession of faith, upon reaffirmation of faith in Jesus Christ, or upon satisfactory certification of transfer of church membership, provided that membership shall not be denied any person because of race, economic or social circumstances, or any other reason not related to profession of faith;

c. to lead the congregation in participation in the mission of the whole Church in the world, in accordance with G-3.0000;

d. to provide for the worship of the people of God, including the preaching of the Word, the sharing of the Sacraments, and for the music program, in keeping with the principles in the Directory for Worship, and to appeal to the presbytery for a duly trained and authorized elder under the provisions of G-11.0103 in those extenuating circumstances where an ordained minister of the Word and Sacrament is not available to meet the needs for the administration of the Lord's Supper;

e. to provide for the growth of its members and for their equipment for ministry through personal and pastoral care, educational programs including the church school, sharing in fellowship and mutual support, and opportunities for witness and service in the world;

f. to develop and supervise the church school and the educational program of the church;

g. to lead the congregation in ministries of personal and social healing and reconciliation in the communities in which the church lives and bears its witness;

h. to challenge the people of God with the privilege of responsible Christian stewardship of money and time and talents, developing effective ways for encouraging and gathering the offerings of the people and assuring that all offerings are distributed to the objects toward which they were contributed;

i.   to establish the annual budget, determine the distribution of the church's benevolences, and order offerings for Christian purposes, providing full information to the congregation of its decisions in such matters;

j.   to lead the congregation continually to discover what God is doing in the world and to plan for change, renewal, and reformation under the Word of God;

k.   to engage in a process for education and mutual growth of the members of the session;

l.   to instruct, examine, ordain, install, and welcome into common ministry elders and deacons on their election by the congregation and to inquire into their faithfulness in fulfilling their responsibilities;

m.   to delegate and to supervise the work of the board of deacons and the board of trustees and all other organizations and task forces within the congregation, providing for support, report, review, and control;

n.   to provide for the administration of the program of the church, including employment of nonordained staff, with concern for equal employment opportunity, fair employment practices, personnel policies, and the annual review of the adequacy of compensation for all staff, including all employees;

o.   to provide for the management of the property of the church, including determination of the appropriate use of church buildings and facilities, and to obtain property and liability insurance coverage to protect the facilities, programs, and officers, including members of the session, staff, board of trustees, and deacons;

p.   to maintain regular and continuing relationship to the higher governing bodies of the church, including

(1) electing commissioners to presbytery and receiving their reports; sessions are encouraged to elect commissioners to the presbytery for at least one year, preferably two or three;

(2) nominating to presbytery elders who may be considered for election to synod or General Assembly;

(3) in both the above responsibilities, implementing the principles of participation and inclusiveness to ensure fair representation in the decision making of the church;

(4) observing and carrying out the instructions of the higher governing bodies consistent with the *Constitution of the Presbyterian Church (U.S.A.)*;

(5) welcoming representatives of the presbytery on the occasions of their visits;

(6) proposing to the presbytery and, through it, to the synod and the General Assembly such measures as may be of common concern to the mission of the whole church;

(7) sending annually to the stated clerk of the presbytery statistical and other information according to the requirements of the presbytery.

q. to establish and maintain those ecumenical relationships necessary for the life and mission of the church in its locality;

r. to serve in judicial matters in accordance with the Rules of Discipline;

s. to keep an accurate roll of the membership of the church, in accordance with G-10.0302, and to grant certificates of transfer to other churches, which when issued for parents shall include the names of their children specifying whether they have been baptized, and which when issued for an elder or deacon shall include the record of ordination.

G-10.0103
Moderator

a. The pastor of the church shall be the moderator of the session and the session shall not meet without the pastor except as hereunder provided. In congregations where there are co-pastors, they shall, when present, alternately preside in the session. When it may appear advisable for prudential reasons that some minister other than the pastor should preside, the pastor may, with the concurrence of the session, invite a minister of the same presbytery to do so. In addition, the moderator of the session of a church with a vacant pulpit may request an elder who is a member of the presbytery's committee on ministry, the stated clerk, executive presbyter, or associate executive presbyter, to preside; such elder may not moderate the session of the church of which that elder is a member. In the case of the sickness or absence of the pastor the same expedient may be adopted; or the session, after having obtained the approval of the pastor, may convene and elect another of its own members to preside.

When Without a
Pastor

b. When a church is without a pastor, the moderator of the session shall be the minister appointed for that purpose by the presbytery, or a minister of the same presbytery invited by the session to preside on a particular occasion. When it is impossible for such a minister to attend, the session may elect one of its own members to preside.

Judicial Cases

c. In all judicial cases, the moderator of the session shall be a minister of the presbytery to which the church belongs.

G-10.0200

G-10.0201
Meetings

2. Meetings

The session shall hold stated meetings at least quarterly. The moderator of the session may call a special meeting of the session when he or she judges it necessary and shall do so when requested in writing by any two members of the session. The session shall also meet when directed to do so by presbytery. Reasonable notice of all special meetings must be given when other than routine business is to be transacted. The session may invite members of the congregation to attend and observe its meetings if it so desires, without restricting its right to meet in executive session whenever circumstances indicate the wisdom of doing so.

G-10.0202
Quorum

A quorum of the session shall be the pastor or other presiding officer and one third of the elders but no fewer than two, except for the reception and dismission of members, when the quorum shall be the moderator and two members of the session. The session may fix its own quorum at any higher number.

G-10.0300

G-10.0301
Minutes

3. Minutes and Records

Each session shall keep a full and accurate record of its proceedings which shall be submitted at least once each year to the presbytery for its general review and control. (G-11.0103x, G-9.0407-.0411) The minutes shall state the composition of the session with regard to racial ethnic members, women, men, age groups, and persons with disabilities, and how this corresponds to the composition of the congregation. Minutes and other official records of the session, which shall include minutes of congregational meetings and records of the board of deacons and the board of trustees of the particular church, are the property of the session, and the clerk shall be responsible for their preservation. They shall be available to the presbytery upon request and may be stored with the denomination's historical agency.

G-10.0302
Rolls and
Registers

Every session shall maintain rolls of members as defined by G-5.0200, and registers as provided below.

a. Membership Rolls. The names of the members shall be placed upon, removed, or deleted from the rolls of the church only by order of the session whenever the session is fully satisfied that such action is justified.

G-10.0302a. (1)
Baptized
Members

(1) Baptized Members' Roll. The baptized members' roll shall list the names of those persons baptized in the particular church who have not made a profession of faith in Jesus Christ as Lord and Savior, and children of active members or of ministers of the Word and Sacrament related to the particular church, when such children have been baptized elsewhere.

G-10.0302a. (2) (a)
Active Members

(2) (a) Active Members' Roll. The active members' roll shall list the names of those who have been received

into the membership of the church and who are active in the church's work and worship. The number of members on this roll shall be reported to the General Assembly annually.

G-10.0302a. (2) (b)
Affiliate Members
Certified

(b) An active member who has temporarily moved from the community may become an affiliate member of another church of this denomination or of a denomination in correspondence with the General Assembly, in which case the session may issue a certificate of good standing. (G-15.0201) The certificate shall be directed to a particular church named therein, shall commend the member to its pastoral care, and shall be valid for two years. Upon the issuance of the certificate, the session shall retain the name of the member on the active roll of the church until the person is received into membership in the other church.

G-10.0302a. (2) (c)
When Active
Members Move

(c) When a member moves and can no longer be active in the work and worship of the church of membership, it shall be that person's duty to become an active member of a church in the community where that person is living. The session of the church of membership shall inform the person of this duty as soon as practicable and shall notify a church in the new community and request it to provide pastoral care with a view to membership. In addition, notice shall be sent to either the presbytery office or to the stated clerk of the presbytery, or both.

G-10.0302a. (3) (a)
Inactive Members

(3) (a) Inactive Members' Roll. The inactive members' roll shall list the names of those who have been removed from the active members' roll because of their failure, in the judgment of the session, to participate in the church's work and worship. No member shall be transferred from the active to the inactive roll until that member shall have failed intentionally to participate in the work and worship of the church for a period of one year and until the session shall have made diligent effort to discover the cause of the member's nonparticipation and to restore the member to activity in the church's work and worship. Any member whose name is so transferred shall be notified of this action.

G-10.0302a. (3) (b)
Nonresident Member

(b) A nonresident member to whom the notice required above has been given may after one year be placed on the inactive members' roll. The session shall then advise the person at the last known address to request a certificate of transfer to a Christian church in the community of residence.

G-10.0302a. (4)
Affiliate Members
Received

(4) Affiliate Members' Roll. The affiliate members' roll shall list the names of those who have been received into affiliate membership by the session and who are active in

the church's work and worship. Affiliate membership must be renewed every two years.

G-10.0302b.
Deletion from Rolls

b.   The session may delete names from the rolls of the church in the following circumstances:

G-10.0302b. (1)
Certificate of
Transfer

(1)   When requested, the session shall issue a certificate of transfer to a particular church setting forth the membership status of the person. The church receiving the certificate shall determine whether to receive the person as a member and the conditions upon which that person shall be received. When a certificate of transfer has been issued, the name of the member shall be retained on the appropriate roll by the church issuing the certificate until the person is received into membership in the other church. As soon as the person is received, the receiving church shall notify the session issuing the certificate of the member's reception, whereupon the session shall delete the name.

G-10.0302b. (2)
When Church Is
Dissolved

(2)   When a church is dissolved, the presbytery of jurisdiction shall take possession of its records, have jurisdiction over its members, and grant them certificates of transfer to other churches.

G-10.0302b. (3)
Request
Termination

(3)   When a member, whether active or inactive, requests that membership be terminated, the session, after making diligent effort to persuade the member to retain membership, may delete that person's name from the active or inactive roll.

G-10.0302b. (4)
Joins Another
Church

(4)   When a member joins another church without a regular transfer or renounces the jurisdiction of this church, the session shall delete the member's name from any rolls on which it has been listed.

G-10.0302b. (5)
Nonresident
Member Inactive

(5)   When a nonresident member has been given the notices required above, and that member's name has been on the inactive roll for one year, the session may delete that person's name from the roll without further notice.

G-10.0302b. (6)
Moved and
Unknown

(6)   When a member moves and the session is unable, after due and diligent search, to ascertain the member's place of residence, the session, after one year of absence, may delete that person's name from any roll on which it has been listed.

G-10.0302b. (7)
Inactive Roll for
Two Years

(7)   When a resident church member has been transferred from the active to the inactive roll, it shall be the duty of the session to provide that member pastoral care. If pastoral care for a period of two years fails to accomplish that person's restoration as an active member, the session may without further notice delete the person's name from the roll.

G-10.0302b. (8)
Member Dies

G-10.0302c.
Registers of
Marriages,
Baptisms, Officers

(8) When a member dies, the session shall record the date of death and delete the name from the roll.

c.   Registers. The session shall keep complete registers of

(1) Marriages, including marriages of all members of the church, all marriages conducted by the ministerial staff of the church, and all marriages performed on church property;

(2) Baptisms

(a) Infant Baptisms. Include name, parents' names, and date of birth of those being baptized and the names of persons presenting the children for Baptism.

(b) Adult Baptisms. Include name, parents' names, and date of birth of those being baptized.

(3) Elders, with the name of the church in which each was ordained, the date of ordination, terms of active service, and the record of removals;

(4) Deacons, with the name of the church in which each was ordained, the date of ordination, terms of active service, and the record of removals;

(5) Pastors, co-pastors, associate pastors, assistant pastors, interim pastors, stated supplies, and parish associates serving the church, with dates of service.

4.   Church Finances

The treasurer shall be elected annually by the session, if permitted by the state in which the church is located, and his or her work shall be supervised by the session, or by specific assignment to the board of deacons or trustees. Those in charge of the various funds in the church shall report at least annually to the session, and more often when requested. The following minimum standards of financial procedure shall be observed:

a.   The counting and recording of all offerings by at least two duly appointed persons, or a fidelity bonded person;

b.   The keeping of adequate books and records to reflect all financial transactions, open to inspection by authorized church officers at reasonable times;

c.   Periodic reporting of the financial activities to the board or boards vested with financial oversight at least annually, preferably more often;

d.   A full financial review of all books and records relating to finances once each year by a public accountant or public accounting firm or a committee of members versed in accounting procedures. Such auditors should not be related to the treasurer (or treasurers). Terminology in this section is meant to provide general guidance and is not intended to require or not require specific audit procedures or practices as understood within the professional accounting community.

G-11.0000   **CHAPTER XI. THE PRESBYTERY**

G-11.0100   **1. General**

G-11.0101   Presbytery is a corporate expression of the church consisting
Membership   of all the churches and ministers of the Word and Sacrament within
                    a certain district. When a presbytery meets, each church shall be
                    represented by an elder commissioned by the session with the fol-
                    lowing additional provisions:

                    a.   Churches with membership over 500 shall be represented
                    as follows:

                         501-1000—2 elders

                         1001-1500—3 elders

                         1501-2000—4 elders

                         2001-3000—5 elders

                    From 3,001 members there shall be an additional elder repre-
                    sentative for each 1,000 additional active members or major
                    fraction thereof.

                    b.   Annually, during the first week of January, the stated clerk
                    of each presbytery shall ascertain the number of resident min-
                    isters who are members of the presbytery and the number of
                    elders which the churches are entitled to send as commission-
                    ers to presbytery meetings. When the number of ministers is
                    larger, the stated clerk shall bring the imbalance to the atten-
                    tion of the presbytery at its first meeting of the year. The pres-
                    bytery shall redress the imbalance by inviting sessions of par-
                    ticular churches to elect additional elder commissioners or on
                    some other basis acceptable to the presbytery, with special at-
                    tention to the concerns of G-9.0104.

                    c.   Each elder elected moderator shall be enrolled as a mem-
                    ber of the presbytery for the term of office, whether or not com-
                    missioned by his or her session. Each elder elected an officer
                    (other than moderator), a chairperson of a standing committee,
                    or a member of the council of presbytery may be enrolled as a
                    member of the presbytery for the term of office, whether or not
                    commissioned by his or her session. Each elder elected by a
                    presbytery as executive presbyter, associate executive pres-
                    byter, or other exempt staff position, may be enrolled as a mem-
                    ber of the presbytery for the duration of service in such staff po-
                    sition, whether or not commissioned by his or her session.

G-11.0102   In each presbytery the minimum number of ministers shall be
Minimum   twelve and the minimum number of churches shall likewise be
                    twelve. In an isolated area, upon recommendation of the synod, the
                    General Assembly may permit a presbytery to be organized with

fewer than these minimums, provided that there shall be at least five ministers in each presbytery.

G-11.0103
Responsibilities

The presbytery is responsible for the mission and government of the church throughout its geographical district. It therefore has the responsibility and power

a.   to develop strategy for the mission of the church in its area consistent with G-3.0000;

b.   to coordinate the work of its member churches, guiding them and mobilizing their strength for the most effective witness to the broader community for which it has responsibility;

c.   to initiate mission through a variety of forms in light of the larger strategy of the synod and the General Assembly;

d.   to implement, consistent with G-9.0104, the principles of participation, inclusiveness, and affirmative action in employing its personnel and in establishing the membership of its committees, councils, boards, and other policy-making and policy-recommending bodies, in order to assure fair representation in its decision making and in the election of commissioners to synod and the General Assembly. Its committee on representation shall report directly to the presbytery, and shall be empowered to make recommendations to correct situations of unbalanced representation, including the recommendation that the nominating committee reconsider its nominations;

e.   to counsel with a particular church where the various constituencies of the congregation are not represented on a session;

f.   to provide encouragement, guidance, and resources to its member churches in the areas of leadership development, church officer training, worship, nurture, witness, service, stewardship, equitable compensation, personnel policies, and fair employment practices;

g.   to provide pastoral care for the churches and members of presbytery, visiting sessions and ministers on a regular basis (G-11.0502c);

h.   to organize new churches and to receive and unite churches in consultation with their members. When two or more churches of a presbytery unite, the pastor or pastors of the former churches may continue as or become pastor or pastors of the united church if the uniting churches agree and specify those relationships in the plan of union, with the concurrence of the presbytery;

i.   to divide, dismiss, or dissolve churches in consultation with their members;

j.   to control the location of new churches and of churches desiring to move;

k.   to take special oversight of churches without pastors, including the authority to select, train, examine, and commission lay pastors and may authorize them to administer the Lord's Supper (G-14.0516);

l.   to enter into covenant relationship with those preparing to become ministers of the Word and Sacrament by enrolling them as inquirers, and to receive inquirers as candidates;

m.   to elect elder and minister readers of examinations for candidates for ordination at the request of the Presbyteries' Cooperative Committee on Examinations for Candidates;

n.   to ordain, receive, dismiss, install, remove, and discipline ministers, to plan for the integration of new ministers into the life and work of presbytery, to establish minimum compensation requirements for all pastoral calls (G-14.0506e) and guidelines for compensation and benefits for Certified Christian Educators employed by the churches of the presbytery (G-14.0705b(2)), to provide services of recognition for Certified Christian Educators (G-14.0705b(1)), and to find in order, approve, and record in the presbytery minutes the full terms of all calls, and changes of calls approved by the presbytery;

o.   to establish the pastoral relationship and to dissolve it at the request of one or both of the parties, or when it finds that the church's mission under the Word imperatively demands it;

p.   to designate ministers to work as teachers, evangelists, administrators, chaplains, and in other forms of ministry recognized as appropriate by the presbytery. Such ministers may administer the Sacraments at times and places approved by a governing body, or in conformity to other conditions specified by a governing body. The applicable provisions of W-2.3000, W-2.4000, and W-3.3600 shall be followed;

q.   to receive under its care persons preparing for professional service in the church, and to commission them when appropriate (G-14.0102);

r.   to serve in judicial matters in accordance with the Rules of Discipline;

s.   to assume original jurisdiction in any case in which it determines that a session cannot exercise its authority. Whenever, after a thorough investigation, and after full opportunity to be heard has been accorded to the session in question, the presbytery of jurisdiction shall determine that the session of a particular church is unable or unwilling to manage wisely the affairs of its church, the presbytery may appoint an administrative commission (G-9.0503) with the full power of a session. This commission shall assume original jurisdiction of the existing session, if any, which shall cease to act until such time as the presbytery shall otherwise direct;

t. to maintain regular and continuing relationship to the higher governing bodies of the church, including

(1) electing commissioners to the synod and to the General Assembly and receiving their reports,

(2) seeing that the orders of higher governing bodies are observed and carried out,

(3) proposing to the synod or the General Assembly such measures as may be of common concern to the mission of the whole church;

u. to establish and maintain those ecumenical relationships which will enlarge the life and mission of the church in its district;

v. to establish and superintend the agencies necessary for its work, including a presbytery council, providing for the regular review of the functional relationship between presbytery's structure and its mission. The presbytery may, by its own established rules, assign to its council responsibility for action between meetings of presbytery on such specific areas of its responsibilities as it shall deem appropriate, assign to its committee on ministry those powers specified in G-11.0502h, and assign to its committee on preparation for ministry authority to dismiss candidates and enroll inquirers, with the provision that all such actions be reported to the next stated meeting of the presbytery (G-9.0403, G-14.0507);

w. to establish a nominating committee composed of equal numbers of ministers, laymen, and laywomen (i.e., one third each);

x. to review session minutes and records at least once each year;

y. to consider and act upon requests from congregations for permission to take the actions regarding real property as described in G-8.0000;

z. to authorize specific elders for periods not exceeding one year at a time, to administer or preside at the Lord's Supper in specific circumstances and with proper instruction by presbytery in the doctrine and administration of the Lord's Supper, when it deems it necessary to meet the needs for the administration of the Sacrament of the Lord's Supper that cannot otherwise be met;

aa. to deal with prevailing, emerging, and emergency issues of racism, racial violence, and racial injustices, as well as with any ideology that promotes racial oppression in the church and in the surrounding political and social contexts.

G-11.0200

G-11.0201
Meetings

2. Meetings

The presbytery shall hold stated meetings at least twice each year. The moderator shall call a special meeting at the request, or with the concurrence, of two ministers and two elders, the elders being of different churches. Should the moderator be unable to act, the stated clerk shall, under the same conditions, issue the call. If both moderator and stated clerk are unable to act, any three ministers and three elders, the elders being of different churches, may call a special meeting. The synod may direct the presbytery to convene a special meeting for the transaction of designated business. Notice of a special meeting shall be sent not less than ten days in advance to each minister and to the session of every church. The notice shall set out the purpose of the meeting, and no other business than that listed in the notice shall be transacted.

G-11.0202
Quorum

A quorum of the presbytery shall be any three minister members and the elder members present, provided that at least three churches are represented by elders. The presbytery may fix its own quorum at any higher number.

G-11.0203
Corresponding
Members

Presbyters (ministers of the Word and Sacrament or elders) in good standing in other governing bodies of this church or in any other Christian church, who are present at any meeting of the presbytery, may be invited to sit as corresponding members, with voice but without vote. A presbytery may invite ministers of other presbyteries who are laboring within its bounds to sit as corresponding members with voice but without vote for the period of their service.

G-11.0300

G-11.0301
Participation

3. Other Provisions

In electing members to its council and permanent committees, the presbytery shall adhere to the principle of participation and representation expressed in G-9.0104, et seq.

G-11.0302
Committee on
Representation

The presbytery's committee on representation shall advise presbytery's nominating committee of any need for nominations in particular categories needing increased representation and shall regularly inform the presbytery of its progress toward fair representation of the categories of persons listed in G-4.0403.

G-11.0303
Staff

The presbytery may authorize the administrative staff services of an executive presbyter and other staff as needed. For purposes of coordination, the presbytery shall consult through its council (or other appropriate committee or representative) with the synod (or its council or other committee or representative) concerning the overall mission needs of synod, as well as the need for financial assistance in maintaining presbytery staff services. (G-12.0302) In the employment of all personnel, including administrative staff, the presbytery shall observe the practice of consultation set forth in G-9.0404, and the provisions of the churchwide plan for affirmative action and equal employment opportunity. (G-13.0201b)

G-11.0304
Budget

The presbytery shall have a presbytery general mission budget to support the church's mission within its area. As the presbytery raises and expends these funds, it shall do so in light of the priorities of the whole church. The presbytery shall make its plans and determine its general mission budget after receiving recommendations from the synod and in light of the comprehensive strategy of the whole church as represented in the synod and the General Assembly.

G-11.0305
Records

a. The presbytery shall keep a full and accurate record of its proceedings, which shall be submitted at least once each year to the synod for its general review and control. It shall report to the synod and to the General Assembly every year the condition and progress of the church within its bounds during the year and all important changes which have taken place including ordinations; the receiving, dismissing, and deaths of ministers; and the organizing, uniting, dividing, or dissolving of churches.

Property of
Presbytery

b. Minutes and other official records of the presbytery are the property of the presbytery, and the stated clerk is responsible for their preservation.

G-11.0306
Annual Report

The presbytery shall send annually to the Stated Clerk of the General Assembly lists of its ministers and churches and statistical and other information according to the requirements of the General Assembly.

G-11.0307
Audit

The presbytery shall have a full financial review of all books and records relating to finances once a year by a public accountant or public accounting firm or a committee of church members versed in accounting procedures. Such auditors should not be related to the treasurer (or treasurers). Terminology in this section is meant to provide general guidance and is not intended to require or not require specific audit procedures or practices as understood within the professional accounting community.

G-11.0308
Insurance

The presbytery shall obtain property and liability insurance coverage to protect its facilities, programs, staff, and elected and appointed officers.

G-11.0400

4. **Minister Members**

G-11.0401
Membership of
Ministers

a. Every minister shall ordinarily be a member of the presbytery where his or her work is situated. A minister called to work not under the jurisdiction of a presbytery may apply for reception to the presbytery in which he or she will be resident, or to another presbytery, or retain membership in the presbytery where he or she was formerly a member. The presbytery may grant a minister permission to engage in work which is outside its geographic bounds or which is not under its jurisdiction, but no presbytery shall permit a minister to engage in work which is within the geographic bounds of another presbytery and which is properly within the responsibility of another presbytery without consent of that presbytery. Such permission and consent shall be reviewed and renewed annually. The stated clerk of the presbytery shall inform ministers who seek permission to labor outside the bounds of the presbytery of their membership that they must first seek permission to labor within the bounds of the other presbytery. In January of each year the stated clerk of the presbytery of which the ministers are members shall correspond with those other presbyteries in which such ministers labor, informing them of the ministers' addresses. A minister who is serving as a minister in a church outside the United States may, with the approval of presbytery, accept ministerial membership in that church for the period of such service without affecting his or her membership in the presbytery of this church. (G-11.0410)

Authority to Labor

b.   The authority for granting permission to labor within or outside the bounds of the presbytery may be delegated by presbytery to its council or committee on ministry, with the provision that all such actions be reported to the next stated meeting of the presbytery.

G-11.0402 Minister Seeking Membership

The presbytery, through its appropriate committee, shall examine each minister or candidate who seeks membership in it on his or her Christian faith and views in theology, the Sacraments, and the government of this church, except as provided in G-14.0314. Every minister seeking membership in a presbytery shall have a call to a pastoral relation within the presbytery, or from a governing body or agency as defined in G-11.0410, or be entering a work defined in G-11.0411, for which the receiving presbytery shall give its permission, or shall be honorably retired as defined in G-11.0412.

G-11.0403 Criteria for Ministry of Continuing Members

A presbytery shall determine the ministers of the Word and Sacrament who shall be its continuing members. In making this determination the presbytery shall be guided by written criteria developed by the presbytery for validation of ministries within its bounds. These criteria shall be based upon the description of the nature of ordained office found in G-6.0100 and G-6.0200 and the following standards:

a.   The ministry of continuing members shall be in demonstrable conformity with the mission of God's people in the world as set forth in Holy Scripture, *The Book of Confessions*, and the *Book of Order* of this church.

b.   The ministry shall be one that serves others, aids others, and enables the ministries of others.

c.   The ministry shall give evidence of theologically informed fidelity to God's Word. This will normally require the Master of Divinity degree or its equivalent and the completion of the requirements for ordination set forth in G-14.0402.

d.   The ministry shall be carried on in accountability for its character and conduct to the presbytery and to organizations, agencies, and institutions.

e.   The ministry shall include responsible participation in the deliberations and work of the presbytery and in the worship and service of a congregation.

G-11.0404
Ministers of Other
Denominations:
Reformed Churches

Ministers of other denominations may be received by the presbytery as follows:

a.   Ministers of Reformed churches holding the Presbyterian Order in correspondence with the General Assembly shall, when applying for membership in a presbytery, furnish satisfactory credentials of (1) ordination by a presbytery or classis, (2) present good standing, and (3) dismissal to the particular presbytery. They shall also submit satisfactory evidence of possessing the qualifications of character and scholarship required of candidates of this church and shall be examined by the presbytery in their Christian faith, in theology, and in the system of government of this church, and at the discretion of the presbytery in other subjects, and shall answer in the affirmative questions (1) to (9) contained in G-14.0405b. Such ministers ordained for five or more years shall be exempted by a two-thirds vote of presbytery from some or all of the provisions of G-14.0508a(3). Presbyteries, prior to receiving ministers from other Reformed churches, shall confer with the Stated Clerk of the General Assembly for advice and assistance.

Hold Word and
Sacrament in
Fundamental
Integrity

b.   When a minister of another denomination, which is judged by the presbytery to hold the Word and Sacraments in their fundamental integrity, has evidence of a call to a work properly under the jurisdiction of the presbytery, presents a proper dismissal from the ecclesiastical body to which the minister belongs, including attestation of present good standing, and requests to be received by that presbytery as a minister, the presbytery shall, after the constitutional conditions have been satisfied, recognize the minister's previous ordination to the office of minister upon the expression of the minister's acceptance of the obligation in the ordination vows required of a minister in the Constitution of this church. (G-14.0405)

In
Correspondence
With

c.   A minister of the Word and Sacrament of another denomination in correspondence with the General Assembly, whose ecclesiastical relations have been certified by that denomination, who is serving a Presbyterian congregation in a temporary, noninstalled pastoral relationship (G-14.0513) other than organizing pastor, who has become a minister of a congregation or larger parish composed of denominational units, at least one of which is associated with the Presbyterian Church (U.S.A.), or who has become a minister serving a cooperative specialized ministry in which this church shares the sponsorship, or who has been jointly called to an administrative office by more than one denomination, one of which is this church, or a minister of a church outside the United States that is in correspondence with the General Assembly who is serving in a ministerial capacity in this church, may be enrolled for the period of this service as a member of a presbytery and have temporarily the rights and privileges of membership.

d. A minister of another denomination, with whom the Presbyterian Church (U.S.A.) is in full communion (G-15.0201), may be called, examined, approved (G-14.0508a(1), (4), (5)) and installed as pastor or may serve in another ministerial capacity in this denomination and may be enrolled for the period of this service as a member of a presbytery with the rights and privileges of membership. The minister shall participate in the benefits plan of one of the denominations. If the minister is already participating in one plan, membership in that plan shall be retained. If the minister is not a member of any plan, one or another of the churches' plans shall be chosen by the minister. The congregation or other employing body shall pay the fees, dues, or premiums required by the plan to which the minister belongs.

G-11.0405
Enrollment

When a minister of another denomination seeks membership in a presbytery of this church, that person shall, before being enrolled, furnish the presbytery with satisfactory evidence of having been removed from the roll of ministers of any and all other denominations with which the minister has previously been associated.

G-11.0406
Continuing
Members

The ministers of the Word and Sacrament who are continuing members of a presbytery of the Presbyterian Church (U.S.A.) include active members, members-at-large, and inactive members.

Active Member

a. An active member is a minister of the Word and Sacrament who has been admitted to the presbytery in accordance with G-11.0401, and is now engaged in ministry that complies with all of the criteria in G-11.0403 without exception. An active member may be engaged in a validated ministry within congregations of the church (G-11.0409), in a validated ministry in other service of this church (G-11.0410), in a validated ministry in service beyond the jurisdiction of this church (G-11.0411), or may be honorably retired (G-11.0412). An active member is entitled to take part in the meetings of the presbytery and to speak, vote, and hold office.

Member-at-Large

b. A member-at-large is a minister of the Word and Sacrament who has previously been admitted to the presbytery or another presbytery as an active member, and who now, without intentional abandonment of the exercise of ministry, is no longer engaged in a ministry that complies with all the criteria in G-11.0403. A minister may be designated a member-at-large because he or she is limited in his or her ability to engage in a ministry fulfilling all of the criteria for a validated ministry because of family responsibilities or other individual circumstances which presbytery recognizes as important. A member-at-large shall comply with as many of the criteria in G-11.0403 as possible and shall be encouraged to become a parish associate in a congregation. A member-at-large is entitled to take part in the meetings of the presbytery and to speak, vote, and hold office. The status of each member-at-large may be granted by the presbytery upon the minister's application and shall be reviewed annually.

Inactive Member

c. An inactive member is a minister of the Word and Sacrament who has previously been admitted to the presbytery or another presbytery as an active member, but is now voluntarily engaged in an occupation that does not comply with all of the criteria in G-11.0403. The presbytery may, at the minister's request or on its own initiative after notifying the minister in person or by certified mail at the last known address, determine that the minister's category of membership is that of inactive member. An inactive member is not entitled to take part in the meetings of the presbytery or to speak, vote, hold office, or serve on committees, except that the inactive member may speak when the matter under consideration concerns that minister. The continued status of each inactive member shall be reviewed annually up to three years. If at the end of three years the minister has not been restored to active membership or membership-at-large, the presbytery shall delete that person's name from the appropriate roll of presbytery and may give that person a certificate of membership to a particular church. (G-11.0414)

G-11.0407
Rolls

The stated clerk shall maintain four rolls, one listing the names of all the ministers of the Word and Sacrament who are continuing members of the presbytery and who are active members, one listing the names of all the ministers of the Word and Sacrament who are continuing members of the presbytery and who are members-at-large, one listing the names of all the ministers of the Word and Sacrament who are continuing members of the presbytery and who are inactive members, one listing all Certified Christian Educators within the bounds of the presbytery who are entitled to the privilege of the floor with voice at all presbytery meetings, and a fifth roll listing those who have been deleted from the other rolls. On or before December 31 of each year, the presbytery shall determine the category of membership of each continuing member in accordance with the relevant sections of this chapter and cause appropriate record of such determination to be made.

G-11.0408
Validated
Ministries

A minister of the Word and Sacrament who is an active member of presbytery may be engaged (1) in a validated ministry within congregations of this church, (2) in a validated ministry in other service of this church, (3) in a validated ministry in service beyond the jurisdiction of this church, or may be (4) honorably retired.

G-11.0409
Service in
Congregations of
This Church

An active member engaged in a validated ministry within congregations of this church shall serve a particular church or churches as pastor, co-pastor, associate pastor, assistant pastor, stated supply, temporary supply, interim pastor, or interim associate pastor, as provided in G-6.0202 and G-14.0513.

G-11.0410
In Other Service
of This Church

An active member engaged in a validated ministry in other service of this church shall serve as a staff member of a presbytery, a synod, or the General Assembly of this church or of an organization related to one of these governing bodies; as a minister serving an organization sponsored by two or more denominations, one of which is this church, such as a federated church, a specialized ministry, an administrative office, or an interdenominational agency; as a partner in mission in connection with a church outside the United States of America. Before entering upon such service, the minister shall request and obtain the approval of the presbytery of membership. Changes in the terms of the call or dissolution of the relationship shall be reported to the presbytery.

G-11.0411
In Service
Beyond the
Jurisdiction of the
Church

An active member engaged in a validated ministry in service beyond the jurisdiction of the church may be engaged in a ministerial calling consonant with the mission of the presbytery in an organization, agency, or institution in which this church has no official participation or may serve temporarily as pastor or in some other capacity in another denomination, and may, with the approval of presbytery, accept ministerial membership in that church for the period of such service without forfeiting his or her membership in the Presbyterian Church (U.S.A.) presbytery in which he or she holds membership. Before entering upon such service the minister shall request permission of the presbytery of membership. The committee on ministry of the presbytery shall make a thorough review of the proposed ministerial function and report its recommendations to the presbytery. The committee shall determine and report whether the service complies with all of the criteria enumerated in G-11.0403, without exception. If the presbytery grants the permission requested, such permission shall be subject to review and renewal annually.

G-11.0412
Honorably
Retired

a.   A presbytery may designate an active minister as an honorably retired minister if that minister is in good and regular standing, or is granted the status of being in good and regular standing, at the time the minister is designated as an honorably retired minister. The status of being an honorably retired minister may be granted because of physical or mental disability, or age. The procedure for electing a new pastor is set out in G-14.0502. Presbytery may also grant the status of being an honorably retired minister to a minister member who has been granted retirement by an agency described in G-11.0410 or G-11.0411, or upon the completion of twenty years of cumulative service as an active and (or) at-large member.

Presbytery Membership of Honorably Retired Ministers

b. Honorably retired ministers are encouraged to transfer their membership to the presbytery in which they live and the presbytery is encouraged to receive them. If they are active in presbytery, additional elders may be elected to keep a proper balance between ministers and lay persons at the presbytery meetings. (G-11.0101b) Presbyteries should encourage honorably retired ministers to use their experience and skills in creative and meaningful ways. Those who are able and willing to reengage in ministry and service to others should relate to a particular church or presbytery. For those who do not or cannot, the presbytery should provide nurture and support.

G-11.0413 Members-at-Large and Inactive Members

Members-at-large and inactive members remain under the care, oversight, and discipline of the presbytery. They may be transferred in their current category of membership to another presbytery with the permission of both presbyteries. All of the minister's records shall be transmitted to the receiving presbytery. The committee on ministry shall confer with each member-at-large and inactive member annually and make a recommendation to the presbytery as to whether the member should continue in the present category, be assigned another category, or be released from the exercise of ordained office. Such action may be initiated by the presbytery or at the request of the minister.

G-11.0414 Release from the Exercise of Ordained Office

a. If a minister concerning whom no inquiry has been initiated pursuant to D-10.0102 and D-10.0201, against whom no charges have been filed, and who otherwise is in good standing, shall make application to be released from the exercise of the ordained ministry, the presbytery shall delete that person's name from the appropriate roll of presbytery and give that person a certificate of membership to a particular church. **In addition, when a presbytery releases a minister under G-11.0406c or G-11.0413, the presbytery shall delete that person's name from the appropriate roll of presbytery and may give that person a certificate of membership to a particular church.** The presbytery shall retain a roll of persons so deleted with date of deletions, date of ordination, and place of ordination. No judgment of failure on the part of the minister is implied in this action.

Discontinuance of Functions

b. Release from the exercise of the ordained office of a minister of the Word and Sacrament requires a discontinuance of all functions of that office. The designations reverend, minister, pastor, or other similar term shall not be used. The status of a minister who has been so released shall be the same as any church member.

Desire to Be Restored

c.   Should a person released under this section later desire to be restored to continuing membership in presbytery, that person shall make application to the presbytery that granted the release, and upon approval of that presbytery, the reaffirmation of ordination vows, and resumption of a ministry that qualifies that person for continuing membership in presbytery, the person shall be restored to the exercise of the ordained office without reordination.

G-11.0415
Minister to Be Placed on Inactive Roll

a.   If a minister shall be absent from the sessions of the presbytery of membership for a period of one year and shall neglect to report to that presbytery concerning residence and work, the presbytery, after making an effort to locate and counsel with the minister, shall then, without prejudice to the minister, place that minister's name on the inactive roll.

Within Other Bounds

b.   A minister of the Word and Sacrament who has received permission to labor outside the bounds of the presbytery of membership but has not received permission to labor within the bounds of the presbytery of labor shall, after a period of two years, be placed on the inactive roll.

G-11.0416
Minister Joining Another Denomination

When a minister of this church continues or accepts membership of any character in another denomination, except as provided in G-11.0411, the presbytery shall record the fact, delete the minister's name from the roll, and take such other action of an administrative character as may be required by the Constitution.

G-11.0500

5.   **Committee on Ministry**

G-11.0501
Nature and Membership

a.   Each presbytery shall elect a committee on ministry to serve as pastor and counselor to the ministers of the presbytery, to facilitate the relations between congregations, ministers, and the presbytery, and to settle difficulties on behalf of presbytery when possible and expedient.

Membership and Quorum

b.   This committee shall consist of equal numbers of elders and ministers with a membership of at least six. Its quorum shall be set by presbytery and shall be at least a majority of the membership of the committee. Membership shall be for a term of three years and replacement of a member whose term has not expired shall be for the remainder of that term. Members shall be ineligible to serve more than two consecutive terms or consecutive portions of terms.

The committee shall serve the presbytery in the following ways:

G-11.0502
Responsibilities

a.   It shall visit regularly and consult with each minister of the presbytery. It shall report to the presbytery annually the type of work in which each minister of the presbytery is engaged. It shall require an annual report from every minister performing work which is not under the jurisdiction of the presbytery or a higher governing body of the church.

b.   It shall make recommendations to presbytery regarding calls for the services of its ministers. Every call for the services of a minister or candidate in a pastoral relationship shall be placed in its hands and presented by it to the presbytery, with a report as to the call being in order and recommendation as to whether the call shall be placed in the hands of the minister or candidate. Every request by a minister or candidate for the presbytery's approval of a task appropriate to the ministry, though not a pastoral relationship to a particular church, shall be made by the minister or candidate through the committee and shall be reported by it to the presbytery with recommendation for presbytery's action.

c.   It shall visit with each session of the presbytery at least once every three years, discussing with them the mission and ministry of the particular church and encouraging the full participation of each session and congregation in the life and work of presbytery and of the larger church. (W-1.4002)

d.   It shall counsel with churches regarding calls for permanent pastoral relations, visiting and counseling with every committee elected to nominate a pastor or associate pastor. It shall advise with the committee regarding the merits, availability, and suitability of any candidate or minister whose name is contemplated for nomination to the congregation, and shall have the privilege of suggesting names to the committee. No call to a permanent pastoral relationship shall be in order for consideration by the presbytery unless the church has received and considered the committee's counsel before action is taken to issue a call. (G-14.0502) A call to a permanent pastoral relationship shall not be issued until it has been approved by the presbytery. In the case of a church receiving aid in supporting a pastor, it shall confer with both the church and that agency of presbytery charged with arranging such aid before it shall recommend to the presbytery that a call to such a church be placed in the hands of a minister. The proper agency of the presbytery shall present to the committee a statement of the presbytery's anticipated support of a pastor, which shall be attached to the call of the church.

e.   It shall counsel with churches regarding the advisability of calling a designated pastor as defined in G-14.0501.

f.   It shall counsel with sessions regarding stated supplies, interim pastors, interim co-pastors, interim associate pastors, and temporary supplies when a church is without a pastor, and it shall provide lists of pastors, commissioned lay pastors, and qualified lay persons who have been trained and commissioned by the presbytery to supply vacant pulpits. Concurrence of the presbytery through its committee on ministry is required when a session invites an interim pastor, interim co-pastor, or interim associate pastor as provided for in G-14.0513b and c.

g.   It shall provide for the implementation of equal opportunity employment for ministers and candidates without regard to race, ethnic origin, sex, age, marital status, or disability. In the case of each call, it shall report to the presbytery the steps in this implementation taken by the calling group.

h.   It may be given authority by the presbytery to find in order calls issued by churches, to approve and present calls for services of ministers, to approve the examination of ministers transferring from other presbyteries required by G-11.0402, to dissolve the pastoral relationship in cases where the congregation and pastor concur, to grant permission to labor within or outside the bounds of the presbytery, and to dismiss ministers to other presbyteries, with the provision that all such actions be reported to the next stated meeting of the presbytery. (G-9.0403, G-14.0507)

i.   It shall serve as an instrument of presbytery for promoting the peace and harmony of the churches, especially in regard to matters arising out of the relations between ministers and churches. Its purpose shall be to mediate differences and reconcile persons, to the end that the difficulties may be corrected by the session of the church if possible, that the welfare of the particular church may be strengthened, that the unity of the body of Christ may be made manifest.

j.   It shall exercise wise discretion in determining when to take cognizance of information concerning difficulties within a church, proceeding with the following steps:

(1) It may take the initiative to bring the information which has come to it to the attention of the session of the church involved, counseling with the session as to the appropriate actions to be taken in correcting the reported difficulties.

(2) It may offer its help as a mediator in case the session either finds itself unable to settle the problems peaceably or takes no steps toward settlement.

(3) It may act to correct the difficulties if requested to do so by the parties concerned, or if this authority is granted by the presbytery for the specific case. When so doing, the committee shall always hold hearings which afford procedural safeguards as in cases of process, following the procedures outlined in the Rules of Discipline.

G-11.0503
Open
Communication
          The committee shall be open to communication at all times with the ministers, elders who are members of sessions, sessions of the presbytery, and Certified Christian Educators within the bounds of the presbytery.

G-11.0504
Synod and
General
Assembly
Agencies

The presbytery's committee on ministry may look to synod and the General Assembly for information and assistance in the matter of ministers and pastoral relations. Synods shall create the necessary agency to coordinate the work of presbytery committees. The General Assembly shall create the necessary agency to facilitate and support the work of the presbyteries and the synods in this matter.

G-12.0000   **CHAPTER XII. THE SYNOD**

G-12.0100

1. General

G-12.0101
Membership

Synod is the unit of the church's life and mission which consists of not fewer than three presbyteries within a specific geographic region. When a synod meets it shall be composed of commissioners elected by the presbyteries. The synod shall determine, with the consent of a majority of its presbyteries, the basis of election and the ratio of commissioners to members represented in the presbyteries, as well as its method to fulfill the principles of participation and representation found in G-9.0104 and G-9.0105. The commissioners from each presbytery shall be divided equally between elders and ministers of the Word and Sacrament. Each person elected moderator shall be enrolled as a member of the synod until a successor is elected and installed, and then shall be enrolled as a corresponding member of the synod.

G-12.0102
Responsibilities

Synod is the intermediate governmental unit responsible for the mission of the church throughout its region. It therefore has the responsibility and power

a. to develop, in conjunction with its presbyteries, a broad strategy for the mission of the church within its bounds in accord with G-3.0000;

b. to initiate mission through a variety of forms in light of the larger strategy of the General Assembly;

c. to develop, in conjunction with its presbyteries, joint plans and objectives for the fulfillment of mission, providing encouragement and guidance to its presbyteries and overseeing their work;

d. to implement, consistent with G-9.0104, the principles of participation and inclusiveness in employing its personnel and in establishing the membership of its committees, councils, boards, and other policy-making and policy-recommending bodies, in order to ensure fair representation in its decision making;

e. to develop and provide resources as needed to facilitate the mission of its presbyteries, as well as guidelines and criteria for evaluation;

f. to consult with its member presbyteries with regard to their general mission budgets, the establishment of administrative staff positions, equitable compensation, personnel policies, and fair employment practices;

g. to coordinate the work of presbyteries' committees on ministry and assist its member presbyteries in matters related to the calling, ordaining, and placement of ministers;

h.   to facilitate communication among its presbyteries and between its presbyteries and the General Assembly;

i.   to facilitate joint action in mission with other denominations and agencies in its region;

j.   to provide services and programs for presbyteries, sessions, congregations, and members within its area that can be performed more effectively from a broad regional base;

k.   to organize new presbyteries and to divide, unite, or otherwise combine presbyteries or portions of presbyteries previously existing, subject to the approval of the General Assembly;

l.   to serve in judicial matters in accordance with the Rules of Discipline;

m.   to warn or bear witness against error in doctrine or immorality in practice in the area of its jurisdiction;

n.   to review the records of its presbyteries and to take care that they observe the Constitution of the church;

o.   to maintain regular and continuing relationship to the General Assembly, including

(1)   seeing that the orders and instructions of the General Assembly are observed and carried out,

(2)   proposing to the General Assembly such measures as may be of common concern to the mission of the whole church;

p.   to establish and maintain those ecumenical relationships which will enlarge the life and mission of the church in its region;

q.   to provide a system of administrative services to fulfill its objectives and programs;

r.   to establish and superintend the agencies and task forces necessary for its work, including a synod council when the synod deems one is necessary to provide for the regular review of the functional relationship between synod's structure and its mission;

s.   to establish a nominating committee composed of equal numbers of ministers, laywomen, and laymen (i.e., one third each). (G-9.0801, G-11.0501, G-12.0102d, G-13.0111, G-13.0202)

t.   to deal with prevailing, emerging, and emergency issues of racism, racial violence, and racial injustices, as well as with any ideology that promotes racial oppression in the church and in the surrounding political and social contexts.

G-12.0200

G-12.0201
Meetings

2.   **Meetings**

The synod shall hold a stated meeting at least biennially. The moderator shall call a special meeting at the request or with the concurrence of ten ministers and ten elders, representing at least three presbyteries, all of whom must have been commissioners to the last preceding stated meeting of the synod. Should the moderator be unable to act, the stated clerk shall, under the same conditions, issue the call. If both the moderator and the stated clerk are unable to act, the most recent moderator shall, under the same conditions, issue the call. The General Assembly may direct the synod to convene a special meeting for the transaction of designated business. Commissioners to the special meeting shall be the commissioners elected to the last preceding stated meeting of the synod or their alternates. A presbytery may, however, elect a commissioner or alternate to replace one who has died or changed presbytery membership. Notice of a special meeting shall be sent not less than fifteen days in advance to each commissioner elected to the last preceding stated meeting of the synod and to the stated clerk of each presbytery. The notice shall set out the purpose of the meeting and no other business than that listed in the notice shall be transacted.

G-12.0202
Quorum

A quorum of the synod shall be twenty commissioners, at least ten of whom shall be elders and at least ten of whom shall be ministers representing at least three presbyteries, or three quarters of the commissioners eligible to serve at a meeting of the synod representing at least three presbyteries, whichever is the lesser number. The synod may fix its own quorum at any higher number.

G-12.0203
Corresponding
Members

Presbyters in good standing in other governing bodies of this church or in any other Christian church, who are present at any meeting of the synod, may be invited by the synod to sit as corresponding members, with voice but without vote.

G-12.0204
Participation

Each presbytery shall have a part in the synod's responsibilities and service through its elected commissioners in the synod, and through the membership of at least one elder or minister from each presbytery, nominated by the presbytery and elected by the synod, on the synod council when there is a council and, where feasible, on each permanent committee of the synod. The synod may provide that the members from the presbytery on the council and permanent committees shall alternate, with a minister succeeding an elder and vice versa. The synod's nominating committee shall coordinate this process, keeping in mind the need for presbytery representatives and members from the church at large, and seeing that adherence is given to the principles of participation and representation expressed in G-9.0104.

G-12.0300

3. Other Provisions

G-12.0301
Committee on
Representation

Each synod shall establish a committee on representation, as required by G-9.0105, which shall advise synod's nominating committee of any need for nominations in particular categories needing increased representation. The committee on representation shall report at least biennially to synod progress toward fair representation of the categories of persons listed in G-4.0403.

G-12.0302
Staff

The synod may authorize the administrative staff services of a synod executive and may establish other staff positions as needed. The executive shall be nominated to the synod by its council or by a special representative nominating committee elected for that purpose. In the employment of all personnel, including administrative staff, the synod shall observe the principles of fair representation and consultation set forth in G-9.0404, and the provisions of the churchwide plan for equal employment opportunity and affirmative action. (G-13.0201b) The synod may authorize synod administrative staff services for a presbytery at the request of the presbytery. (G-11.0303)

G-12.0303
General Mission
Budget

The synod shall have a synod general mission budget to support the church's mission within its region. As the synod raises and expends those funds, it shall do so in the light of the priorities of the whole church. The synod shall make its plans and determine its general mission budget after receiving recommendations from the General Assembly and in light of the comprehensive strategy of the whole church.

G-12.0304
Records

The synod shall keep a full and accurate record of its proceedings which shall be submitted to the next succeeding meeting of the General Assembly for its general review and control. It shall report to the General Assembly the number of its presbyteries and, in general, all important changes that have occurred within its bounds.

G-12.0305
Audit

The synod shall have a full financial review of all books and records relating to finances once a year by a public accountant or public accounting firm. Such auditors should not be related to the treasurer (or treasurers). Terminology in this section is meant to provide general guidance and is not intended to require or not require specific audit procedures or practices as understood within the professional accounting community.

G-12.0306
Insurance

The synod shall obtain property and liability insurance to protect its facilities, programs, staff, and elected and appointed officers.

G-13.0000   **CHAPTER XIII. THE GENERAL ASSEMBLY**

G-13.0100   **1. The General Assembly**

G-13.0101   The General Assembly is the highest governing body of this
Definition   church and is representative of the unity of the synods, presbyter-
                   ies, sessions, and congregations of the Presbyterian Church
                   (U.S.A.).

G-13.0102   The General Assembly shall consist of equal numbers of el-
Membership   ders and ministers from each presbytery, in the following propor-
                   tion: Each presbytery consisting of not more than 10,000 members
                   shall elect one elder and one minister; and each presbytery con-
                   sisting of more than 10,000 members shall elect one elder and one
                   minister for each additional 10,000 members, or for each additional
                   fractional number of members not less than 5,000; and these per-
                   sons, so elected, shall be called commissioners to the General As-
                   sembly. Each person elected Moderator shall be enrolled as a mem-
                   ber of the General Assembly until a successor is elected and
                   installed, and then shall be enrolled as a corresponding member of
                   the General Assembly.

G-13.0103   The General Assembly constitutes the bond of union, commu-
Responsibilities   nity, and mission among all its congregations and governing bod-
                   ies. It therefore has the responsibility and power

                   a.   to set priorities for the work of the church in keeping
                   with the church's mission under Christ as described in
                   G-3.0000;

                   b.   to develop overall objectives for mission and a compre-
                   hensive strategy to guide the church at every level of its life;

                   c.   to provide the essential program functions that are appro-
                   priate for overall balance and diversity within the mission of
                   the church;

                   d.   to establish and administer national and worldwide min-
                   istries of witness, service, growth, and development;

                   e.   to provide a system of administrative services to fulfill its
                   objectives and program;

                   f.   to provide services for the whole church that can be per-
                   formed more effectively from a national base;

                   g.   to establish and maintain an office of the General As-
                   sembly;

                   h.   to establish and superintend the agencies and task forces
                   necessary for its work, including a General Assembly Council,
                   providing for the regular review of the functional relationship
                   between the General Assembly's structure and its mission;

i.   to adopt the comprehensive annual budget of the General Assembly, providing full information to the whole church of its decision in such matters;

j.   to provide for communication within the church;

k.   to oversee the work of the synods and to facilitate their participation in the mission of the church;

l.   to review the records of the synods and to take care that they observe the Constitution of the church;

m. to organize new synods and to divide, unite, or otherwise combine synods or portions of synods previously existing;

n.   to approve the organization, division, uniting, or combining of presbyteries or portions of presbyteries by synods;

o.   to serve in judicial matters in accordance with the Rules of Discipline;

p.   to warn or bear witness against error in doctrine or immorality in practice in or outside the church;

q.   to decide controversies brought before it and to give advice and instruction in cases submitted to it, in conformity with the Constitution;

r.   to provide authoritative interpretation of the *Book of Order* which shall be binding on the governing bodies of the church when rendered in accord with G-13.0112 or through a decision of the Permanent Judicial Commission in a remedial or disciplinary case. The most recent interpretation of a provision of the *Book of Order* shall be binding;

s.   to establish and maintain those ecumenical relationships that will enlarge the life and mission of the church;

t.   to correspond with other churches;

u.   to receive under its jurisdiction, with the consent of two thirds of the presbyteries, other ecclesiastical bodies whose life is consistent with the faith and order of this church;

v.   to authorize synods to exercise similar power in receiving ecclesiastical bodies suited to become constituents of those governing bodies and lying within their geographic bounds;

w.   to unite with other churches in accordance with the procedures set forth in this Constitution. (G-15.0300)

x.   to review the work of the Office of the General Assembly in consultation with the Stated Clerk of the General Assembly.

G-13.0104
Meetings

The General Assembly shall hold a stated meeting at least biennially. The Moderator shall call a special meeting at the request or with the concurrence of twenty-five elders and twenty-five ministers, representing at least fifteen presbyteries, under the jurisdiction of at least five synods, all of whom must have been commissioners to the last preceding stated meeting of the General Assembly. Should the Moderator be unable to act, the Stated Clerk shall, under the same conditions, issue the call. If both the Moderator and the Stated Clerk are unable to act, the most recent Moderator shall, under the same conditions, issue the call. Commissioners to the special meeting shall be the commissioners elected to the last preceding stated meeting of the General Assembly or their alternates. A presbytery may, however, elect a commissioner or alternate instead of one who has died or changed presbytery membership. Notice of a special meeting shall be sent not less than sixty days in advance to each commissioner elected to the last preceding stated meeting of the General Assembly and to the stated clerk of each presbytery. The notice shall set out the purpose of the meeting and no other business than that listed in the notice shall be transacted.

G-13.0105
Quorum

A quorum of the General Assembly shall be one hundred commissioners, fifty of whom shall be elders and fifty of whom shall be ministers, representing presbyteries of at least one fourth of its synods.

G-13.0106
Corresponding Members

The General Assembly may by its own rules determine whom it will invite to sit as corresponding members.

G-13.0107
Synod Participation

Each synod shall have part in the General Assembly's mission structure through the membership of at least one elder or minister from each synod, proposed for nomination by the synod after consultation with the General Assembly Nominating Committee, and elected by the General Assembly, on the General Assembly Council, and on each permanent committee of the General Assembly. The General Assembly Nominating Committee shall coordinate this process, keeping in mind the need for synod representatives and members-at-large, and seeing that special attention is given to the principles of participation and representation expressed in G-9.0104, G-13.0111, and G-13.0202.

G-13.0108
Committee on Representation

The General Assembly shall establish a permanent Committee on Representation as required by G-9.0105, which shall advise the General Assembly Nominating Committee of any need for nominations in particular categories needing increased representation. The Committee on Representation shall report to each meeting of the General Assembly (other than special or adjourned meetings) regarding progress toward fair representation of the categories of persons listed in G-4.0403.

G-13.0109
Staff

Executive or administrative staff positions of the agencies of the General Assembly shall be established and filled in accordance with the provisions of G-9.0404, G-9.0703, and G-9.0704, and those of the churchwide plan for equal employment opportunity. (G-13.0201b) Provision shall be made for the regular review of each administrative staff member.

G-13.0110
Records

The General Assembly shall keep a full and accurate record of its proceedings.

G-13.0111
General
Assembly
Nominating
Committee

a.   To ensure careful nomination of members of such boards, agencies, and committees as the General Assembly shall from time to time designate, the General Assembly Nominating Committee shall propose nominees to the General Assembly for such bodies. Consideration shall be given to the nomination of equal numbers of ministers (both women and men), laymen, and laywomen. The committee shall consist of members equal in number to the synods of the church, each member resident in a different synod, and members distributed so that there are one third ministers (both women and men), one third laymen, and one third laywomen. (G-9.0801, G-11.0501, G-12.0102d, G-13.0202) Members shall be appointed for a term of five years, and the terms shall be so arranged as to provide that one fifth of the members shall complete their service at the conclusion of each regular meeting of the General Assembly. Within thirty days prior to the regular meeting of the General Assembly, the Moderator of the preceding General Assembly shall appoint persons to fill the vacancies occurring at the adjournment of the ensuing General Assembly. The Moderator shall also appoint persons to fill vacancies during the year caused by death, resignation, or inability to act. These appointments shall be in consultation with the synod through its regular nominating process and shall reflect the commitment of the inclusive policies of the General Assembly. Such appointments shall be limited to the unexpired portion of the term of the original appointee and shall not prevent appointment of the same person to a full term. No person who has served a full term of five years on the committee shall be eligible for reappointment or for appointment or nomination to a body for which the committee has submitted nominations to the General Assembly during that person's term until four years have passed since the expiration of the person's term on the committee.

Election of
Officers

b.   The committee shall elect its own officers at the last meeting prior to the regular meeting of the General Assembly. The existence of this committee shall not limit or abridge the right of any commissioner to the General Assembly to nominate any eligible person in addition to the nominees presented by the committee.

G-13.0112
Advisory
Committee on the
Constitution

a.   The General Assembly shall establish an Advisory Committee on the Constitution composed of nine persons, ministers and elders in numbers as nearly equal as possible. The Stated Clerk of the General Assembly shall be a member ex officio without vote. The nine voting members shall be former members of the Permanent Judicial Commission of the General Assembly, stated clerks or former stated clerks of synods or presbyteries, or other qualified persons with knowledge of and experience with the Constitution and polity of the church. Voting members shall be nominated by the General Assembly Nominating Committee and elected by the General Assembly and shall serve terms of three years in three classes. Members shall be eligible to serve not more than two successive terms.

Meet at Least Annually

b. The Advisory Committee on the Constitution shall meet at least annually in time to submit its report and recommendations no later than sixty days prior to the convening of the next session of the General Assembly.

Questions 120 Days Prior to General Assembly

c. All questions requiring an interpretation by the General Assembly of the *Book of Order* arising from governing bodies of the church or from individuals shall be communicated in writing to the Stated Clerk of the General Assembly no later than 120 days prior to the convening of the next session of the General Assembly.

Pending Before Judicial Commissions

d. The Stated Clerk shall refer all such questions of interpretation to the Advisory Committee on the Constitution, except those pertaining to matters pending before a judicial commission. The Advisory Committee shall report its findings to the General Assembly along with its recommendations. Such recommendations may include proposals for constitutional change. The General Assembly shall vote on the recommendations, and may amend or decline to approve them.

At General Assembly

e. At least three members of the Advisory Committee on the Constitution, appointed by the moderator of the committee, shall be present at the session of the General Assembly. All items introduced as new business that touch upon constitutional matters, including requesting rulings by the Moderator on questions of order involving constitutional matters, shall be referred in writing to these persons. They shall act as the full committee and shall consider each matter referred to them and make recommendations directly to the General Assembly through the Moderator.

G-13.0200

G-13.0201 Responsibilities

2. General Assembly Council

The General Assembly shall create an Assembly Council which shall have the following responsibilities:

a. to cultivate and promote the spiritual welfare of the whole church;

b. to institute and coordinate a churchwide plan for equal employment opportunity and affirmative action for members of racial ethnic groups, for women, for various age groups, for persons regardless of marital condition (married, single, widowed, or divorced), and for persons with disabilities;

c. to engage in churchwide planning to propose, for General Assembly determination, the mission directions, goals, objectives, and priorities of the church;

d.   to coordinate the work of General Assembly agencies and bodies, synods and presbyteries, in light of these mission directions, goals, objectives, and priorities;

e.   to review the work of General Assembly agencies and bodies in light of General Assembly mission directions, goals, objectives, and priorities;

f.   to prepare and submit a comprehensive budget to the General Assembly in accordance with the provisions of G-9.0404b;

g.   to correspond or consult with presbyteries, synods, and their councils in matters relating to churchwide planning, budget development, and the coordination of the work of the church;

h.   to act, in matters of administrative staff, with synod councils and General Assembly agencies, as provided in G-9.0701, G-9.0702, and G-9.0703;

i.   to consult with the synods with regard to equitable compensation, personnel policies, and fair employment practices;

j.   [This section was stricken by action of the 206th General Assembly (1994).]

k.   to act in those specific matters assigned to the General Assembly Council by the General Assembly or this Constitution, acting always according to previously enacted General Assembly policies, reporting fully to each subsequent General Assembly its actions;

l.   to perform such additional responsibilities and duties as may be assigned by the General Assembly.

G-13.0202
Membership

The membership, terms of office, and officers of the General Assembly Council shall be governed by Articles 5.1, 5.2, and 5.3 of the Articles of Agreement until the end of the respective applicability periods specified in those Articles, at which times the following provisions shall commence taking effect automatically, in stages or phases consistent with the provisions of such Articles:

Voting Members

a.   The General Assembly Council shall consist of the following voting members, each of whom shall be an active member of a congregation, or a continuing member of a presbytery, of the Presbyterian Church (U.S.A.):

(1) The Moderator of the General Assembly and the Moderator's two most recent living predecessors.

(2) One (1) member proposed for nomination by each synod, after consultation with the General Assembly Nominating Committee in order to ensure inclusiveness and needed skills, elected by the General Assembly for a three-year term and eligible for one additional term.

(3) One (1) member proposed for nomination by each of those presbyteries constituting the number of presbyteries established in the Manual of Operations of the General Assembly Council as approved by the General Assembly, after consultation with the General Assembly Nominating Committee in order to ensure inclusiveness and needed skills, elected by the General Assembly for a three-year term and eligible for one additional term. Presbyteries chosen to propose nominations will be selected on a rotation system to be established by the General Assembly Nominating Committee.

(4) The number of members-at-large constituting the members-at-large established in the Manual of Operations of the General Assembly Council as approved by the General Assembly nominated by the General Assembly Nominating Committee, elected by the General Assembly for a three-year term, and eligible for one additional term.

(5) Two (2) youth/young adult members, younger than twenty-six years of age when elected, nominated by the General Assembly for a three-year term and eligible for an additional term.

(6) The moderator of Presbyterian Women.

Advisory Members

b. In addition to the voting members, the General Assembly Council shall include the following advisory members, who shall have the privilege of the floor but not the right to vote:

(1) Four (4) Ecumenical Advisory Members from other churches in the United States and from partner churches in other countries, nominated by the General Assembly Nominating Committee on recommendation of the coordinating body for ecumenical involvement and elected by the General Assembly for a one-year term, with eligibility for two additional one-year terms. However, the General Assembly, on the recommendation of the General Assembly Council, may, from time to time, increase or decrease the number of Ecumenical Advisory Members.

(2) [This section was stricken by action of the 206th General Assembly (1994).]

Corresponding Members

c. The Stated Clerk of the General Assembly and the Executive Director of the General Assembly Council shall be corresponding members of the General Assembly Council and have the right to speak but not vote; and the General Assembly Council may designate other persons to function in the same manner.

Nominating Committee of General Assembly and

d. In the nominating process, the General Assembly Nominating Committee shall consult with the General Assembly Council to identify needed skills, and shall provide for diversity and inclusiveness in accordance with G-4.0403. It will maintain a goal of at least twenty percent racial ethnic membership for the General Assembly Council. It will also follow the provisions of G-9.0104, G-9.0105, and G-13.0111 and shall ensure that, exclusive of the Moderator and predecessor Moderators, one third of the members are ministers of the Word and Sacrament (both women and men), one third laymen, and one third laywomen. The committee will also provide that members be nominated in such a manner as to provide three classes of approximately equal size. Any vacancy occurring during a term shall be filled pursuant to General Assembly policies.

Chair, Vice-Chair, Recording Secretary

e. The General Assembly Council shall elect annually its chair and vice-chair from among its voting members. The Stated Clerk of the General Assembly shall be the Recording Secretary of the General Assembly Council.

G-13.0203
Manual of
Operations

The council shall develop, in consultation with the synods, a manual of operations that shall include design for administrative staff and provisions for size, and for specific representation of council membership, providing for diversity and inclusiveness. (G-9.0104) The manual shall be approved by the General Assembly.

G-14.0000

CHAPTER XIV. ORDINATION, CERTIFICATION, AND COMMISSIONING

G-14.0100

G-14.0101
Ordination

1. Ordination for Church Office

The persons elected by the church to service in the offices of the church (G-6.0000) shall be ordained to these offices by the church. Ordination is the act by which the church sets apart persons to be presbyters (ministers of the Word and Sacrament or elders) or deacons, and is accompanied with prayer and the laying on of hands. Ordination to the office of minister of the Word and Sacrament is an act of the presbytery. Ordination to the offices of elder and deacon is an act of the session, except in the case of the organization of a new church. (G-7.0202)

G-14.0102
Commissioning

Other persons called to perform special services in the church or in the world may be commissioned by the appropriate governing body of the church through a service of dedication.

G-14.0103
Servant Style

The purpose and pattern of leadership in the church in all its forms of ministry shall be understood not in terms of power but of service, after the manner of the servant ministry of Jesus Christ.

G-14.0200

G-14.0201
Election
Provisions

2. Electing and Ordaining Elders and Deacons

Every congregation shall elect men and women from among its active members, giving fair representation to persons of all ages and of all racial ethnic members and persons with disabilities who are members of that congregation, to the office of elder and to the office of deacon, or either of them, in the mode most approved and in use in that congregation, subject, however, to the following provisions:

Terms

a.   No elder or deacon on a board of deacons shall be elected for a term of more than three years, nor shall an elder or deacon on a board of deacons serve for consecutive terms, either full or partial, aggregating more than six years. An elder or deacon having served a total of six years shall be ineligible for reelection to the same board for a period of at least one year. A particular church may provide for a period of ineligibility after one full term. There shall always be no fewer than two and no more than three classes of elders in the session and no fewer than two and no more than three classes of deacons on the board of deacons if the congregation chooses to have deacons. The classes shall be as nearly equal in number as possible, of which only one shall expire each year. Terms shall ordinarily be for two years if there are two classes of elders and/or deacons, and for three years, if there are three classes of elders and/or deacons, except when it is necessary to elect some elders or deacons for shorter terms in order to equalize the numbers in the classes or to fill vacancies, provided, however, a congregation may by vote in a congregational meeting choose to elect one or more persons under twenty-five years of age to the office of elder or deacon, to serve on the session or board of deacons for a term of one, two, or three years. All other factors of election, ordination, and service shall apply to such elders or deacons. Terms of elders or deacons shall expire when their successors have been ordained and installed.

Nominations

b.   Nominations shall be made by a representative nominating committee of active members of the church, which shall itself include both women and men, giving fair representation to persons of all age groups and of all racial ethnic members and persons with disabilities who are members of that congregation. At least two members of this committee shall be elders designated by the session, one of whom shall be currently on the session and serve as moderator of the committee. At least one member of this committee shall be designated by and from the board of deacons, if the church has deacons. Other members of the committee, in sufficient number to constitute a majority thereof (exclusive of the pastor), shall be chosen by the congregation or by such organizations within the church as the congregation may designate, none of whom may be in active service on the session or in active service on the board of deacons. The pastor shall be a member of this committee, serving ex officio and without vote. The nominating committee shall be chosen annually and no member of the committee shall serve more than three years consecutively.

When a Small
Church

c.   Any congregation of fewer than seventy members may choose, at a regular congregational meeting, to elect a small church nominating committee which shall consist of one member of the session, appointed by the session to be the moderator, and at least two members of the congregation not in active service on the session. The provisions of G-14.0201b, regarding fair representation, length of service on the committee, and membership of the pastor, shall apply.

Principles

d.   All nominating procedures shall be subject to the principles of participation and representation as stated in G-4.0403 and G-9.0104.

Floor
Nominations

e.   Full opportunity shall always be given to the congregation for nominations by any active member of the church.

G-14.0202
Exemptions for
Certain
Congregations

a.   There may be exemptions for certain congregations as follows:

Waiver

(1) If in any church the nomination and election process results in the choice of elders or deacons that does not conform to the above requirement of the election of "men

and women from among its active members, giving fair representation to persons of all ages and of all racial ethnic members and persons with disabilities who are members of that congregation" (G-14.0201), the church shall apply for a waiver of the requirements. Presbytery shall satisfy itself that effort is being made to move toward compliance. A three-fourths vote of the presbytery is required to grant exemption. Such exemption shall be granted for not more than three years at a time but shall be subject to renewal by a three-fourths vote and to revocation at any time by a majority vote.

Waiver

(2) If in any church it is impossible because of limited membership to provide for the rotation of terms, the congregation may request a waiver of the requirements of G-14.0201a. The presbytery may grant the exemption by majority vote. Such exemption shall be granted for not more than three years at a time but shall be subject to renewal or to revocation at any time by a majority vote.

G-14.0203
Office Is
Perpetual

The limitations placed by G-14.0201a, upon the period for which elders or deacons may be elected and may serve, apply to active service on the session or board of deacons. In all other respects the office of elder or deacon is perpetual and no one can lay it aside at pleasure or be divested of it except as provided in the Rules of Discipline. Elders or deacons being once ordained are not divested of office by the circumstance of not being reelected to serve on the session or board of deacons of a particular church, or by ceasing to be a member of that church. Elders shall be entitled to represent in presbytery the particular church of which they are members if appointed by its session, and to serve as a member of the synod or the General Assembly when duly elected whether or not they are in active service on the session.

G-14.0204
Congregational
Meeting

a.   The election of elders and deacons shall ordinarily take place at the annual meeting of the congregation called for that purpose by the session. (G-7.0302)

Nominating and
Voting
Requirements

b.   The moderator shall explain the purpose of the meeting and then put the question: "Are you now ready to proceed to the election of elders and deacons?" If the congregation is ready, the election may proceed. In every case, procedures must allow for nominations from the floor by any member present. When the number of nominees equals the number of elders and deacons to be elected, the congregation may vote by voice vote or show of hands. When the number of nominees is greater than the number of elders and deacons to be elected, the congregation shall vote by secret ballot. A majority of all the voters present and voting shall be required to elect.

G-14.0205
Preparation for
Office

When persons have been elected to the office of elder or deacon, the session shall confer with them as to their willingness to undertake the office. The minutes of session shall record the completion of a period of study and preparation, after which the session shall examine them as to their personal faith; knowledge of the doctrine, government, and discipline contained in the Constitution of the church; and the duties of the office. If the examination is approved, the session shall appoint a day for the service of ordination and installation. If the examination is not approved for one or more elected officers, the session shall report its action to the congregation's nominating committee, which shall bring nomination(s) to a special meeting of the congregation for any office(s) not filled.

G-14.0206
Service of
Ordination and
Installation

The service of ordination and installation shall focus upon Christ and the joy and responsibility of serving him through the mission and ministry of the church, and shall include a sermon appropriate to the occasion. The minister presiding shall state briefly the nature of the offices of elder and deacon.

G-14.0207
Constitutional
Questions to
Officers

The minister shall ask those preparing to be ordained or installed to stand before the congregation and to answer the following questions:

a.   Do you trust in Jesus Christ your Savior, acknowledge him Lord of all and Head of the Church, and through him believe in one God, Father, Son, and Holy Spirit?

b.   Do you accept the Scriptures of the Old and New Testaments to be, by the Holy Spirit, the unique and authoritative witness to Jesus Christ in the Church universal, and God's Word to you?

c.   Do you sincerely receive and adopt the essential tenets of the Reformed faith as expressed in the confessions of our church as authentic and reliable expositions of what Scripture leads us to believe and do, and will you be instructed and led by those confessions as you lead the people of God?

d.   Will you fulfill your office in obedience to Jesus Christ, under the authority of Scripture, and be continually guided by our confessions?

e.   Will you be governed by our church's polity, and will you abide by its discipline? Will you be a friend among your colleagues in ministry, working with them, subject to the ordering of God's Word and Spirit?

f.   Will you in your own life seek to follow the Lord Jesus Christ, love your neighbors, and work for the reconciliation of the world?

g.   Do you promise to further the peace, unity, and purity of the church?

h.   Will you seek to serve the people with energy, intelligence, imagination, and love?

i.   (For elder) Will you be a faithful elder, watching over the people, providing for their worship, nurture, and service? Will you share in government and discipline, serving in governing bodies of the church, and in your ministry will you try to show the love and justice of Jesus Christ?

j.   (For deacon) Will you be a faithful deacon, teaching charity, urging concern, and directing the people's help to the friendless and those in need? In your ministry will you try to show the love and justice of Jesus Christ?

G-14.0208
Constitutional
Questions to
Congregation

The elders- and deacons-elect having answered in the affirmative, an elder shall stand with them before the congregation and shall ask the congregation to answer the following questions:

a.   Do we, the members of the church, accept (names) _____ as elders or deacons, chosen by God through the voice of this congregation to lead us in the way of Jesus Christ?

b.   Do we agree to encourage them, to respect their decisions, and to follow as they guide us, serving Jesus Christ, who alone is Head of the Church?

G-14.0209
Prayer and
Laying on
of Hands

a.   The members of the church having answered these questions in the affirmative, those to be ordained shall kneel, if able, for prayer and the laying on of hands by the session. Those previously ordained ordinarily shall stand, along with the congregation, if able, for the prayer of installation. The session may invite other elders and ministers of the Word and Sacrament to participate in the laying on of hands.

Statement

b.   The moderator shall say to those who have thus been ordained and installed:

You are now elders and deacons in the Church of Jesus Christ and for this congregation. Whatever you do, in word or deed, do everything in the name of the Lord Jesus, giving thanks to God the Father through him. Amen.

Session
Welcomes

c.   Then the members of the session, and others as may be appropriate, shall welcome the newly ordained and installed, or newly installed, elders and deacons into their fellowship in ministry.

Congregation
Greets

d.   After the service, it is appropriate for the members of the congregation to greet their new elders and deacons, showing affection and support.

G-14.0210
Dissolution of
Relationship

An elder or deacon may resign from the session or board of deacons for good cause, with the session's consent. On ceasing to be an active member of a particular church, an elder or deacon ceases to be a member of its session or board. When an elder or deacon, because of change of residence or disability, is unable to perform the duties of the office for a period of one year, the active relationship shall be dissolved by the session unless there is good reason not to do so, which reason should be recorded.

G-14.0211
Release from the
Exercise of
Ordained Office

a.   If an elder or deacon against whom no inquiry has been initiated pursuant to D-10.0100 and D-10.0200, against whom no charges have been filed, and who otherwise is in good standing, shall make application to the session of the church in which he or she holds membership to be released from the exercise of the ordained office, the session, upon granting the release, shall delete that person's name from the appropriate register of the church. No judgment of failure on the part of the elder or deacon is implied in this action.

b.   Release from the exercise of the ordained office of elder or deacon requires a discontinuance of all functions of that office. The designation of elder or deacon shall not be used. The status of an elder or deacon so released shall be the same as any church member.

c.   Should a person released under this section later desire to be restored to the ordained office, that person shall make application to the session that granted the release, and upon approval of that session, the person shall be restored to the exercise of the ordained office without reordination.

G-14.0300

3.   Preparation for the Office of Minister of the Word and Sacrament

G-14.0301
Presbytery
Responsibility

It is important that those who are to be ordained as ministers of the Word and Sacrament receive full preparation for their task under the direction of the committee on preparation for ministry. (G-9.0902) For this purpose, presbyteries shall enter into covenant relationship with those preparing to become ministers of the Word and Sacrament. This relationship shall be divided into the two phases of inquiry and candidacy.

G-14.0302
Inquiry Defined

The purpose of the inquiry phase is to provide an opportunity for the church and for those who believe themselves called to ministry of the Word and Sacrament to explore that call together in such a way that a decision regarding the inquirer's suitability for ministry of the Word and Sacrament will be based on knowledge and experience of one another.

G-14.0303
Inquiry Phase

The process and requirements for the inquiry phase shall be as follows:

a.   A person desiring to become an inquirer shall indicate to the session of the particular church a desire to explore the personal implications of becoming a minister of the Word and Sacrament.

b.   The person shall have been an active member of that particular church for at least six months.

c.   The session shall contact the committee on preparation for ministry for orientation to the process used in that presbytery.

d.   The session shall consult with the person and, if the individual requests to be enrolled as an inquirer, shall make a recommendation to presbytery through the stated clerk with respect to the request.

e.   Upon receipt of the recommendation of the session, the committee on preparation for ministry shall recommend to the presbytery whether to enroll the person as an inquirer. The committee on preparation for ministry shall interview the person before making its recommendation. The date of the presbytery's action to enroll shall be the beginning of the covenant relationship. This period shall be at least two years, at least one year of which shall be as a candidate, required in G-14.0401. (See G-14.0313c for exception.) A presbytery may assign to its committee on preparation for ministry the power to enroll inquirers, with the provision that the action be reported to the next stated meeting of the presbytery. (G-9.0403)

f.   The phase of inquiry shall be of sufficient length for the inquirer, the session, and the committee on preparation for ministry to decide whether the inquirer should apply to become a candidate. During this time, the committee on preparation for ministry shall make use of resources such as information provided by the inquirer, personal references, and reports from counseling services, the session, and the inquirer's institution of learning, if the inquirer is a student.

g.   By the end of the inquiry phase, each inquirer shall demonstrate adequate promise for ministry by presenting

(1) a statement of his or her understanding of Christian vocation in the Reformed tradition and how it relates to his or her sense of call;

(2) a statement of personal faith which incorporates an understanding of the Reformed tradition;

(3) an analysis of at least one concept from the personal faith statement regarding what it suggests about God, humanity, and their interrelationships;

(4) a statement of what it means to be Presbyterian, indicating how that awareness grows out of participation in the life of a particular church;

(5) a statement of self-understanding which reflects the inquirer's personal and cultural background and includes a concern for maintaining spiritual, physical, and mental health;

(6) a statement of his or her understanding of the task ministers of the Word and Sacrament perform, including an awareness of his or her specific gifts for ministry of the Word and Sacrament and of areas in which growth is needed.

**G-14.0304
Candidacy
Defined**

The purpose of the candidacy phase is to provide for the full preparation of persons to serve the church as ministers of the Word and Sacrament. This shall be accomplished through the guidance and evaluation of candidates, using learning contacts within a context of supportive relationships.

**G-14.0305
Candidacy
Process**

The process for the candidacy phase is as follows:

a. An inquirer shall apply to the presbytery through the stated clerk to become a candidate for the office of minister of the Word and Sacrament through the session of his or her church.

b. The session shall confer with the inquirer, review the evidence of the inquiry phase, and make recommendations to the presbytery through the stated clerk with respect to the application.

c. The committee on preparation for ministry shall confer with the inquirer and review the evidence which indicates whether the inquirer is ready to proceed to candidacy.

d. The committee on preparation for ministry shall make a definite recommendation to the presbytery with respect to whether the inquirer should be received as a candidate. Presbytery shall act on every committee recommendation regarding application for candidacy.

e. The presbytery shall receive the report and recommendation of its committee and shall examine the inquirer in person with respect to his or her Christian faith, forms of Christian service undertaken, and motives for seeking the ministry.

f. If the examination is approved, the presbytery shall receive the inquirer as a candidate after the following manner. The moderator shall propose the following questions to the inquirer:

(1) Do you believe yourself to be called by God to the ministry of the Word and Sacrament?

(2) Do you promise in reliance upon the grace of God to maintain a Christian character and conduct, and to be diligent and faithful in making full preparation for this ministry?

(3) Do you accept the proper supervision of the presbytery in matters that concern your preparation for this ministry?

(4) Do you desire now to be received by this presbytery as a candidate for the ministry of the Word and Sacrament in the Presbyterian Church (U.S.A.)?

g.　If these questions are answered in the affirmative, a brief charge shall be given, the candidate's name shall be recorded on the presbytery's roll of candidates, and the proceedings shall close with prayer.

h.　A presbytery may provide, at the request of the candidate and her or his session, for the service of reception to be conducted by a commission of the presbytery in the presence of the candidate's congregation.

i.　The phase of candidacy lasts until the candidate receives an approved call and is examined and ordained, or until the candidate's name is removed from the roll of candidates in accord with G-14.0312.

j.　By the end of the candidacy phase, each candidate to be ordained shall demonstrate readiness to begin ministry of the Word and Sacrament by

(1) presenting evidence of competence in the fields of theology, Bible, polity, and worship and Sacraments, ordinarily attested by completion of the requirements of G-14.0310; and evidence of ministerial skill attested in the supervised practice of ministry;

(2) presenting evidence of readiness to participate in a calling presbytery's plan for transition and of plans for continuing study and growth (G-11.0103n and G-14.0506, last sentence);

(3) expressing theological views compatible with the confessional documents of the church;

(4) expressing understanding of the meaning of the questions required for ordination (G-14.0405) informed by knowledge of the church in diverse settings;

(5) revealing commitment to the ministry of the Word and Sacrament within the discipline of the Presbyterian Church (U.S.A.) with personal maturity, spiritual depth, and a capacity to respond to the needs of others, including colleagues in ministry;

(6) presenting a written sermon, together with a description of the contemporary need to which it was addressed and an exegetical interpretation of the biblical material out of which the sermon arose. This sermon shall be preached before the calling presbytery or a committee thereof as a part of the appearance of the candidate as set forth in G-14.0402.

The duties of presbytery and sessions shall be as follows:

G-14.0306
Duties of
Presbytery and
Session

(a) (1) The committee on preparation for ministry shall seek to instruct sessions on their role in the inquiry and candidacy process. Particular direction shall be given a session which has endorsed an inquirer or candidate. This work could best be done by the committee on preparation for ministry.

(2) During the phases of inquiry and candidacy the individual continues to be an active member of his or her particular church and subject to the concern and discipline of the session. In matters relating to preparation for the ministry, the individual is under the oversight of the presbytery through the committee on preparation for ministry. It shall be the duty of the presbytery to exercise responsibility for the spiritual growth of inquirers and candidates, to support them with an understanding and sympathetic interest, and to give guidance in regard to courses of study, familiarity with the Bible and with the confessions, practical training and plans for education, including the choice of institutions, field education, and the inquirer's or candidate's financial need. The presbytery shall also seek to give guidance and instruction to the inquirer or candidate in the faith and polity of the church. (G-6.0108)

Support by
Session

b. The session shall function in a supportive role during the phases of inquiry and candidacy to assure that care is provided on a continuous basis. The session shall appoint an elder from the church to be a liaison person with the inquirer or candidate and the appropriate presbytery committee. The session should consider the provision of financial support for the inquirer or candidate.

G-14.0307
Service in
Covenant
Relationship

The inquirer or candidate shall be encouraged to engage in some form of service to the church with the approval and under the guidance of the inquirer's or candidate's committee on preparation for ministry. Field education assignments that are under the supervision of a theological institution do not require presbytery approval; however, field education assignments that place an inquirer or candidate as the student intern having sole pastoral responsibility for the life of a church require the counsel and oversight of the committee on ministry having jurisdiction over the church. An inquirer or candidate shall not undertake to serve a church, even as a temporary supply, without the approval of the presbytery having jurisdiction over the church as well as the approval of the inquirer's or candidate's presbytery. Under no circumstances may an inquirer or candidate, who has not been previously ordained as an elder, serve as moderator of a session, administer the Sacraments, or perform a marriage ceremony. A previously ordained elder who becomes an inquirer or candidate may be authorized to administer the Lord's Supper in accordance with G-6.0304 and G-11.0103z, but may not serve as moderator of a session nor perform a marriage ceremony, except as may be provided in G-10.0103 and G-7.0306. A previously commissioned lay pastor who becomes an inquirer or candidate may continue to be authorized to administer sacraments in accordance with the presbytery's previous grant of authority under G-14.0801c.

G-14.0308
Annual Report

The presbytery shall require the inquirer or candidate to make an annual written report concerning progress in studies and service to the church, including a report from the individual's institution of learning.

G-14.0309
Consultation and
Guidance

a.   The committee on preparation for ministry shall provide for an annual consultation with each person on the rolls of inquirers and candidates. The purpose of the consultation shall be for the evaluation and nurture of inquirers and candidates. Such consultation may be held by the entire committee or may be carried out by persons appointed by the committee either from its own membership or with similar responsibilities in a presbytery within which the inquirer or candidate is pursuing a course of study or engaged in other approved service, except in the case of the final assessment, which should be conducted by the committee on preparation for ministry of the candidate's presbytery. Presbytery, together with the session and the inquirer or candidate, shall bear the necessary expenses of the annual consultation, which shall be concerned with the spiritual growth and needs of the individual, the financial planning for his or her educational program, and with his or her relation to the church and progress in the program of study leading to ordination for ministry. Each consultation shall include a decision, made by the whole committee, whether to continue or terminate the period of inquiry or candidacy. This decision shall be reported to presbytery.

Written Report

b.   There shall be a written report of each annual consultation, including a statement of the individual's strengths and areas of needed growth, prepared jointly by the committee or its representative and the inquirer or candidate. The presbytery shall be notified of receipt of these reports and the reports themselves shall be submitted to the individual, the sponsoring session, and the theological institution.

Content

c.   The content of these annual consultations shall include, but need not be limited to, assessment of the inquirer's or candidate's development in terms of the outcomes for the appropriate phase and the following in the appropriate years:

Prior to Theological Education

(1) In the years prior to entering theological education, discussion of the inquirer's or candidate's preparation for theological education and for personal growth;

First Year Theological Education

(2) For annual consultations which cover the time period of the first year of theological education, a general assessment of her or his experience and the implications this has for future professional ministry. The primary focus of this consultation(s) shall not be one of formal examination but of guidance and counseling with the inquirer and candidate. At this consultation(s) the student may ask the committee on preparation for ministry to present to the presbytery any request for an exemption from formal educational requirements of G-14.0310b(2) and b(3), such as language provisions. Should the presbytery be willing to make such an exception, the procedures of G-14.0313a shall be followed;

Second Year Theological Education

(3) For annual consultations which cover the time period of the second year of theological education, an assessment of the inquirer's or candidate's experience similar to that held in the previous year(s). In addition, the consultation(s) shall include a discussion with the individual on progress in preparation for ordination, including a preliminary statement of faith, a review of all grades, field education reports, and other appropriate evaluations. The presbytery also shall satisfy itself of the individual's thorough knowledge of the Bible. To this end, the presbytery shall accept a certificate of passing grade on the Bible Content examination of G-14.0310c(2). The committee on preparation for ministry and the inquirer or candidate shall discuss the means by which any deficiencies are to be removed.

Negotiation for Service

d. In no case shall an inquirer or candidate be excused from these annual consultations. Prior to the completion of two full years of theological education or its equivalent, prior to that year's annual consultation, and prior to the successful completion of all ordination exams or to the presbytery's certification of readiness according to the provisions of G-14.0313b, no inquirer or candidate shall enter into negotiation with a church for his or her ministerial services except by a three-fourths vote of the members of presbytery present, with the reasons therefor recorded in the minutes of presbytery.

G-14.0310 Final Assessment

a. In the final year of theological education or when a candidate has satisfied the requirements of G-14.0310, and before a candidate may receive a call, the committee on preparation for ministry of the candidate's presbytery shall conduct a final assessment of the candidate's readiness to begin ministry. This consultation shall focus on the outcomes of inquiry (G-14.0303g) and candidacy (G-14.0305j) and shall include each of the requirements of certification set forth in G-14.0310b–e. A summary of this assessment shall be reported to the presbytery and shall be transmitted to a calling presbytery when requested. The committee on preparation for ministry shall report to the presbytery when it has certified a candidate ready for examination for ordination, pending a call. (See G-14.0507.)

Requirements to Be Certified Ready for Examination

b.   The candidate's presbytery shall require a candidate to fulfill the following requirements to be certified as to be ready for examination for ordination, pending a call:

(1)   demonstration of readiness to begin ministry of the Word and Sacrament as required in G-14.0305j;

(2)   presentation of a transcript showing satisfactory grades at a regionally accredited college or university, together with a diploma;

Educational Requirements

(3)   presentation of a transcript from a theological institution accredited by the Association of Theological Schools acceptable to the presbytery, the transcript showing satisfactory grades, and presentation of a plan to complete the theological degree including Hebrew and Greek and exegesis of the Old and New Testaments using Hebrew and Greek texts;

Examination Requirements

(4)   presentation of satisfactory grades together with the examination papers in the five areas covered by the Presbyteries' Cooperative Committee on Examinations for Candidates.

Bible Content Examination

c.   Inquirers or candidates are encouraged to take the Bible Content Examination in their first year of seminary. The other four examinations may be taken by inquirers or candidates after completion of two full years of theological education. These four examinations shall only be taken upon approval by the committee on preparation for ministry of the inquirer's or candidate's presbytery.

Areas of Examination

d.   The areas of these examinations are:

(1)   *Open Book Bible Exegesis.* This examination shall assess the candidate's ability to find and state the meaning of an assigned passage of Scripture, demonstrating working knowledge of the original language of the text and ability to understand its historical situation.

The candidate shall have access to any or all of the following:

Hebrew and Greek texts, translations, commentaries, and other exegetical tools, including those which presuppose knowledge of the biblical languages. Using these, he or she shall be asked to state the meaning of the passage, show how he or she arrived at this interpretation, and suggest how this passage might be used in the contemporary life of the church.

(2) *Bible Content.* This examination shall assess the candidate's knowledge of the form and content of the Bible.

(3) *Theological Competence.* This examination shall assess the candidate's capacity to make effective use of the classical theological disciplines and of the confessional documents of the church in relating the gospel to the faith of the church in the contemporary world.

(4) *Worship and Sacraments.* This examination shall assess the candidate's understanding of the meaning and purpose of corporate worship and the Sacraments, familiarity with the Directory for Worship and *The Book of Confessions* and their application to the life of worshiping communities.

(5) *Church Polity.* This examination shall assess the candidate's working knowledge of the constitutional structure of the Presbyterian Church (U.S.A.) and the method by which differences are properly resolved and programs to fulfill the mission of the church are determined.

How Graded

e.   The examinations required in the five specified areas shall be graded by representatives of the presbyteries under the supervision of the Presbyteries' Cooperative Committee on Examinations for Candidates as provided in G-11.0103m.

G-14.0311
Transfer of
Covenant
Relationship

A presbytery may transfer the covenant relationship of an inquirer or candidate to another presbytery, but only with the approval of the receiving presbytery and the inquirer or candidate. An inquirer or candidate shall not transfer her or his membership to a particular church under the jurisdiction of another presbytery without the approval of the presbytery responsible for the person's preparation for ministry. Whenever a presbytery approves such a transfer, it shall send to the other presbytery a certificate of its approval, its records concerning the individual, and the reasons for the request for transfer. Failure of an inquirer or candidate to follow this procedure shall result in the forfeiture of standing as an inquirer or candidate. No presbytery may restore such a person's status except by beginning again under the provisions of G-14.0303.

G-14.0312
Removal from
Covenant
Relationship

An inquirer or candidate may, after consultation with the session and the committee on preparation for ministry, withdraw from covenant relationship. Upon receiving such a request transmitted through the committee on preparation for ministry, the stated clerk shall remove the individual's name from the roll of inquirers or candidates and report the removal to presbytery. A presbytery may also, for sufficient reasons, remove an individual's name from the roll of inquirers or candidates, reporting this action and the reasons to the session, to the individual, and, if appropriate, to the educational institution in which the individual is enrolled. In both instances, prior to final action, the committee on preparation for ministry shall make a reasonable attempt to give the inquirer or candidate and other parties of interest an opportunity to be heard by that committee. The presbytery may arrange for the continued guidance and support of those who withdraw or are removed from the roll of inquirers or candidates.

G-14.0313
Extraordinary
Circumstances

All of the requirements of G-14.0310 shall be met except in the following extraordinary circumstances:

Educational
Requirements

a.   If the inquirer's or candidate's presbytery judges that there are good and sufficient reasons why certain of the educational requirements of G-14.0310b(2) or b(3) should not be met by an inquirer or candidate, it shall make an exception only by three-fourths vote of the members of presbytery present. A full account of the reasons for such an exception shall be included in the minutes of presbytery and shall be communicated to the presbytery to which the inquirer or candidate may be transferred. (G-14.0311 and G-14.0314) The successful completion of the course of study specified in such an exception shall fulfill the requirements of G-14.0310b(2) or b(3).

Examination
Requirements

b.   The examination requirements of G-14.0310b(4) shall not be waived until an inquirer or candidate has failed on two attempts to receive a satisfactory grade. If the presbytery believes at this time that the person should be certified as ready for examination for ordination, pending a call, it shall authorize an exception only by a three-fourths vote of the members of the presbytery present, and must determine an alternate means whereby it will satisfy itself of competence in the area(s) of failure. When the individual successfully completes the alternate pattern, the presbytery may certify readiness in the usual manner. The minutes of the presbytery shall contain a full record of the reasons for the exception and the alternate pattern for determining competence. Presbyteries shall submit to the synod the process by which a candidate, who has failed one or more ordination exams twice, would be examined. Once that process has been approved, presbyteries may proceed with particular candidates, and note such exemptions in their minutes each occasion. Such processes will be reviewed every three years.

Time
Requirements

c.   The time requirements of G-14.0303 shall not be waived unless the presbytery judges that there are good and sufficient reasons why the time requirement should not be met by an inquirer or candidate. It shall make an exception only by three-fourths vote of the members of the presbytery present. A full account of the reasons for such an exception shall be included in the minutes of presbytery and shall be communicated to the presbytery to which the inquirer or candidate may be transferred. (G-14.0311) Under no circumstances shall the time requirement be less than one year. (See G-14.0303e.)

Confirmation of
Action

d.   The foregoing exceptions shall hold if the presbytery has received the inquirer or candidate from another presbytery that approved the exemption of any of these requirements, the reception of the candidate having confirmed the action of the dismissing presbytery.

G-14.0314
Location of
Ordination

a.   The presbytery placing the call to a candidate for ministry shall ordinarily examine and, contingent upon the candidate's successful completion of that examination and all requirements in G-14.0402, the presbytery responsible for the candidate's preparation for ministry shall ordinarily ordain the candidate.

Other Reformed
Bodies

b.   When a candidate is called to work under the jurisdiction of some other Reformed body, he or she may be dismissed as a candidate by certification. Likewise, candidates may be received for this purpose from other Reformed bodies by transfer of certificate.

G-14.0400

G-14.0401
Ordination of
Candidates

4.   Ordination for the Ministry of the Word and Sacrament

Ordination for the office of minister of the Word and Sacrament is an act of the whole church carried out by the presbytery, setting apart a person to the ministry of the Word and Sacrament. Such a person shall have been in covenant relationship with a presbytery or presbyteries for a period of at least two years including at least one year as a candidate (see G-14.0313c for exception), met the requirements of G-14.0310 together with the completion of the theological degree, and received a call for service to a church or other work in the mission of the church that is acceptable to the candidate and the presbytery.

G-14.0402
Examination for
Ordination

a.   The candidate shall appear before the presbytery in which he or she shall make a brief statement of personal faith and of commitment to the ministry of the Word and Sacrament except as provided in G-14.0314. The presbytery, having received certification of a diploma from a theological institution accredited by the Association of Theological Schools and acceptable to the presbytery, having heard the candidate and his or her sermon preached before the presbytery or a committee thereof (G-14.0305j(6)), and having received the recommendation of its responsible committee (G-11.0402), shall conduct any further examination of his or her Christian faith and views in theology, the Bible, the Sacraments, and the government of this church as it deems necessary.

Vote to Proceed

b.   If the presbytery is fully satisfied of the candidate's qualifications, it shall vote to proceed to his or her ordination, appointing a time and place for the service of ordination.

G-14.0403
Extraordinary
Circumstances

The presbytery shall not omit any of the requirements for ordination except in the case of extraordinary circumstances as provided in G-14.0313.

G-14.0404
Place of
Ordination

a.   The ordination of candidates to the ministry of the Word and Sacrament shall ordinarily take place in the presence of the congregation in which the candidate is a member, and in the place for the regular worship of that congregation.

Place of
Installation

b.   A service of installation (G-14.0510) shall be held by the presbytery within whose bounds the candidate has been called to minister.

G-14.0405
Ordination
Service

a.   The presbytery or commission appointed for this purpose shall convene and shall call the congregation to worship. The service shall focus upon Christ and the joy and responsibility of the mission and ministry of the church, and shall include a sermon appropriate to the occasion. The member named to preside shall state briefly the proceedings of the presbytery preparatory to the ordination and shall point out its nature and importance.

Constitutional
Questions

b.   The member presiding shall then ask the candidate to answer the following questions:

> (1) Do you trust in Jesus Christ your Savior, acknowledge him Lord of all and Head of the Church, and through him believe in one God, Father, Son, and Holy Spirit?
>
> (2) Do you accept the Scriptures of the Old and New Testaments to be, by the Holy Spirit, the unique and authoritative witness to Jesus Christ in the Church universal, and God's Word to you?
>
> (3) Do you sincerely receive and adopt the essential tenets of the Reformed faith as expressed in the confessions of our church as authentic and reliable expositions of what Scripture leads us to believe and do, and will you be instructed and led by those confessions as you lead the people of God?
>
> (4) Will you be a minister of the Word and Sacrament in obedience to Jesus Christ, under the authority of Scripture, and continually guided by our confessions?
>
> (5) Will you be governed by our church's polity, and will you abide by its discipline? Will you be a friend among

your colleagues in ministry, working with them, subject to the ordering of God's Word and Spirit?

(6) Will you in your own life seek to follow the Lord Jesus Christ, love your neighbors, and work for the reconciliation of the world?

(7) Do you promise to further the peace, unity, and purity of the church?

(8) Will you seek to serve the people with energy, intelligence, imagination, and love?

(9) Will you be a faithful minister, proclaiming the good news in Word and Sacrament, teaching faith, and caring for people? Will you be active in government and discipline, serving in the governing bodies of the church; and in your ministry will you try to show the love and justice of Jesus Christ?

Installation

c. [This section was stricken by action of the 206th General Assembly (1994).]

Prayer and Laying on of Hands

d. The candidate, having answered the questions in the affirmative, shall kneel, if able, and the presbytery shall, with prayer and the laying on of hands, ordain the candidate to the office of minister of the Word and Sacrament. The member presiding shall then say:

(Name)_____, you are now ordained a minister of the Word and Sacrament in the Church of Jesus Christ. Whatever you do, in word or deed, do everything in the name of the Lord Jesus, giving thanks to God the Father through him. Amen.

Welcome

e. Then the members of the presbytery, and others as may be appropriate, shall welcome the new minister into the ministry of the Word and Sacrament. At the conclusion of the ordination service, the new minister may make a brief statement and shall pronounce the benediction.

G-14.0406
Ordination
Recorded

The presbytery shall record the ordination as a part of its official records along with the acceptance and subscription of the new minister to the obligations undertaken in the ordination vows. It shall also be the duty of the stated clerk of the presbytery to enroll the newly ordained minister as a member of the presbytery and to notify the session of the particular church of which the candidate has been a member, so that the session may record the fact that the candidate is now ordained and has been transferred to the roll of the presbytery.

G-14.0500

5. Calling and Installing Ministers of the Word and Sacrament

G-14.0501
Pastors,
Co-Pastors,
Associate Pastors,
and Assistant
Pastors

a. Every church should have the pastoral services of a minister of the Word and Sacrament. The pastoral relations which may exist between a particular church and a minister of the Word and Sacrament are permanent, designated, or temporary relations. The permanent pastoral relations are those of pastor, co-pastor, associate pastor, and assistant pastor. The only designated pastoral relationships are pastor and co-pastor. The temporary relations are stated supply, organizing pastor, interim pastor, interim co-pastor, interim associate pastor, and temporary supply. Those persons serving as assistant pastors on December 31, 1985, may continue in that pastoral relation so long as the individual holding such relationship continues that relationship to the same particular church.

Pastor or
Associate
Pastor

b. A pastor or associate pastor shall be elected by the vote of the congregation and the relationship between them shall be established by the presbytery. The call extended to a pastor or associate pastor shall be approved by the presbytery and cannot be changed except by consent of the presbytery, at the request of the pastor or associate pastor, or at the request of the church by action of the congregation.

Co-Pastors

c. Co-pastors are ministers who are called and installed with equal responsibility for pastoral ministry. Each shall be considered a pastor and they may share duties within the congregation as agreed upon by the session and approved by the presbytery. When a particular church has two pastors serving as co-pastors and the relationship of one of them is dissolved, the other remains as pastor of the church.

Assistant Pastor

d. Any formal change in the relationship of an assistant pastor entered into prior to December 31, 1985, must be approved by presbytery, and the relationship may be dissolved by presbytery on its own initiative or upon the request of the assistant pastor or of the session.

Assistant Called
as Associate

e. An assistant pastor shall be eligible to serve as associate pastor within the same congregation. When a minister has served in a church as assistant pastor for at least one year, that person may be called as an associate pastor in the following manner:

The session, in consultation with the committee on ministry of the presbytery, may nominate the assistant pastor as an associate pastor at a meeting of the congregation called for that purpose. The action of the congregation, if favorable, shall be presented to the presbytery for its concurrence. The presbytery may concur in the call if the minister is judged suitable for the increased responsibility. Upon its concurrence, the presbytery shall make arrangements for the installation of the minister as associate pastor.

Cannot
Immediately
Succeed the
Pastor

f.   The official relationship of an associate or assistant pastor to a church is not dependent upon that of a pastor, but an associate or assistant pastor is not eligible to succeed immediately the pastor in a church which they have served together, nor may either be called as pastor to serve as co-pastor of that church, except in churches which currently have a co-pastor model which has been in effect for at least three years and the congregation desires to continue such model. In such churches, an associate or assistant pastor may be called as pastor to serve as co-pastor of that church with a three-fourths affirmative vote of presbytery. The call to an associate or assistant pastor shall specify the particular functions to be fulfilled. An associate or assistant pastor shall be directed in his or her work by the pastor in consultation with the session.

Designated Pastor

g.   A designated pastor or co-pastor(s) is a minister of the Word and Sacrament approved by the committee on ministry to be elected for a term of not less than two nor more than four years by the vote of the congregation. The relationship shall be established by the presbytery. The only designated pastoral relationships are pastor and co-pastor. Such a pastor or co-pastor(s) shall be nominated by the congregation's pastor nominating committee only from among those designated by the committee on ministry of the presbytery. The congregation and the minister both must volunteer to be considered for a designated term relationship. Such a call may be established only with the prior concurrence of the committee on ministry of the presbytery. The terms of the call shall be approved by the presbytery. The minister shall be installed by the presbytery. When the minister is pastor, he or she shall be moderator of the session. The sections on calling and installing a pastor shall apply. (G-14.0502-.0507) (See G-14.0501a.) If there has been an open search process conducted by the committee on ministry and after two years of the designated pastor relationship, upon the concurrence of the committee on ministry, the designated pastor, and the session, acting in place of the pastor nominating committee for the single purpose of calling the designated pastor as pastor, a congregational meeting may be held to call the designated pastor as pastor. The session, with the concurrence of the committee on ministry, may call a congregational meeting to elect a pastor nominating committee to conduct a full pastoral search or to prosecute the call to the designated pastor to become pastor. The action of the congregation shall be reported to the presbytery. If the congregational action is affirmative, the presbytery, after voting to approve the new pastoral relationship, shall install the designated pastor as pastor.

G-14.0502
Election of a
Pastor

a.   When a church is without a pastor, or after the effective date of the dissolution of the pastoral relationship, the congregation shall, with the guidance and permission of the committee on ministry, G-11.0502d, proceed to elect a pastor in the following manner. The session shall call a congregational meeting to elect a nominating committee, which shall be representative of the whole congregation. This committee's duty shall be to nominate a minister to the congregation for election as pastor. Public notice of the time, place, and purpose of the meeting shall be given at least ten days in advance, which shall include two successive Sundays.

Work of the
Committee

b.   The nominating committee shall confer with the committee on ministry as provided in G-11.0502d and when seeking an associate pastor or co-pastor, with the pastor or any continuing co-pastors. Care must be taken to consider candidates without regard to race, ethnic origin, sex, marital status, age, or disabilities.

Report of the
Committee

c.   When the committee is ready to report, it shall notify the session, which shall call a congregational meeting, giving public notice as required in the paragraph a. above, for the purpose of acting on the report of the nominating committee. The same procedure shall be followed in the selection of an associate pastor. The action of the congregation, if favorable, shall be presented to the presbytery for its concurrence. If the presbytery concurs, it shall make arrangements for the minister's installation. A call to a permanent pastoral relationship shall not be issued until it has been approved by the presbytery. (G-11.0502d)

G-14.0503
Congregational
Meeting

a.   When a congregation is convened for the election of a pastor (associate pastor), the moderator of the session appointed by presbytery or some other minister of the presbytery shall preside.

Vote by
Ballot

b.   Following prayer for the guidance of God, the moderator shall call for the report of the nominating committee. Following the report, the moderator shall then put the question: "Are you ready to proceed to the election of a pastor (associate pastor)?" If they are ready the moderator shall declare the name submitted by the nominating committee to be in nomination. The vote shall be upon the question whether the congregation, under the will of God, shall call the person nominated to be its pastor (associate pastor), and it shall be taken by ballot. In every case a majority of the voters present and voting shall be required to elect.

G-14.0504
Larger Parish

When two or more churches established by presbytery as a larger parish unite in calling a pastor, the call must specify the support promised by each church. With the approval of presbytery, such a call may be issued by a larger parish council providing for the approval of the churches given in properly called meetings of their congregations, for payment of a total salary from a common parish treasury along with an explanation of the financial agreement between the churches of the parish, and for the annual review of the pastor's salary by the parish council with provision for a vote thereon by each congregation. When such a call has been issued by a parish council, and approved by the presbytery, each participating church shall be obligated to continue its financial support of the parish for the duration of the pastorate, unless excused by the other participating churches with the approval of the presbytery. The call shall specify that the minister is called to be pastor (associate pastor) of the churches constituting the parish.

G-14.0505
Dissent

On the election of a pastor (associate pastor), if it appears that a substantial minority of the voters are averse to the nominee who has received a majority of the votes, and that they cannot be persuaded to concur in the call, the moderator shall recommend to the majority that they not prosecute the call. If the congregation is nearly unanimous, or if the majority insist upon their right to call a pastor (associate pastor), the moderator shall forward the call to the presbytery, certifying the number of those who do not concur in the call and any other facts of importance. The moderator shall also inform the person being called of the nature and circumstances of the decision.

G-14.0506
The Call

a.   Persons shall be elected by the vote of the congregation to sign the call and to present and prosecute the call before the presbytery. The moderator of the meeting shall certify to the presbytery that those signing the call were properly elected and that the call was in all other respects prepared as constitutionally required.

Form

b.   The call shall be in the following or like form:

The _____ Presbyterian Church (U.S.A.) of (Location) _____ belonging to _____ Presbytery, being well satisfied with your qualifications for ministry and confident that we have been led to you by the Holy Spirit as one whose service will be profitable to the spiritual interests of our church and fruitful for the Kingdom of our Lord, earnestly and solemnly calls you, (Name) _____, to undertake the office of pastor (or associate pastor) of this congregation, promising you in the discharge of your duty all proper support, encouragement, and allegiance in the Lord.

That you may be free to devote yourself full time (part time) to the ministry of the Word and Sacrament among us, we promise and obligate ourselves to pay the following (those agreed upon are to be filled in):

Annual salary
     (in regular monthly payments) . . . . . .$ _____
Use of the manse . . . .$ _____
Housing allowance . . . .$ _____
Utilities allowance . . . .$ _____
Other medical insurance . . . .$ _____

Professional expenses

     Automobile expenses . . . .$ _____
     Continuing education expenses . . . . . .$ _____
     Book expenses . . . .$ _____

Personal business expenses . . . .$ _____
Other (specify) . . . .$ _____
Moving costs . . . .$ _____
Vacation of (time period) . . . .   _____
Continuing Education (time period) . . . . .   _____

and we will pay regularly in advance to the board responsible for benefits a sum equal to that requisite percent of your salary which may be fixed by the General Assembly of the Presbyterian Church (U.S.A.) for participation in the Benefits Plan of the Presbyterian Church (U.S.A.), including both pension and medical coverage, or any successor plan approved by the General Assembly, during the time of your being and continuing in the pastoral relationship set forth in this call to this church. We further promise and obligate ourselves to review with you annually the adequacy of this compensation. In testimony whereof we have subscribed our names this _____ day of _____, A.D. _____.

(Signatures)

Allowances and Amounts

c.   The call shall specify all and only those allowances and amounts which are undertaken as part of the call. If the minister is obligated to fulfill military commitments during a period of pastoral service, an agreement between the minister and the calling agency may be added to the terms of call for that obligation and potential mobilization of the minister, and become an element in the terms of call when approved by presbytery. If the call is for less than full time, the precise terms of the contract shall be indicated.

Certification

d.   The certification by the moderator shall be as follows:

Having moderated the congregational meeting which extended a call to (Name) _____ for ministerial services, I do certify that the call has been made in all respects according to the rules laid down in the Form of Government, and that the persons who signed the foregoing call were authorized to do so by vote of the _____ _____ Presbyterian Church (U.S.A.).

(Signed) _____
Moderator of the Meeting

Minimum Requirements

e.   The terms of the call shall always provide for compensation that meets or exceeds any minimum requirements of the presbytery in effect when the call is made and shall thereafter be adjusted annually as required to conform to such requirement.

Integration

f.   Every call to a candidate shall be accompanied by a description of the presbytery's plan for the integration of new ministers into the life and work of presbytery. (G-11.0103n)

G-14.0507 Call Presented and Received

a.   If the presbytery finds the call in order and determines that it is for the good of the whole church, it shall inform the person being called of its decision and shall proceed to present the call through the presbytery having jurisdiction over the minister or candidate.

Call Through
Own Presbytery

b. No minister or candidate shall receive a call except through the hands of his or her own presbytery. When a church in one presbytery extends a call to a minister or candidate of another presbytery, the stated clerk of the calling presbytery shall transmit the call to the stated clerk of the other presbytery, with certification that the call has been found in order by the presbytery. The stated clerk of the minister's or candidate's presbytery shall deliver the call to the committee on ministry (G-11.0502b), which shall inform the presbytery of the receipt of the call and shall recommend to presbytery what action should be taken with respect to it. If the presbytery thinks it wise to release the minister from the present charge, it may present the call to her or him with permission to transfer to the presbytery having jurisdiction over the church, there to be examined and received. If the presbytery thinks it wise for the candidate to accept the call, it may present the call to her or him with the permission to be examined by the presbytery having jurisdiction over the church. If the examination is not sustained, the minister or candidate remains under the jurisdiction of his or her own presbytery. The presbyteries shall deal directly with each other through their stated clerks in certifying both the call of the church and the credentials of the minister or candidate.

Call, Delegation
of Authority

c.   The authority for finding calls in order, for approving and presenting calls, for approving the examination of ministers transferring from other presbyteries required by G-11.0402, for dissolving the pastoral relationship in cases where the congregation and pastor concur, and for dismissing ministers to other presbyteries may be delegated by presbytery to its council or committee on ministry, with the provision that all such actions be reported to the next stated meeting of the presbytery. (G-9.0403, G-11.0103v, and G-11.0502h)

G-14.0508
Call to a Minister
of Another
Denomination

a.   When a church extends a call to a minister of another denomination, the minister shall apply for membership in the presbytery, requesting the denominational body of jurisdiction to send his or her credentials of good standing to the presbytery. Such a minister shall be required

(1) to have been called to appropriate work in this church;

(2) to present a baccalaureate degree or its equivalent from an accredited college or university and a theological degree from an institution acceptable to the presbytery and requiring not less than three years' residence;

(3) to answer satisfactorily the questions on the examinations required of candidates for ordination (G-14.0310b(4));

(4) to articulate their Christian faith and to demonstrate an acceptable knowledge of theology (G-14.0310d(3)) and of the government of this church (G-14.0310d(5));

(5) to answer in the affirmative before the presbytery the questions asked of candidates at their ordination. (G-14.0405)

Requirements Waived

b.   The presbytery shall not waive any of the foregoing requirements except in extraordinary cases, in which the presbytery shall follow the same procedure required in G-14.0313, for extraordinary circumstances.

G-14.0509 Installation of Minister

a.   When a call is presented to a minister or candidate, it shall be viewed as a sufficient petition from the congregation for his or her installation.

Acceptance of Call

b.   The acceptance of a call by a minister or candidate shall likewise be considered a request to be installed. The presbytery shall, therefore, appoint a time and place for the service of installation.

G-14.0510 Installation Service

a.   On the day designated for the installation, the presbytery or commission appointed for this purpose shall convene and shall call the congregation gathered to worship. The service shall have the same focus and form as the service of ordination and the person being installed shall be asked to answer the questions asked at the time of ordination. (G-14.0405) Following the affirmative answers to the questions asked of the person being installed, an elder shall face the congregation along with the pastor-elect (associate pastor-elect) and shall ask them to answer the following questions:

(1) Do we, the members of the church, accept (Name) _____ as our pastor (associate pastor), chosen by God through the voice of this congregation to guide us in the way of Jesus Christ?

(2) Do we agree to encourage him (her), to respect his (her) decisions, and to follow as he (she) guides us, serving Jesus Christ, who alone is Head of the Church?

(3) Do we promise to pay him (her) fairly and provide for his (her) welfare as he (she) works among us; to stand by him (her) in trouble and share his (her) joys? Will we listen to the word he (she) preaches, welcome his (her) pastoral care, and honor his (her) authority as he (she) seeks to honor and obey Jesus Christ our Lord?

Prayer and Laying on of Hands

b.   The members of the congregation having answered these questions in the affirmative, a candidate being ordained and installed shall kneel, if able, and the presbytery shall, with prayer and the laying on of hands, ordain the candidate to the office of minister of the Word and Sacrament and install him or her in the particular pastoral responsibility. A minister, previously ordained, who is being installed ordinarily shall stand, if able, for the prayer of installation.

Statement

c. The member presiding shall then say:

(Name) _____, you are now a minister of the Word and Sacrament in the Church of Jesus Christ and for this congregation. Whatever you do, in word or deed, do everything in the name of the Lord Jesus, giving thanks to God the Father through him. Amen.

(For a minister previously ordained say only: You are now a minister of the Word and Sacrament in and for this congregation. Whatever you do, . . . etc.)

Welcome

d. Then the members of the presbytery, and others as may be appropriate, shall welcome the newly ordained and installed or newly installed minister into their fellowship in the ministry of the Word and Sacrament.

Brief Charges

e. Persons invited by the presbytery may then give brief charges to the pastor (associate pastor) and to the congregation to be faithful in their relationship and in their reciprocal responsibilities.

Benediction

f. At the conclusion of the service, the newly installed minister may make a brief statement and shall pronounce the benediction.

Record Service

g. The presbytery shall duly record the service of installation.

G-14.0511
Welcome

After the installation service, the officers and members of the church should come forward to their pastor (associate pastor) and give him or her an appropriate expression of cordial reception and affectionate regard.

G-14.0512
More Than
One Church

The installation of a minister as pastor or associate pastor of more than one church may take place in a joint service, provided each church is present and answers for itself the constitutional questions set forth in G-14.0510.

G-14.0513
Temporary
Pastoral
Relations

When a church does not have a pastor, or while the pastor is unable to perform her or his duties, the session should obtain the services of a minister of this denomination in a temporary pastoral relation. When a congregation employs more than one pastor, or a pastor and one or more associate pastors, and there is a vacancy in one of these positions, it may obtain the services of a minister in a temporary pastoral relation. No formal call shall be issued by the congregation and no formal installation shall take place. Temporary pastoral relations are those of stated supply, interim pastor, interim co-pastor, interim associate pastor, temporary supply, or organizing pastor:

Stated Supply

a. A stated supply is a minister appointed by the presbytery, after consultation with the session, to perform the functions of a pastor in a church which is not seeking an installed pastor. The relation shall be established only by the presbytery and shall extend for a period not to exceed twelve months at a time. A stated supply shall not be reappointed until the presbytery, through its committee on ministry, has reviewed her or his effectiveness. A stated supply may, with presbytery's approval, serve as moderator of the session.

Interim Pastor

b.   An interim pastor is a minister invited by the session of a church without an installed pastor to preach the Word, administer the Sacraments, and fulfill pastoral duties for a specified period not to exceed twelve months at a time, while the church is seeking a pastor. An interim co-pastor is a minister invited by the session of a church without an installed co-pastor which had a co-pastor model which was in effect for at least three years and where the congregation desires to continue such model of permanent ministerial relationship, to preach the Word, administer the Sacraments, and fulfill pastoral duties for a specified period not to exceed twelve months at a time, while the church is seeking a co-pastor. The session may not secure or dissolve a relationship with an interim pastor or interim co-pastor without the concurrence of the presbytery through its committee on ministry. A minister may not be called to be the next installed pastor, co-pastor, or associate pastor of a church served as interim pastor or interim co-pastor.

Interim Associate Pastor

c.   An interim associate pastor is a minister invited by the session to serve in this position while the church is seeking a new associate pastor or is seeking a pastor to serve as co-pastor in accord with G-6.0202. The session may not secure or dissolve a relationship with an interim associate pastor without the concurrence of the presbytery through its committee on ministry. An interim associate pastor shall serve for a specified period not to exceed twelve months at a time and may not be called to be the next installed pastor or associate pastor of a church served as interim associate pastor.

Temporary Supply

d.   A temporary supply may be a minister, a candidate, a commissioned lay pastor, or an elder secured by the session to conduct services when there is no pastor or the pastor is unable to perform pastoral duties. The session shall seek the counsel of presbytery through its committee on ministry before securing a temporary supply. A temporary supply may not be called to be a pastor or associate pastor of a church served as temporary supply, unless six months have elapsed since the end of the temporary supply relationship.

Inquirer or Candidate as Temporary Supply

e.   When a church is without a pastor or when the pastor is unable to perform pastoral duties, the session, after obtaining the approval of the presbytery having jurisdiction over the church through its committee on ministry, may secure the services of an inquirer or candidate to serve as temporary supply. Appropriate guidance and supervision for such an inquirer or candidate serving as temporary supply must be assured by the presbytery having jurisdiction over the church and approved by the inquirer's or candidate's committee on preparation for ministry.

Organizing Pastor

f. An organizing pastor is a minister **or commissioned lay pastor** appointed by the presbytery to serve as pastor to a group of people who are in the process of organizing a new Presbyterian church. An organizing pastor may be designated a member of the presbytery administrative staff and is to be hired in accordance with the principles of G-9.0702, G-9.0704, and G-4.0403. This relationship as organizing pastor shall terminate when the new church is formally organized by the presbytery. At that time the new church may, with the approval of the committee on ministry and the presbytery, call the organizing pastor to be its pastor without being required to elect a pastor nominating committee and conduct a pastoral search, or it may choose to elect a pastor nominating committee and conduct a full pastoral search as provided in the Form of Government.

G-14.0514
Ministers of
Other Churches

Ordained ministers of other Christian churches may be employed by the session of a particular church in a temporary pastoral relationship, provided that such ministers present to the presbytery credentials of good standing in the ecclesiastical body to which they belong, and provided that presbytery gives its approval to the temporary pastoral relationship.

G-14.0515
Parish Associate

a. A parish associate is a minister who serves in some validated ministry other than the local parish, or is a member-at-large, or is retired, but who wishes to maintain a relationship with a particular church or churches in keeping with ordination to the ministry of the Word and Sacrament. Such persons, already qualified as continuing members of presbytery, may serve as parish associates. The relation shall be established, upon nomination by the pastor, between the parish associate, the session, and the presbytery. The parish associate shall be responsible to the pastor, as head of staff, on an "as needed, as available" basis and with or without remuneration. A parish associate may not be called to be the next installed pastor or associate pastor of a church served as parish associate unless at least six months have elapsed since the end of the parish associate relationship.

Designation
Made Under
Supervision of
Committee on
Ministry

b. The designation of parish associate shall be made under the supervision of the committee on ministry at the request of the session of a particular church, the consent of the parish associate, and the approval of the presbytery. No formal call shall be involved. Any change in relationship must be approved by the presbytery. Ordinarily no more than one parish associate will be related to a particular church.

Annual Review

c.   The committee on ministry shall review the designation once each year to insure

(1) that the time and energy required as a parish associate will not interfere unduly with the work of the person in his or her principal function;

(2) that installed leadership of the particular church be protected in its effective functioning;

(3) that the parish associate continue to meet the criteria for continuing membership in the presbytery based on other than this relationship to a particular church.

When Pulpit
Is Vacant

d.   The agreement between the session and the parish associate shall, whenever a pulpit becomes vacant, be terminated upon due notice by the session or the parish associate with the approval of the presbytery.

G-14.0516

[This section was stricken and the text moved to G-14.0801 by the 208th General Assembly (1996).]

G-14.0517
Validated
Ministry: Call,
Installation,
Recognition

a.   A call to a validated ministry in other service of this church (G-11.0410) or in service beyond the jurisdiction of the church (G-11.0411) shall ordinarily be in a form which includes a description of the goals and working relationships, financial terms, and the signatures of the minister, a representative of the presbytery, and where possible, a representative of the employing agency.

Service

b.   It is appropriate for presbytery to conduct a service of installation similar to that found in G-14.0510, or a service of recognition, at the inauguration of this ministry.

G-14.0600

6.   Dissolution of Pastoral Relationships

G-14.0601
By Presbytery

The pastoral relationship between a pastor, associate pastor, or assistant pastor and a church may be dissolved only by presbytery. (See G-6.0202c)

G-14.0602
Request by
Minister

The minister may request the presbytery to dissolve the pastoral relationship. The minister must also state her or his intention to the session. In the case of a pastor or associate pastor, the session shall call a congregational meeting to act upon the request and to make recommendations to presbytery. The presbytery may grant authority to its committee on ministry to dissolve the pastoral relationship and to inform the presbytery in cases in which the congregation and the pastor concur. If the congregation does not concur, the presbytery shall hear from the church, through the congregation's elected commissioners, the reasons why the presbytery should not dissolve the pastoral relationship. If the church fails to appear, or if its reasons for retaining the relationship are judged insufficient, the request of the minister may be granted and the pastoral relationship dissolved.

G-14.0603
Request by
Congregation

If any church desires the pastoral relationship to be dissolved, a similar procedure shall be observed. A congregation, after a duly called congregational meeting, may request presbytery to dissolve its relationship with its pastor. The pastor shall moderate the congregational meeting (in accordance with G-7.0306) unless he or she deems it to be impractical. The presbytery may grant authority to its committee on ministry to dissolve the relationship and to inform the presbytery in cases in which the pastor and the congregation concur. If the pastor does not concur, the presbytery shall hear from him or her the reasons why the presbytery should not dissolve the relationship. If the pastor fails to appear, or if the reasons for maintaining the relationship are judged insufficient, the relationship may be dissolved.

G-14.0604

[This section was stricken by action of the 200th General Assembly (1988).]

G-14.0605
Pastor Emeritus,
Emerita

When any pastor or associate pastor retires, and the congregation is moved by affection and gratitude to continue an association in an honorary relationship, it may, at a regularly called congregational meeting, elect him or her as pastor emeritus or emerita, with or without honorarium, but with no pastoral authority or duty. This action shall be taken only after consultation with the committee on ministry of the presbytery concerning the wisdom of this relationship for the peace of the church. This action shall be subject to the approval of presbytery, and may take effect upon the formal dissolution of the pastoral or associate pastoral relationship or anytime thereafter.

G-14.0606
Officiate by
Invitation Only

Former pastors, associate pastors, and assistant pastors may officiate at services for members of a particular church, or at services within its properties, only upon invitation from the moderator of the session or, in case of the inability to contact the moderator, from the clerk of session.

G-14.0607

[This section was stricken by action of the 200th General Assembly (1988).]

G-14.0700

7. Certified Christian Educator

G-14.0701
Christian
Educators

a.   Christian educators are persons called to and employed in the ministry of education in a particular church, churches, or governing bodies. Christian educators are persons who demonstrate their faith in and love for Jesus Christ, are dedicated to the life of faith and are serious in purpose, honest in character, and joyful in service.

b.   Christian educators serving particular congregations, with the session and pastor(s) share the responsibility of providing for the spiritual growth of members for their ministry as specified in G-6.0202-.0203 and G-10.0102. Christian educators will perform a variety of tasks including teaching the Bible, recommending curriculum materials and resources, training and supporting lay workers, and planning and administering the educational program of their congregations. Christian educators are accountable to the session and under the supervision of the pastor.

c.   Christian educators shall be persons with skills and training in biblical interpretation, Reformed theology, human development, religious educational theory and practice, and the polity, programs, and mission of the Presbyterian Church (U.S.A.). Christian educators shall be encouraged by their session and presbytery to meet, or be prepared to meet, the certification requirements defined in G-14.0703.

G-14.0702
The Certified
Christian
Educator

a.   Certification is a means whereby the church recognizes the gifts, preparation, and effective service of those persons called to and employed in the ministry of education in the church.

b.   The highest level of certification shall be the Certified Christian Educator.

G-14.0703
Certification

The General Assembly shall provide an accrediting process which evaluates the educator's academic preparation and work experience and examines competency in the following knowledge and skill areas:

a.   *Biblical Interpretation.* This examination shall assess the educator's ability to interpret Scripture using accepted exegetical processes and resources and to apply the Scripture in a contemporary teaching situation.

b.   *Reformed Theology.* This examination shall assess the educator's understanding of theology consistent with the confessional documents of the church, as expressed in educational theory and practice.

c.   *Human Development.* This examination shall assess the educator's understanding of the theories of human development and faith development and their application in the educational ministry of the church.

d.   *Religious Education Theory and Practice.* This examination shall assess the educator's ability to integrate religious educational theory and practice in the church's educational ministry.

e.   *Polity.* This examination shall assess the educator's working knowledge of the *Constitution of the Presbyterian Church (U.S.A.).*

f.   *Program and Mission of the Presbyterian Church (U.S.A.).* This examination shall assess the educator's knowledge of the program and mission of the Presbyterian Church (U.S.A.) and the ability to interpret this program and mission in the educational ministry of the church.

G-14.0704
Educator
Certification
Council

a.   The accrediting process shall be administered by and certification granted by the Educator Certification Council on behalf of the General Assembly Council.

b. The Educator Certification Council shall

(1) establish certification standards;

(2) designate Educator Certification Advisors in consultation with presbyteries;

(3) evaluate certification examinations;

(4) grant certificates and report to the General Assembly Council (through the National Ministries Division).

G-14.0705
Presbytery

a. The presbytery shall support the certification process by

(1) encouraging educators to seek certification;

(2) providing guidance through the Educator Certification Advisor;

(3) encouraging sessions to make continuing education funds and time available to educators seeking certification.

b. The presbytery shall provide the following support to the Certified Christian Educator:

(1) service of recognition; (G-11.0103n)

(2) guidelines for compensation and benefits; (G-11.0103n)

(3) access to the committee on ministry. (G-11.0503)

c. The presbytery shall grant the privilege of the floor to the Certified Christian Educator at all its meetings with voice. (G-11.0407)

8. Other Certified Employees

G-14.0800

G-14.0801
Commissioned
Lay Pastor

a. The commissioned lay pastor is an elder of the Presbyterian Church (U.S.A.), who is granted a local commission by the presbytery to lead worship and preach the gospel, watch over the people, and provide for their nurture and service. This commission is valid only in one or more congregations, **new church development, or other validated ministries of the presbytery** designated by the presbytery. Such an elder is selected by and receives training approved by the presbytery. The elder shall be instructed in Bible, Reformed Theology and Sacraments, Presbyterian Polity, preaching, leading worship, pastoral care, and teaching. The elder shall be examined by the appropriate committee of presbytery as to personal faith, motives for seeking the commission, and the areas of instruction mentioned previously. An elder who has been commissioned and later ceases to serve in a particular congregation may continue to be listed as available to serve, but is not authorized to perform the functions of a commissioned lay pastor until appointed again to a particular congregation by the presbytery.

Period
Valid

b. The commission shall be valid for a period up to three years as determined by the presbytery. It may be renewed at expiration or terminated at any time at the discretion of the presbytery. Presbytery shall regularly provide resources for the person's spiritual and intellectual development. A review of the work of the commissioned lay pastor shall be conducted annually. Presbytery shall revoke the commission of any lay pastor who does not abide by these provisions or whose work is evaluated as not adequate to meet the needs of the particular congregation or the presbytery.

Authorization
to Perform
Functions

c.   When a presbytery, in consultation with the session or other responsible committee, determines that its strategy for mission in a local church requires it, and after additional instruction deemed necessary by the presbytery has been provided, a presbytery may authorize a commissioned lay pastor to perform any or all of the following functions described in (1)–(6) below.

(1)   Administer the Lord's Supper.

(2)   Administer the Sacrament of Baptism.

(3)   Moderate the session of the congregation under the supervision of and when invited by the moderator of the session appointed by the presbytery.

(4)   Have a voice in meetings of presbytery.

(5)   Have a vote in meetings of the presbytery (such vote to be counted as an elder commissioner for purposes of parity).

(6)   Perform a service of Christian marriage when invited by the session or other responsible committee, and when allowed by the state.

Supervision

d.   The commissioned lay pastor shall work under the supervision of the presbytery through the moderator of the session of the church being served or through the committee on ministry. A minister of the Word and Sacrament shall be assigned as a mentor and supervisor.

Questions Asked

e.   When the presbytery is satisfied with the qualifications of an applicant it shall ask the applicant the following questions:

(1) Do you trust in Jesus Christ your Savior, acknowledge him Lord of all and Head of the Church, and through him believe in one God, Father, Son, and Holy Spirit?

(2) Do you accept the Scriptures of the Old and New Testaments to be, by the Holy Spirit, the unique and authoritative witness to Jesus Christ in the Church universal, and God's Word to you?

(3) Do you sincerely receive and adopt the essential tenets of the Reformed faith as expressed in the confessions of our church as authentic and reliable expositions of what Scripture leads us to believe and do, and will you be instructed and led by those confessions as you lead the people of God?

(4) Will you fulfill your commission in obedience to Jesus Christ, under the authority of Scripture, and be continually guided by our confessions?

(5) Will you be governed by our church's polity, and will you abide by its discipline? Will you be a friend among your colleagues in ministry, working with them, subject to the ordering of God's Word and Spirit?

(6) Will you in your own life seek to follow the Lord Jesus Christ, love your neighbors, and work for the reconciliation of the world?

(7) Do you promise to further the peace, unity, and purity of the church?

(8) Will you seek to serve the people with energy, intelligence, imagination, and love?

(9) Will you be a faithful commissioned lay pastor, watching over the people, providing for their worship? In your ministry, will you try to show the love and justice of Jesus Christ? (G-14.0207)

Prayer and Statement

f.   The applicant having answered these questions in the affirmative, the moderator shall pray and say to the applicant:

(Name) _____, you are now a lay pastor commissioned to lead worship and preach for the time and in the place set by this presbytery. The grace of the Lord Jesus Christ be with you. Amen.

**G-14.0802
Other Certified
Lay Employees**

a.   Other certified lay employees have been called to service within particular churches, governing bodies, and church-related entities. These individuals endeavor to reflect their faith through their work and to strengthen the church through their dedication. To that end, groups of professionals have organized for community, support, and professional development. Several of these associations have entered into formal liaison relationships with General Assembly entities. These groups include the Administrative Personnel Association, the Presbyterian Association of Musicians, and the Presbyterian Church Business Administrators Association.

b.   Members of the Administrative Personnel Association (APA) include secretaries, administrative assistants, bookkeepers and support staff in church-related settings. Certification is granted by APA; the requirements for certification are approved by the Division of National Ministries. Requirements include attendance at association conferences as well as a total of forty hours of instruction in polity, in Reformed theology, in church history, and in one's area of expertise.

c.   Members of the Presbyterian Association of Musicians (PAM) include choir directors, organists, ministers, and other persons interested in the quality and integrity of music in the worship experience. Certification is granted by the association. Requirements include a Master of Music degree and additional courses in polity, Bible, worship, human faith and development, and music education. Those who earn certification are advised by a reference group and are examined for proficiency in the areas of study. This association has a liaison relationship with the Division of Congregational Ministries.

d.   Members of the Presbyterian Church Business Administrators Association include pastors and lay persons serving primarily as administrators in particular churches and church-related entities. Certification is granted by the association; requirements for certification are approved by the Division of National Ministries. These include attendance at two ten-day seminars and completion of an approved research project in church administration. Areas of study in the seminars include: property management, finance and investments, personnel management, church history, theology, communication and information systems, legal/tax matters, stewardship, accounting, office procedures, polity, and other management skills.

**G-14.0803
Notification of
Status**

Names of those who have earned certification through these associations shall be transmitted to the Office of Certification in the Division of National Ministries, who will forward them to the Office of the General Assembly and to the stated clerk of the presbyteries in which those persons labor.

**G-14.0804
Recognition by
Presbytery**

The presbytery shall affirm the skill and dedication of these certified lay employees by providing for recognition at presbytery at the time of their certification and by inviting these employees to presbytery meetings, granting them the privilege of the floor.

CHAPTER XV. RELATIONSHIPS

G-15.0000

G-15.0100

1. Ecumenical Commitment

G-15.0101
Openness

The Presbyterian Church (U.S.A.) seeks to manifest more visibly the unity of the church of Jesus Christ and will be open to opportunities for conversation, cooperation, and action with other ecclesiastical bodies and secular groups.

G-15.0102
Other Christian
Bodies

The Presbyterian Church (U.S.A.) will seek to initiate, maintain, and strengthen its relations to, and to engage in mission with, other Presbyterian and Reformed bodies and with other Christian churches, alliances, councils, and consortia.

G-15.0103
All Levels

All governing bodies of the church, in consultation with the next higher governing body, shall be authorized to work with other Christian denominations in the creation and strengthening of effective ecumenical agencies for common mission.

G-15.0104
Non-Christian
Religious Bodies

The Presbyterian Church (U.S.A.) will seek new opportunities for conversation and understanding with non-Christian religious bodies in order that interests and concerns may be shared and common action undertaken where compatible means and aims exist.

G-15.0105
Secular Groups

The Presbyterian Church (U.S.A.) will initiate and respond to approaches for conversation and common action with movements, organizations, and agencies of the business, educational, cultural, and civic communities that give promise of assistance toward accomplishing the mission of the Church in the world.

G-15.0200

2. Relations with Other Denominations

G-15.0201
Churches in
Correspondence

The General Assembly of the Presbyterian Church (U.S.A.) is in correspondence with the highest governing body of those churches with which it has had historical relations outside the United States, and of those churches that are members of the ecumenical bodies in which the Presbyterian Church (U.S.A.) holds membership; and is in full communion with those churches so recognized by ecumenical agreements approved by the General Assembly.

G-15.0202
Recognition of
Ordination

When a minister of another Christian denomination is called to a work properly under the jurisdiction of a presbytery, the presbytery, after the constitutional conditions (G-14.0508) have been met, shall recognize the minister's previous ordination to the office of the ministry. Similar procedures shall be followed in dismissing a minister from this denomination to another.

G-15.0203
Reception and
Dismissal of
Churches

a. When a particular church of another denomination requests that it be received by a presbytery of this denomination, the presbytery shall verify that the church has been regularly dismissed by the governing body of jurisdiction, and the advice of the highest governing body of that denomination dealing with relations between denominations has been received, and shall then receive the church in accord with its responsibilities and powers. (G-11.0103h.)

Dismissal of Churches

b.   Similar procedures shall be followed in dismissing a particular church from this denomination to another. (G-11.0103i)

G-15.0204 Federated or Union Churches

a.   A presbytery may authorize a particular church to form a federated or union church with a church or churches of another denomination or denominations, or may organize a federated or union church acting in concert with a comparable governing body of another denomination or denominations. For the formation of a union church see G-16.0000.

Federated Church

b.   A federated church shall conduct its life and work under a plan of agreement between the presbytery and the other governing body or bodies. This plan shall follow provisions of G-16.0000 as clearly as is practicable, and it shall be subject to the constitutions (disciplines or other organic documents) of each church involved. Whenever the constitutions differ, the mandatory provisions of one shall apply in all cases when the others are permissive. Whenever there are conflicting mandatory provisions, petition shall be made to the appropriate governing bodies of the denominations to resolve the conflict either by authoritative interpretation or by constitutional amendment.

G-15.0300

3.   Church Union

G-15.0301 Organic Union

Full organic union of this church with any other ecclesiastical body can be effected in the following manner:

a.   the approval of the proposed union by the General Assembly and its recommendation to the presbyteries;

b.   the approval in writing of two thirds of the presbyteries;

c.   the approval and consummation by the next ensuing General Assembly, or other General Assembly specified in the proposed plan of union.

G-15.0302 Ecumenical Statements

a.   In the search for the unity of Christ's Church, the Presbyterian Church (U.S.A.) may from time to time receive for guidance statements of ecumenical consensus that regularly chosen representatives of this church have helped to formulate. The purpose of receiving such ecumenical statements shall be to guide the particular churches and governing bodies of this church as they share in joint action with other ecclesiastical bodies seeking ways to express the unity of the Church and to discover its possible future form.

Approved by General Assembly

b.   Such an ecumenical statement shall be approved by the General Assembly as a guide for such shared action and shall be submitted to the presbyteries for their affirmative or negative votes together with a statement of the specific purpose and the effect of approving it. When the next ensuing General Assembly shall have received written advice that an ecumenical statement has received the affirmative vote of a majority of the presbyteries, that statement shall serve as guidance for participation in ecumenical activity.

Received
Ecumenical
Statements

c.   Ecumenical statements which have been approved by the General Assembly and a majority of the presbyteries in the manner described in the preceding paragraphs shall be published as "Received Ecumenical Statements of Guidance." Such statements shall not be part of the *Constitution of the Presbyterian Church (U.S.A.)* as defined in G-1.0500 unless adopted as amendments pursuant to Chapter XVIII, "Amendments." Ecumenical activity under the guidance of such received ecumenical statements may be conducted only under provisions of the Constitution thereof.

d.   Governing bodies are encouraged and permitted to discover and engage in opportunities to minister together in mutual affirmation and admonition with churches with whom the Presbyterian Church (U.S.A.) is in full communion.

G-16.0000   **CHAPTER XVI. UNION CHURCHES**

G-16.0100   **1. Particular Churches of Reformed Churches**

G-16.0101
Union with Other
Reformed Bodies

A particular church of this church may unite to form a union church with one or more particular churches which are members of other Reformed churches.

G-16.0200   **2. Plan of Union**

G-16.0201
Plan of Union
General

These provisions shall be included in the Plan of Union with such churches:

     a.   The following Plan of Union is adopted by the _____ _____ Presbyterian Church of _____ _____ and the _____ Church of _____ effective as of the date when each of the congregations has approved the plan by a two-thirds majority of those present at a regularly called congregational meeting with such notice and quorum as is required by the Constitution of each church, and when the presbytery (or comparable governing body) of each church has approved the particular union and this Plan of Union.

Purpose

     b.   The purpose of this union is to provide for the worship of Almighty God, instruction in the Christian religion, and participation in the mission of the church in the world, by a union congregation which will share the property, real and personal, of the uniting churches and provide for the services of a minister or ministers for the union church.

Name

     c.   The union church shall be known as the _____ _____ church of _____.

Subjection

     d.   The union church shall be subject to the Constitution of each church involved as set forth in subsections r, s, u, and v below.

Review of
Records

     e.   The session (or comparable governing body) shall submit its records annually, and whenever requested, to each governing body of jurisdiction.

Membership

     f.   The membership of the union church shall consist of those who were members of the uniting churches, plus those received by the session of the union church.

Report of
Membership

     g.   The session of the union church shall report an equal share of the total membership to each governing body of jurisdiction and such membership shall be published in the *Minutes* of the General Assembly (or comparable governing body) with a note to the effect that the report is that of a union church, and with an indication of the total actual membership.

A similar report of church school members, baptisms, etc., and financial expenditures shall be made by the session and noted by each General Assembly in its *Minutes*.

Officers

h.   Initially the officers of the union church, elders and deacons, shall be those officers in active service of the uniting churches who will undertake to perform their ordination responsibilities under the Constitution of each church as indicated in subsections d above and r, s, u, and v below.

Election of
Officers

i.   At the first annual meeting subsequent to the effective date of the union, new classes of officers, to replace the officers noted in subsection h above, shall be elected by the union congregation according to the constitutional procedures in force as a consequence of subsection v below.

Ministers of
Union Churches

j.   The pastoral relations of the ministers of the uniting churches shall be dissolved automatically by the action of the presbytery in approving this plan, but they may be eligible to be ministers (pastors, or associate pastors) of the union church according to the will of the union church and subject to the approval of the governing bodies.

Full Members

k.   The minister or ministers of the union church shall be full and responsible members of each governing body of immediate jurisdiction and shall be subject to discipline as provided below in subsection s.

Incorporation

l.   The union church shall cause a corporation to be formed under the appropriate laws of the state where permissible. That corporation shall include in its articles or charter the substance of subsections b, c, and d above.

Property

m.   All property of the uniting churches, real and personal, shall be transferred to the corporation formed in subsection l above. The new corporation shall be the legal successor of the corporations, if any, of the uniting churches, and it shall be bound to administer any trust, property, or moneys received in accordance with the provisions of the original establishment of the trust. All liabilities of the uniting churches shall be liabilities of the union church. In any state where a church corporation is forbidden, the purposes of this paragraph shall be achieved in harmony with the law of the state.

Trustees

n.   Trustees of the corporation (or the unincorporated body) shall be elected in harmony with civil law according to the constitutional provisions outlined in subsection d interpreted by subsection v below.

Benevolences

o.   While recognizing the basic right of any giver to designate the cause or causes to which personal gifts shall go, the session of the union church shall annually propose to the congregation a general mission or benevolence program which shall be divided equitably among the officially approved causes of each denomination. The proportions shall be as the session shall decide in response to the requests of the higher governing bodies.

Per Capita Apportionments

p.   Per capita apportionments or assessments shall be paid to each governing body of jurisdiction on the basis of the total active membership of the union church, equally divided among the denominations involved.

Session

q.   All members of the union church shall be under the discipline of the session according to rules agreed upon in harmony with the Constitution of each denomination where they coincide, and in harmony with the mandatory provisions of the Constitution of one denomination where the others are permissive, and at the choice of the session where they may be contradictory.

Appeals or Complaints

r.   Appeals or complaints against the actions of the session shall be made to one higher governing body only (presbytery or comparable governing body) at the choice of the members and all subsequent appeals or complaints shall be in the governing bodies of the members' original choice, and decisions so finally made shall be binding on the session and on the member.

Judicial Cases

s.   The minister or ministers shall be subject to the discipline of the presbyteries or comparable governing body provided that when either shall begin an action it shall invite a committee from the others to join the commissioner, prosecutor, or prosecuting committee in formulating and pressing the charges. In the event of appeal the case shall be finally decided by the highest governing body to which the appeal is taken in the church which commenced the action, and that decision shall be equally binding on the governing bodies of jurisdiction.

Pension

t.   The minister or ministers shall participate in the denominational pension plan of one of the churches. If the minister is already participating in one plan, membership in that plan shall be retained. If the minister is not a member of any plan, one or the other of the churches' plans shall be chosen.

Administrative Complaints

u.   Complaints against the administrative acts of the session may be taken under the constitutional provisions of only one denomination, according to the choice of the complainant, and once being complained to one higher governing body, no other denomination shall accept jurisdiction in the same manner.

Conflict of Constitutions

v.   Wherever the constitutions of the denominations differ, the mandatory provisions of one shall apply in all cases when the others are permissive. Wherever there are conflicting mandatory provisions (except as provided in subsection q above), the session of the union church shall petition the next higher governing bodies to overture their highest governing bodies to resolve the conflict either by authoritative interpretation or by constitutional amendment.

Dissolution

w. A union church may be dissolved by a two-thirds vote of two congregational meetings, held not less than one year and not more than two years apart, subject to the concurrence of the governing bodies involved. In case of dissolution of a union church, all property of the union church, real and personal, shall be divided equally between the next higher governing bodies.

G-16.0300

G-16.0301
Union with
Other Christian
Churches

3. Particular Churches of Other Christian Bodies

With the approval of the presbytery, and the consent of the General Assembly, particular churches of this church may unite to form union churches with one or more particular churches of churches other than those of the Reformed faith but which recognize Jesus Christ as Lord and Savior, accept the authority of Scripture, and observe the Sacraments of Baptism and the Lord's Supper.

G-16.0400

G-16.0401
Plan of Union

General

4. Plan of Union

The following Plan of Union shall be adopted by the union church so formed:

a. The union church shall be subject to the constitutions of each church involved, as set forth in subparagraphs l, m, o, and p below.

Government of
Church

b. The union church shall be governed by a representative body elected by the congregation from among its members. This governing body shall have the powers of the session. The members of the governing body need not be elders, but if the Plan of Union provides for elders, the governing body shall consist of elders.

Membership

c. Members of the governing body of the union church shall be eligible to membership and office in the higher governing bodies.

Report an Equal
Share

d. The governing body of the union church shall report an equal share of the total membership to each governing body of jurisdiction, and such membership shall be published in the minutes of each church involved with a note to the effect that the report is that of a union church, and with an indication of the total actual membership. A similar report of church school members, baptisms, etc., and financial expenditures shall be made by the governing body and noted by each involved church in its minutes.

Ministers

e. The minister or ministers of the union church shall be full and responsible members of each governing body of immediate jurisdiction and shall be subject to discipline as provided below in subparagraph m.

Incorporation

f.　The union church shall cause a corporation to be formed under the appropriate laws of the state where permissible. That corporation shall include in its articles or charter the substance of subparagraph a above.

Property

g.　All property of the uniting churches, real and personal, shall be transferred to the corporation formed in subparagraph f above. The new corporation shall be the legal successor of the corporations, if any, of the uniting churches, and it shall be bound to administer any trust property or moneys received in accordance with the provisions of the original establishment of the trust. All liabilities of the uniting churches shall be liabilities of the union church. In any state where a church corporation is forbidden, the purposes of this subparagraph shall be achieved in harmony with the law of that state.

Trustees

h.　Trustees of the corporation (or the unincorporated body) shall be elected in harmony with civil law according to constitutional provisions outlined in subparagraph a above as interpreted by subparagraph p below.

Benevolences

i.　While recognizing the basic right of any giver to designate the cause or causes to which a personal gift shall go, the governing body of the union church shall annually propose to the congregation a general mission or benevolence program which shall be divided equitably among the officially approved causes of each denomination. The proportions shall be as the governing body shall decide in response to the requests of the higher governing bodies.

Per Capita
Apportionments

j.　Per capita apportionments or assessments shall be paid to each governing body of jurisdiction on the basis of the total active membership of the union church, equally divided among the denominations involved.

Discipline

k.　All members of the union church shall be under the discipline of the governing body according to rules agreed upon in harmony with the Constitution of each denomination where they coincide, and in harmony with the mandatory provisions of the Constitution of one denomination where the others are permissive, and at the choice of the governing body where they may be contradictory.

Appeals or
Complaints

l.　Appeals or complaints against the actions of the governing body shall be made to one higher governing body only at the choice of the members and all subsequent appeals or complaints shall be in the governing bodies of the members' original choice, and decisions so finally made shall be binding on the governing body and on the members.

Judicial Cases

m.   The minister or ministers shall be subject to the discipline of the governing body of jurisdiction provided that when one shall begin an action, it shall invite a committee from the others to join the commissioner, prosecutor, or prosecuting committee in formulating and pressing the charges. In the event of appeal the case shall be finally decided by the highest governing body to which the appeal is taken in the church which commenced the action and that decision shall be equally binding on the governing bodies of jurisdiction.

Pension

n.   The minister or ministers shall participate in the denominational pension plan of one of the several churches. If the minister is already participating in one plan, membership in that plan shall be retained. If the minister is not a member of any plan, one or the other of the churches' plans shall be chosen.

Administrative
Complaints

o.   Complaints against the administrative acts of the governing body may be taken under the constitutional provisions of only one denomination, according to the choice of the complainant, and once being complained to one denomination, no other denomination shall accept jurisdiction in the same matter.

Conflict of
Constitutions

p.   Wherever the constitutions of the denominations differ, the mandatory provisions of one shall apply in all cases when the others are permissive. Wherever there are conflicting mandatory provisions (except as provided in subparagraph k above), the governing body of the union church shall petition the governing bodies of immediate jurisdiction to overture their highest governing bodies to resolve the conflict either by authoritative interpretation or by constitutional amendment.

Dissolution

q.   A union church may be dissolved by a two-thirds vote of two congregational meetings, held not less than one year and not more than two years apart, subject to the concurrence of the governing bodies involved. In case of dissolution of a union church, all property of the union church, real and personal, shall be divided equally between the governing bodies of jurisdiction.

G-16.0500

G-16.0501
No Change in
Constitution

5.   Exception

No provision in Sections 1, 2, 3, and 4 above shall be construed as modifying or amending the Constitution of this church in its application to any but union churches organized under this chapter, their members, officers, or ministers.

G-17.0000

CHAPTER XVII. UNION GOVERNING BODIES

G-17.0100

1. Authorization

G-17.0101
Authorization

A presbytery of this church may unite to form a union presbytery with one or more comparable governing bodies, each of which is a member of another Reformed body, with the approval of the synod or comparable governing body of which each is a part.

G-17.0200

2. Plan of Union

G-17.0201
Plan of Union

The following Plan of Union shall be adopted by each presbytery (or comparable governing body) involved:

General

a. This plan of union is adopted by the Presbytery of _____ _____ and the Presbytery of _____ _____ effective as of _____ (date), the presbyteries having each approved the plan by a two-thirds majority of those present at a stated meeting of the presbytery, the matter having been published beforehand on its docket and the union and this plan having been approved by the synod (or comparable governing body) of jurisdiction over each.

Purpose

b. The purpose of the union shall be the furtherance of a united witness and mission, the administration of a single program of nurture, sustenance, and growth of the church within the union presbytery, and the oversight of all churches within its bounds by a union presbytery that will hold title to the properties of the uniting governing bodies and provide the functions and fulfill the duties of a presbytery as specified in the Constitution of each church.

Constitutional
Requirements

c. The union presbytery shall be subject to the Constitution of each denomination as set forth below:

Records

(1) The presbytery shall submit its records annually and whenever requested to each synod (or comparable governing body) of jurisdiction.

Benevolences

(2) The presbytery shall be fully and equally responsible to each church. The presbytery shall adjust its benevolence or general mission askings of the particular churches annually, to the end that the presbytery shall equitably support the program of each denomination.

Per Capita
Apportionments

(3) Per capita apportionments or assessments shall be paid to each governing body of jurisdiction on the basis of the active member strength of the union presbytery, equally divided among the denominations involved. In the event that such a procedure proves inequitable, an alternative

basis may be adopted subject to approval by the governing body of jurisdiction of each denomination. Such an alternative if adopted shall be subject to periodic review.

Standing Rules

(4) The union presbytery shall be under the discipline of the synods and General Assemblies (or comparable governing bodies) according to standing rules agreed upon in harmony with the constitutions of the denominations where they coincide, and in harmony with the mandatory provisions of the laws of each church where the others are permissive, and at the choice of the presbytery where they may be contradictory.

Appeals or Complaints

(5) Appeals or complaints against the actions of the presbytery shall be made only to the synod of one denomination. That denomination shall be determined by the presbytery, and all subsequent appeals or complaints in the same action shall be in the governing bodies of the original determination, and decisions so reached shall be binding on all the parties to such action.

Administrative Complaints

(6) Complaints against administrative acts of the presbytery may be taken under the constitutional provisions of only one denomination, according to the determination of the presbytery; and, once being complained to one governing body, governing bodies of the other denomination may not accept jurisdiction in the same matter.

Conflict of Constitutions

(7) Wherever the constitutions of the denominations differ, any mandatory provisions of one shall apply in all cases where the others are permissive. Where there are conflicting mandatory provisions (except as provided in (4) above), the union presbytery shall overture the highest governing body of the denominations involved to resolve the conflict either by authoritative interpretation or by constitutional amendment.

Exemption

(8) The provision of G-8.0500 of the Presbyterian Church (U.S.A.) shall apply only to a union church organized subsequent to the formation of a union presbytery, and to a union church entering the union governing body, which church had previously been under a similar explicit constitutional provision.

Membership of Union Presbytery

d. The membership of the union presbytery shall consist of all minister members of each uniting presbytery and all the churches (elder or lay representatives thereof) of the uniting presbyteries, plus all others received by the union presbytery, subsequent to the effective date of this union. When the constitutions of the churches vary as to elder or lay representation, that provision which confers the largest representation shall apply.

Membership

e.   The churches of a union presbytery shall be considered union churches belonging to each denomination. Each particular church shall be reported to each General Assembly and synod of jurisdiction on the basis of an equal division of its total membership, with a notation to the effect that this has been done.

Ministers

f.   Ministers of the union presbytery shall be full and responsible members of each denomination. They shall be subject to the jurisdiction and discipline of the denominations as provided in this plan. Ministers and elders or lay delegates shall be eligible to serve as commissioners to any General Assembly, as provided in the Constitution of each denomination. Commissioners to the General Assembly shall be elected on the basis of an equal division of the total active membership of the presbytery.

General Mission
Benevolence

g.   The union presbytery shall be responsible to propose to all its churches a general mission and benevolence program which it judges to be an adequate and equitable response to the requests of the General Assemblies, the synods, and to its own needs. Each session shall give the members of its congregation opportunity to support this general mission and benevolence program.

Incorporation

h.   The union presbytery shall cause a corporation to be formed under the appropriate laws of the state. This corporation shall include in its articles or charter the substance of subsections b and c above. All property of the uniting presbyteries, real and personal, shall be transferred to the corporation or corporations formed under this section. The new corporation shall be the legal successor of the corporations, if any, of the uniting presbyteries and it shall be bound to administer any trust property or moneys received in accordance with the provisions of the original establishment of the trust. All liabilities of each uniting presbytery shall be the liabilities of the union presbytery. In any state where a church corporation is forbidden, the purpose of this paragraph shall be achieved in harmony with the laws of the state.

Standing Rules

i.   The union presbytery shall draw up standing rules which shall define the operation of presbytery in such a manner as to fulfill all the functions of a presbytery, as defined in the Constitution of each denomination. (G-17.0201c(4))

Pension Plan

j.   Each minister who may be subject to the call of presbytery or any of its constituent churches in the exercise of that minister's vocation, or who may be an employee of presbytery, shall participate in the denominational pension plan of one of the churches. If the minister is already participating in one plan, membership shall be retained in that plan. If the minister is not a member of any plan, membership shall be chosen in one of the churches' plans.

Dissolution

k.   A union presbytery may be dissolved by a two-thirds vote at two stated meetings of presbytery, not less than one year and not more than two years apart, subject to the concurrence of the synods involved.

(1) In case of dissolution of a union presbytery, all the property, real and personal, of the union presbytery shall be divided between the denominations or their governing bodies of jurisdiction on the basis of the origin of the property, if such is determinable. If the origin is not determinable, then the property shall be divided equally between the denominations or their governing bodies of jurisdiction, as may be proper.

(2) The particular churches within the dissolved union presbytery shall retain their status as union churches, unless they vote to change that status under the provisions of G-16.0201w.

G-17.0300

G-17.0301
No Change in
Constitution

3. Exception

No provision in this plan of union shall be construed as modifying or amending the Constitution of this church in its application to any but union presbyteries organized under this chapter, their churches, or ministers.

CHAPTER XVIII. AMENDMENTS

G-18.0100

G-18.0101
Reform by
Amendment

1. Reform

The Presbyterian Church (U.S.A.) would be faithful to the Lordship of Christ and to its historic tradition of the Church reformed always reforming, by the Spirit of God. In this faith, amendment procedures are understood as a means to faithfulness as God breaks forth yet more light from God's Word.

G-18.0200

G-18.0201
Amendments to
Confessional
Documents

2. Confessional Documents

a. Amendments to the confessional documents of this church may be made only in the following manner:

(1) The approval of the proposed amendment by the General Assembly and its recommendation to the presbyteries;

(2) The approval in writing of two thirds of the presbyteries;

(3) The approval and enactment by the next ensuing General Assembly.

Special
Committee

b. Before such amendments to the confessional documents shall be transmitted to the presbyteries, the General Assembly shall appoint a committee of elders and ministers, numbering not less than fifteen, to consider the proposal, of whom not more than two shall be from any one synod. This committee shall consult with the committee or governing body (or in the latter case an agent thereof) in which the amendment originated, and report its recommendation to the next ensuing General Assembly.

G-18.0300

G-18.0301
Amendments to
the *Book of Order*

3. *Book of Order*

Amendments to the *Book of Order* may be made only in the following manner:

a. All proposals requesting amendment of the *Book of Order* shall be communicated in writing to the Stated Clerk of the General Assembly no later than 120 days prior to the convening of the next session of the General Assembly.

b. The Stated Clerk shall refer all such proposed amendments to the Advisory Committee on the Constitution (G-13.0112), which shall examine the proposed amendment for clarity and consistency of language and for compatibility with other provisions of the *Constitution of the Presbyterian Church (U.S.A.)*. The advisory committee shall report its findings to the General Assembly along with its recommendations, which may include an amended version of any proposed constitutional changes as well as advice to accept or decline the proposals referred to the committee. The General Assembly shall not consider any amendment until it has considered the report and any recommendation from the Advisory Committee on the Constitution.

c.   Proposed amendments must be approved by the General Assembly and transmitted to the presbyteries for their vote.

d.   When the next ensuing General Assembly shall have received written advice that a proposed amendment to the *Book of Order* has received the affirmative votes of a majority of all the presbyteries, the General Assembly shall declare the amendment made.

e.   If the General Assembly shall fail to declare such amendment or amendments made after they have received the affirmative vote of a majority of all the presbyteries, such amendments shall nonetheless take effect upon the adjournment of the General Assembly to which the affirmative votes of a majority of all the presbyteries were reported.

G-18.0302
Provisions Not to
Be Amended

The following limitations on amendment apply as indicated.

a.   The following paragraph of the Form of Government may not be amended:

G-8.0701.

b.   The following paragraph of the Form of Government may not be amended within fifteen years following the establishment of the Presbyterian Church (U.S.A.):

G-14.0202a(2).

G-18.0400

4.   Amending the Special Provisions

G-18.0401
Amending the
Special
Provisions

The special provisions for amending the confessional documents and for effecting full organic union (G-15.0300) can be amended only by the same method which they prescribe.

DIRECTORY
FOR
WORSHIP
[TEXT]

DIRECTORY FOR WORSHIP[1]

PREFACE

a.   This Directory for Worship reflects the conviction that the life of the Church is one, and that its worship, witness, and service are inseparable. The theology is based on the Bible, is instructed by *The Book of Confessions* of the Presbyterian Church (U.S.A.), and seeks to be sensitive to ecumenical discussion. A rich heritage of traditions and a diversity of cultures in the Presbyterian church are reflected and encouraged by this directory. A Directory for Worship is not a service book with fixed orders of worship, a collection of prayers and rituals, or a program guide. Rather it describes the theology that underlies Reformed worship and outlines appropriate forms for that worship. This directory suggests possibilities for worship, invites development in worship, and encourages continuing reform of worship. It sets standards and presents norms for the conduct of worship in the life of congregations and the governing bodies of the Presbyterian Church (U.S.A.). As the constitutional document ordering the worship of the Presbyterian Church (U.S.A.), this Directory for Worship shall be authoritative for this church.

b.   This directory uses language about worship which is simply descriptive.

c.   This Directory for Worship has been written in an intentional effort to listen to the Spirit speaking in Scripture and to be guided by *The Book of Confessions*. When the words have come directly from the Bible or from one of the confessions, that is so noted in the text. References to other sections of this Directory for Worship (W-) or to the Form of Government (G-) and the Rules of Discipline (D-) are included in parentheses in the text to guide those who use the directory. Notes at the bottom of the pages are to identify biblical and confessional sources which have shaped the development of this directory. These notes are also included to guide the reader to Scripture and the confessions in order to enhance the use of this directory as a teaching text and resource at various levels in the life of the church.

---

[1]The following abbreviations are used throughout:

   G - Form of Government
   W - Directory for Worship
   D - Rules of Discipline.

W-1.0000

CHAPTER I. THE DYNAMICS OF
CHRISTIAN WORSHIP

W-1.1000

W-1.1001
Christian Worship

1. Christian Worship: An Introduction

Christian worship joyfully ascribes all praise and honor, glory and power to the triune God. In worship the people of God acknowledge God present in the world and in their lives. As they respond to God's claim and redemptive action in Jesus Christ, believers are transformed and renewed. In worship the faithful offer themselves to God and are equipped for God's service in the world.

W-1.1002
God's Initiative

a. The Spirit of God quickens people to an awareness of God's grace and claim upon their lives. The Spirit moves them to respond by naming and calling upon God, by remembering and proclaiming God's acts of self-revelation in word and deed, and by committing their lives to God's reign in the world.

God's Encounter
with Humans

b. The earliest recollections of the people of God speak of God's encounter with human beings. God takes the initiative in creation and in covenant, in calling to repentance and in offering forgiveness. God plants and plucks up; God judges and blesses. (Jeremiah 1:10)

God's Entrance
Into the Human
Condition

c. In Jesus Christ, God entered fully into the human condition in an act of self-revelation, redemption, and forgiveness. Entering the brokenness of the world, God in Jesus Christ atoned for sin and restored human life. By so entering the created world God brought time and space, matter and human life to fulfillment as instruments for knowing and praising their Creator.

W-1.1003
Jesus Christ

a. In the person and work of Jesus, God and a human life are united but not confused, distinguished but not separated.

Perfect Human
Response

b. Jesus of Nazareth offered the perfect human response to God. The Life that redeems reveals the form and purpose of redeemed life. Jesus' life discloses the character of authentic Christian worship.

The Living God
in Common Life

c. Jesus Christ is the living God present in common life. The One who is proclaimed in the witness of faith is

---

W-1.1001: Isa. 6; Rev. 4:11; Scots Conf. 3.01; 2 Helv.Conf. 5.023, 5.135; West.Conf. 6.112, 6.113; L.Cat. 7.214, 7.215; S.Cat. 7.046, 7.047, 7.050, 7.051; Conf.1967 9.35-9.37
W-1.1002: Rom. 10:13; 1 Cor. 11:26, 12:3; Scots Conf. 3.02, 3.04-3.06, 3.12; Conf.1967 9.07-9.09, 9.18, 9.20
W-1.1003: Jer. 33:1-9; John 1:1-14; Phil. 2:9-11; Heb. 1, 2; Rev. 19:11-16; Scots Conf. 3.06, 3.09-3.11; 2 Helv. Conf. 5.062, 5.064, 5.146; West.Conf. 6.043-6.047; Conf.1967 9.07-9.11, 9.19

    (1) the Word of God spoken at creation,

    (2) the Word of God promising and commanding throughout covenant history,

    (3) the Word of God

       (a) who became flesh and dwelt among us,

       (b) who was crucified and raised in power,

       (c) who shall return in triumph to judge and reign.

W-1.1004
Jesus Christ in Word and Sacrament

Scripture—the Word written, preaching—the Word proclaimed, and the Sacraments—the Word enacted and sealed, bear testimony to Jesus Christ, the living Word. Through Scripture, proclamation, and Sacraments, God in Christ is present by the Holy Spirit acting to transform, empower, and sustain human lives. In Christian worship the people of God

    (1) hear the Word proclaimed,

    (2) receive the Word enacted in Sacrament,

    (3) discover the Word in the world, and

    (4) are sent to follow the Word into the world.

W-1.1005
Christian Response to God in Community

a.   From the beginning God created women and men for community and called a people into covenant. Jesus called, commissioned, and promised to be present to a people gathered in his name. The Holy Spirit calls, gathers, orders, and empowers the new community of the covenant. To each member, that Spirit gives gifts for building up the body of Christ and for equipping it for the work of ministry. A Christian's personal response to God is in community.

Response in Worship and Service

b.   The people of God respond with words and deeds of praise and thanksgiving in acts of prayer, proclamation, remembrance, and offering. In the name of Christ, by the power of the Holy Spirit, the Christian community worships and serves God

    (1) in shared experiences of life,

    (2) in personal discipleship,

    (3) in mutual ministry, and

    (4) in common ministry in the world.

W-1.1004: John 1:14-18; Rom. 10:8; 2 Cor. 4:4b-6; Phil. 2:5-11; Col. 1:15; Barm.Dec. 8.11, 8.14, 8.17; Conf.1967 9.07, 9.20, 9.27, 9.30, 9.35-9.37

W-1.1005: Matt. 28:20; John 14:18 ff.; Rom. 12:6, 8; 1 Cor. 12; Eph. 4:12 ff.; 1 Pet. 4:10; Heid.Cat. 4.055; Conf.1967 9.17-9.19, 9.20, 9.22, 9.31-9.33

W-1.2000

W-1.2001
The Language of
Response to God

W-1.2002
Symbolic
Language

W-1.2003
Old Testament
Symbols

2. The Language of Worship

God brings all things into being by the Word. God offers the Word of grace, and people respond to that divine initiative through the language of worship. They call God by name, invoke God's presence, beseech God in prayer, and stand before God in silence and contemplation. They bow before God, lift hands and voices in praise, sing, make music, and dance. Heart, soul, strength, and mind, with one accord, they join in the language, drama, and pageantry of worship.

When people respond to God and communicate to each other their experiences of God, they must use symbolic means, for God transcends creation and cannot be reduced to anything within it. No merely human symbols can be adequate to comprehend the fullness of God, and none is identical to the reality of God. Yet the symbols human beings use can be adequate for understanding, sharing, and responding to God's gracious activity in the world since God has chosen to accommodate to humanity in self-revelation

    a.   through the created order,

    b.   in the events of covenant history, and

    c.   most fully in the incarnate Word, Jesus Christ.

Symbols spoken or acted are authentic and appropriate for Christian worship to the extent that they are faithful to the life, death, and resurrection of Jesus Christ.

As the people of God worshiped the Holy One, they used symbols out of human experience, speaking of God as creator, covenant-maker, liberator, judge, redeemer, shepherd, comforter, sovereign, begetter, bearer. From the world of nature they ascribed to God the character of rock, well-spring, fire, eagle, hen, lion, or light. Their worship was also filled with the language of symbolic action:

        fasting and feasting,
            rejoicing and wailing,
                marching and resting,
                    dancing and clapping hands,
        purification and dedication,
            circumcisions and anointings,
                burnt offerings and sin offerings,
                doing justice and mercy,
        making music and singing to the Lord.

W-1.2000: 2 Helv.Conf. 5.217; Conf.1967 9.50

W-1.2002: Isa. 40:18-25, 55:8, 9; John 1:1-18; Rom. 11:33-36; Col. 1:15-20; Heb. 1:1-3

W-1.2003: Psalms, Isaiah, and other poetic and prophetic books

W-1.2004
New Testament
Symbols

a.   Jesus used Old Testament symbols and images to speak to and about God. He participated in the symbolic actions of Israel's worship. In many cases, he personalized and gave new depth to the familiar symbols for God, especially as in his intimate use of Abba, Father. He spoke of himself in terms of many Old Testament symbols—the good shepherd, Israel's bridegroom, the Son of Man—and intensified their meanings. He brought new meaning to current religious practices like almsgiving, baptism, and breaking bread. In daily life, Jesus took ordinary acts of human compassion—healing the sick, feeding the hungry, washing feet—and translated them into ways of serving God.

Christ the Focus
of New Symbols

b.   As the Risen Lord, Jesus Christ became the focus of new symbols. The New Testament writers often used Old Testament symbolic language for the new reality as they sought to communicate the good news, describing Christ as the second Adam and as the Lamb of God. They used new symbolic language as well: the eternal Word, the firstborn of all creation, our peace who has broken down the dividing wall of hostility. In hymns and other forms of praise, Jesus Christ was glorified as the true symbol who reveals all that God is to the world. (W-1.1003-.1005)

W-1.2005
Authentic and
Appropriate
Language

The Church in every culture through the ages has used and adapted biblical symbols, images, stories, and words in worship. The Church's use of this language has not always been authentic and appropriate. For the Reformed tradition in its various expressions the historical and cultural use of language proves to be authentic when it reflects the biblical witness to God in Jesus Christ. Language proves to be appropriate when a worshiping community can claim it as its own when offering praise and thanksgiving to God. Appropriate language by its nature

a.   is more expressive than rationalistic,

b.   builds up and persuades as well as informs and describes,

c.   creates ardor as well as order,

d.   is the utterance of the whole community of faith as well as the devotion of individuals.

Appropriate language seeks to recognize the variety of traditions which reflect biblical truth authentically in their own forms of speech and actions. In doing so the church honors and properly uses the language of the tradition. The church is, nonetheless, free to be innovative in seeking appropriate language for worship. While respecting time-honored forms and set orders, the church may reshape them to respond freely to the leading of God's Spirit in every age.

W-1.2004: John 1:1, 36; 1 Cor. 15:45; Eph. 2:14; Col. 1:15

W-1.2006
Inclusive
Language

    a.   Since the Presbyterian Church (U.S.A.) is a family of peoples united in Jesus Christ, appropriate language for its worship should display the rich variety of these peoples. To the extent that forms, actions, languages, or settings of worship exclude the expression of diverse cultures represented in the church or deny emerging needs and identities of believers, that worship is not faithful to the life, death, and resurrection of Jesus Christ.

Diverse Language

    b.   The church shall strive in its worship to use language about God which is intentionally as diverse and varied as the Bible and our theological traditions. The church is committed to using language in such a way that all members of the community of faith may recognize themselves to be included, addressed, and equally cherished before God. Seeking to bear witness to the whole world, the church struggles to use language which is faithful to biblical truth and which neither purposely nor inadvertently excludes people because of gender, color, or other circumstance in life.

W-1.3000

W-1.3010

W-1.3011
Sabbath, Lord's
Day

3.   Time, Space, and Matter

   a.   Time

    (1) Christians may worship at any time, for all time has been hallowed by God. The covenant community worshiped daily. But God set aside one day in seven to be kept holy to the Lord. In the Old Testament the Sabbath was understood as a day totally set aside and offered to the Lord. In the New Testament, believers observed the first day of the week, the day of resurrection, as the time when the new people of the covenant gathered to worship God in Jesus Christ. They came to speak of this as the Lord's Day.

Word and
Sacraments

    (2) From earliest times, the church has gathered on the Lord's Day for the proclamation and exposition of the Word and the celebration of the Sacraments. The Reformed tradition has emphasized the importance of the Lord's Day as the time for hearing the Word and celebrating the Sacraments in the expectation of encountering the risen Lord, and for responding in prayer and service. (W-3.2001; W-5.5001)

W-1.3012
Daily Worship

    (1) In Israel's worship, daily hours were set aside for sacrifices of praise and thanksgiving. Even after the loss of the Temple, morning, noon, and evening were established times for prayer. Jesus set aside regular times for prayer, and the believing

---

W-1.2006: 1 Cor. 9:19-23; 10:23, 24, 31-33; Gal. 3:28; James. 2:1-9

W-1.3011: Gen. 1:3,14 ff.; 2:3; Ex. 20:8-11; Deut. 5:12-15; Acts 20:7; Rev.1:10; Heid.Cat. 4.103; 2 Helv.Conf. 5.223-5.226; West.Conf. 6.118-6.119; S.Cat. 7.060; L.Cat.7.226-7.227

W-1.3012: Acts 1:14; 2:42; 3:1; 10:9; West.Conf. 6.117

community gathered daily for prayer in the Temple, in an upper room, and in their homes. New Testament writers exhorted the Church to pray without ceasing. Through the ages, the Church has maintained special hours for daily prayer, historically known as the daily office.

Prayer and
Scripture

(2) The Reformed tradition adapted the pattern of the daily office, to provide an occasion not only for prayer but also for the public reading and expounding of Scripture. Daily public worship is to be commended as a dimension of the life and witness of the church as it ministers in and to the community. Changing patterns of life have also led to the expression of daily prayer in family and personal devotion, which are encouraged as a part of the regular discipline of the Christian life. (W-3.4000; W-5.2000; W-5.7000)

W-1.3013
Church Year

As God created and appointed days, God created a rhythm of time and appointed seasons for worship. In the Old Testament, people observed seasons of fasting and feasting as occasions for festival worship of God. Jesus kept these festivals. For the Church in the New Testament, the festivals were transformed in meaning and purpose by Jesus' life and teaching, his death and resurrection, and by the gift of the Holy Spirit. Jesus' birth, life, death, resurrection, ascension, and promised return give meaning to the seasons which order the annual rhythm of worship and guide the selection of lessons to be read and proclaimed in the life of the Church. (W-3.2002; W-3.2003)

W-1.3020

b.   Space

W-1.3021
Old Testament

Christians may worship in any place, for the God who created time also created and ordered space. The Old Testament tells us God met with people in many different places. Yet particular locations became recognized as places where people had special encounter with God, so they arranged space in such a way as to remember and enhance that meeting. Whether the stone altars of the patriarchs, the Tent of Meeting for the wandering people of God, the Temple of the Kingdom in Jerusalem, or the house-synagogue worship of the Dispersion, each place was ordered to invite and express God's presence.

W-1.3022
Jesus

Jesus' life reflects the covenant community's understanding of places for worship. He regularly worshiped in the synagogue and in the Temple, in the wilderness and on the hillsides of Galilee. Jesus especially disclaimed the notion that God could be confined to any one place.

W-1.3013: Rom. 14:5, 6; Col. 2:16, 17
W-1.3020: West.Conf. 6.117
W-1.3022: John 4:21-24

W-1.3023
Early Church

Because the identifying reality of Christian worship was neither the place nor the space but the presence of God, the early Christians could worship in the Temple, in synagogues, in homes, in catacombs, and in prisons. Wherever Christ was present among them in the interpretation of the Word and the breaking of bread, that space was hallowed. Yet the Church began to set aside special places for gathering in the presence of the risen Christ and responding in praise and service. To this day, when the Church gathers, it is not the particular place, but the presence of the risen Lord in the midst of the community which marks the reality of worship.

W-1.3024
Arrangement of
Space

When a place is set aside for worship it should facilitate accessibility and ease of gathering, should generate a sense of community, and should open people to reverence before God. It should include a place for the reading of Scripture and the preaching or exposition of the Word. It should provide for the celebration and proper administration of the Sacraments, with a font or pool for Baptism and a table suitable for the people's celebration of the Lord's Supper. The arrangement of space should visibly express the integral relation between Word and Sacrament and their centrality in Christian worship. (W-1.4004)

W-1.3030

c. Matter

W-1.3031
Old Testament

God created the material universe and pronounced it good. The covenant community understood that the material world reflects the glory of God. They also came to see that material realities can be a means for expressing suitable praise and thanksgiving to God. Ark, showbread, woven and embroidered linen, basins, oil, lights, musical instruments, grain, fruit, and animals all became expressions of the community's worship of God. The prophets warned, however, against offering the material as a substitute for offering the self to God.

W-1.3032
Jesus

In Jesus Christ the Word became flesh, and God hallowed material reality. Jesus presented his body as a living sacrifice. In his ministry, he used common things like nets, fish, baskets, jars, ointment, clay, towel and basin, water, bread, and wine. Working in and through these material things, he blessed and healed people, reconciled and bound them into community, and exhibited the grace, power, and presence of the Kingdom of God.

W-1.3033
Church:
Sacraments

(1) The early Church, following Jesus, took three primary material elements of life—water, bread, and wine—to become basic symbols of offering life to God as Jesus had offered his life.

W-1.3024: 2 Helv.Conf. 5.214-5.216
W-1.3031: Amos 5:21-24, Isa. 1:11-17, Mic. 6:6-8; cf. Ps. 50; Conf.1967 9.16
W-1.3033: Scots Conf. 3.21; Heid.Cat. 4.066-4.068; 2 Helv.Conf. 5.169-5.180;
West.Conf. 6.149-6.153; S.Cat. 7.092-7.093; L.Cat. 7.272-7.274

Being washed with the water of Baptism, Christians received new life in Christ and presented their bodies to be living sacrifices to God. Eating bread and drinking wine they received the sustaining presence of Christ, remembered God's covenant promise, and pledged their obedience anew.

Reformed Tradition: Sacraments

(2) The Reformed tradition understands Baptism and the Lord's Supper to be Sacraments, instituted by God and commended by Christ. Sacraments are signs of the real presence and power of Christ in the Church, symbols of God's action. Through the Sacraments, God seals believers in redemption, renews their identity as the people of God, and marks them for service. (W-3.3601)

W-1.3034 Use of Material in Worship

(1) The Church has acknowledged that the lives of Christians and all they have belong to the Creator and are to be offered to God in worship. As sign and symbol of this self-offering, the people of God have presented their creations and material possessions to God. The richness of color, texture, form, sound, and motion has been brought into the act of worship.

Artistic Expressions

(2) The Reformed heritage has called upon people to bring to worship material offerings which in their simplicity of form and function direct attention to what God has done and to the claim that God makes upon human life. The people of God have responded through creative expressions in architecture, furnishings, appointments, vestments, music, drama, language, and movement. When these artistic creations awaken us to God's presence, they are appropriate for worship. When they call attention to themselves, or are present for their beauty as an end in itself, they are idolatrous. Artistic expressions should evoke, edify, enhance, and expand worshipers' consciousness of the reality and grace of God.

W-1.3040 Mission

All time, all space, all matter are created by God and have been hallowed by Jesus Christ. Christian worship, at particular times, in special places, with the use of God's material gifts, should lead the church into the life of the world to participate in God's purpose to redeem time, to sanctify space, and to transform material reality for the glory of God.

W-1.4000

W-1.4001 Responsibility

4. Responsibility and Accountability for Worship

In worship, the church is to remember both its liberty in Christ and the biblical command to do all things in an orderly way. While Christian worship need not follow prescribed forms, careless or

---

W-1.3034: 2 Helv.Conf. 5.020-5.022; Conf.1967 9.50
W-1.3040: Mic. 6:8; Rom. 12:1; Eph. 6:16; James. 1:22-27; West.Conf. 6.174
W-1.4001: Gal. 5:1; 1 Cor. 14

disorderly worship is both an offense to God and a stumbling block to the people. Those responsible for worship are to be guided by the Holy Spirit speaking in Scripture, the historic experience of the Church universal, the Reformed tradition, *The Book of Confessions*, the needs and particular circumstances of the worshiping community, as well as the provisions of the Form of Government and this directory. (W-3.1001; W-3.1002)

W-1.4002
Review and
Oversight

To ensure that these guiding principles are being followed, those responsible on behalf of presbytery for the oversight and review of the ministry of particular worshiping congregations should discuss with those sessions the quality of worship, the standards governing it, and the fruit it is bearing in the life of God's people as they proclaim the gospel and communicate its joy and justice. (G-11.0502c)

W-1.4003
Who May
Participate and
Lead in Worship

In Jesus Christ, the Church is a royal priesthood in which worship is the work of everyone. The people of God are called to participate in the common ministry of worship. No one shall be excluded from participation or leadership in public worship in the Lord's house on the grounds of race, color, class, age, sex, or handicapping condition. Some by gifts and training may be called to particular acts of leadership in worship. It is appropriate to encourage members and ordained officers with such abilities to assist in leading worship.

W-1.4004
Session

In a particular church, the session is to provide for worship and shall encourage the people to participate fully and regularly in it. The session shall make provision for the regular

    a. preaching of the Word,

    b. celebration of the Sacraments,

    c. corporate prayer, and

    d. offering of praise to God in song. (W-2.0000; W-3.0000)

The session has authority

    e. to oversee and approve all public worship in the life of the particular church with the exception of those responsibilities delegated to the pastor alone (W-1.4005)

    f. to determine occasions, days, times, and places for worship.

It is responsible

    g. for the space where worship is conducted, including its arrangement and furnishings,

---

W-1.4003: 1 Pet. 2:9 ff.; Conf.1967 9.39
W-1.4004: Conf.1967 9.50

h.   for the use of special appointments such as flowers, candles, banners, paraments, and other objects of art,

i.   for the overall program of music and other arts in the church,

j.   for those who lead worship through music, drama, dance, and other arts. (G-10.0102d)

W-1.4005
Pastor

a.   The minister as pastor has certain responsibilities which are not subject to the authority of the session. In a particular service of worship the pastor is responsible for

(1)   the selection of Scripture lessons to be read,

(2)   the preparation and preaching of the sermon or exposition of the Word,

(3)   the prayers offered on behalf of the people and those prepared for the use of the people in worship,

(4)   the music to be sung,

(5)   the use of drama, dance, and other art forms

The pastor may confer with a worship committee in planning particular services of worship. (G-6.0202)

Pastor and Choir
Director

b.   Where there is a choir director or other musical leader, the pastor and that person will confer to ensure that anthems and other musical offerings are appropriate for the particular service. The session should see that these conferences take place appropriately and on a regular basis.

W-1.4006
Session and
Pastor

The sequence and proportion of the elements of worship are the responsibility of the pastor with the concurrence of session. The selection of hymnals, song books, service books, Bibles, and other materials for use of the congregation in public worship is the responsibility of the session with the concurrence of the pastor and in consultation with musicians and educators available to the session.

W-1.4007
Session
Responsibility
for Education

In the exercise of its responsibility to encourage the participation of its people in worship, the session should provide for education in Christian worship by means appropriate to the age, interests, and circumstances of the members of the congregation. (W-3.5202; W-6.2000; G-10.0102d, e, f) It shall also provide for the regular study of this directory in the education of church officers. (G-10.0102k, l)

W-1.4008
Accountability to
Presbytery

In fulfilling their responsibilities for worship, pastors and sessions are accountable to presbytery in its exercise of constitutional supervision of its members. (G-11.0502c)

W-1.4005: 2 Helv.Conf. 5.163

W-1.4009
Presbytery
Responsibility
for Education

In the exercise of their responsibility to provide encouragement, guidance, and resources in worship to member churches, presbyteries should arrange appropriate educational events. They shall also provide education in worship through regular use of this directory as they examine candidates for ordination and ministers for continuing membership. (G-11.0103f; G-14.0402; G-14.0508)

W-2.0000

CHAPTER II. THE ELEMENTS OF CHRISTIAN WORSHIP

W-2.1000

W-2.1001
Christian Prayer

1. Prayer

Prayer is at the heart of worship. In prayer, through the Holy Spirit, people seek after and are found by the one true God who has been revealed in Jesus Christ. They listen and wait upon God, call God by name, remember God's gracious acts, and offer themselves to God. Prayer may be spoken, sung, offered in silence, or enacted. Prayer grows out of the center of a person's life in response to the Spirit. Prayer is shaped by the Word of God in Scripture and by the life of the community of faith. Prayer issues in commitment to join God's work in the world.

W-2.1002
Content of Prayer

In prayer we respond to God in many ways. In adoration we praise God for who God is. In thanksgiving we express gratitude for what God has done. In confession we acknowledge repentance for what we as individuals and as a people have done or left undone. In supplication we plead for ourselves and the gathered community. In intercession we plead for others, on behalf of others, and for the whole world. In self-dedication we offer ourselves to the purpose and glory of God.

W-2.1003
Music as Prayer:
Congregational
Song

Song is a response which engages the whole self in prayer. Song unites the faithful in common prayer wherever they gather for worship whether in church, home, or other special place. The covenant people have always used the gift of song to offer prayer. Psalms were created to be sung by the faithful as their response to God. Though they may be read responsively or in unison, their full power comes to expression when they are sung. In addition to psalms the Church in the New Testament sang hymns and spiritual songs. Through the ages and from varied cultures, the church has developed additional musical forms for congregational prayer. Congregations are encouraged to use these diverse musical forms for prayer as well as those which arise out of the musical life of their own cultures.

W-2.1004
Music as Prayer:
Choir and
Instrumental
Music

To lead the congregation in the singing of prayer is a primary role of the choir and other musicians. They also may pray on behalf of the congregation with introits, responses, and other musical forms. Instrumental music may be a form of prayer since words are not essential to prayer. In worship, music is not to be for entertainment or

---

W-2.1000: Heid.Cat. 4.116-4.118; 2 Helv.Conf. 5.218-5.221; West.Conf. 6.114-6.115; S.Cat. 7.098-7.099; L.Cat. 7.264, 7.288-7.296; Conf.1967 9.50

W-2.1003: Eph. 5:19; Col. 3:16

artistic display. Care should be taken that it not be used merely as a cover for silence. Music as prayer is to be a worthy offering to God on behalf of the people. (See also W-2.2008; W-3.3101)

W-2.1005
Enacted Prayer

In the Old and New Testaments and through the ages, the people of God expressed prayer through actions as well as speech and song. So in worship today it is appropriate

    a.   to kneel, to bow, to stand, to lift hands in prayer,

    b.   to dance, to clap, to embrace in joy and praise,

    c.   to anoint and to lay on hands in intercession and supplication, commissioning and ordination.

W-2.2000

2. Scripture Read and Proclaimed

W-2.2001
Centrality of
Scripture

The church confesses the Scriptures to be the Word of God written, witnessing to God's self-revelation. Where that Word is read and proclaimed, Jesus Christ the Living Word is present by the inward witness of the Holy Spirit. For this reason the reading, hearing, preaching, and confessing of the Word are central to Christian worship. The session shall ensure that in public worship the Scripture is read and proclaimed regularly in the common language(s) of the particular church.

W-2.2002
Selection of
Scripture

The minister of the Word and Sacrament is responsible for the selection of Scripture to be read in all services of public worship and should exercise care so that over a period of time the people will hear the full message of Scripture. It is appropriate that in the Service of the Lord's Day there be readings from the Old Testament and the Epistles and Gospels of the New Testament. The full range of the psalms should be also used in worship.

W-2.2003
Lectionaries

Selections for reading in public worship should be guided by the seasons of the church year, pastoral concerns for a local congregation, events and conditions in the world, and specific program emphases of the church. Lectionaries offered by the church ensure a broad range of readings as well as consistency and connection with the universal Church.

W-2.2004
Discipline in
Reading

The people of God should exercise this same principle of selection in their choice of Scripture reading in family and personal worship. (W-5.3000) Those responsible for teaching and preaching the Word have a special responsibility to ensure that in their personal worship they observe a discipline of reading from the fullness of Scripture.

W-2.2000: Scots Conf. 3.18-3.19; 2 Helv.Conf. 5.001-5.007; West.Conf. 6.001-6.010, 6.116; S.Cat. 7.088-7.090; L.Cat. 7.113-7.115, 7.264-7.270; Bar.Dec. 8.11-8.12, 8.26; Conf.1967 9.27-9.30, 9.49

W-2.2005
Versions

The minister of the Word and Sacrament has responsibility for the selection of the version of text from which the Scripture lessons are read in public worship. If paraphrases are used, adaptations are made, or new translations are prepared, the congregation should be informed.

W-2.2006
Public Reading
and Hearing of
Scripture

The public reading of Scripture should be clear, audible, and attentive to the meanings of the text, and should be entrusted to those prepared for such reading. Listening to the reading of Scripture requires expectation and concentration and may be aided by the availability of a printed text for the worshipers. The congregation may read Scripture responsively, antiphonally, or in unison as a part of the service. (W-3.3401)

W-2.2007
Preaching the
Word

The preached Word or sermon is to be based upon the written Word. It is a proclamation of Scripture in the conviction that through the Holy Spirit Jesus Christ is present to the gathered people, offering grace and calling for obedience. Preaching requires diligence and discernment in the study of Scripture, the discipline of daily prayer, cultivated sensitivity to events and issues affecting the lives of the people, and a consistent and personal obedience to Jesus Christ. The sermon should present the gospel with simplicity and clarity, in language which can be understood by the people. For reasons of order the preaching of the Word shall ordinarily be done by a minister of the Word and Sacrament. A minister of the Word and Sacrament or other person authorized by presbytery may be invited by the pastor with the concurrence of the session or, when there is no pastor, by the session. A person may be sent to preach by the presbytery. (G-6.0304; G-11.0103g, k; G-11.0502f; G-14.0307; G-14.0513; G-14.0516)

W-2.2008
Other Forms of
Proclamation

The Word is also proclaimed through song in anthems and solos based on scriptural texts, in cantatas and oratorios which tell the biblical story, in psalms and canticles, and in hymns, spirituals, and spiritual songs which present the truth of the biblical faith. Song in worship may also express the response of the people to the Word read, sung, enacted, or proclaimed. Drama and dance, poetry and pageant, indeed, most other human art forms are also expressions through which the people of God have proclaimed and responded to the Word. Those entrusted with the proclamation of the Word through art forms should exercise care that the gospel is faithfully presented in ways through which the people of God may receive and respond.

W-2.2009
Creeds and
Confessions

The people also express the Word in response to the reading and proclamation of the Word through creeds and confessions. (G-2.0100.) The church confesses its faith in relation to

a.   the Church universal,

b.   its particular historic heritage, and

c.   its local situation.

When the church confesses its faith during the celebration of Baptism and the Lord's Supper the creeds of the universal Church should be used. (W-3.3603) The Word confessed is always judged by the living Word, Jesus Christ, as attested in Scripture.

W-2.2010
Hearing
the Word

The people's participation in the proclamation of the Word is above all to hear:

    a.   to discern Jesus Christ,

    b.   to receive his offered grace,

    c.   to respond to his call with obedience.

Such participation depends upon the illumination of the Holy Spirit, which is to be sought earnestly in prayer. The words "hearing" and "heard" are not intended exclusively to mean acts of sensory perception.

W-2.3000

3. Baptism

W-2.3001
Jesus and
Baptism

Baptism is the sign and seal of incorporation into Christ. Jesus through his own baptism identified himself with sinners in order to fulfill all righteousness. Jesus in his own baptism was attested Son by the Father and was anointed with the Holy Spirit to undertake the way of the servant manifested in his sufferings, death, and resurrection. Jesus the risen Lord assured his followers of his continuing presence and power and commissioned them "Go therefore and make disciples of all nations, baptizing them in the name of the Father and of the Son and of the Holy Spirit, and teaching them to obey everything that I have commanded you. And remember, I am with you always to the end of the age" (Matt. 28:19, NRSV). The disciples were empowered by the outpouring of the Spirit to undertake a life of service and to be an inclusive worshiping community, sharing life in which love, justice, and mercy abounded. (W-1.3033)

W-2.3002
Dying and Rising
in Baptism

In Baptism, we participate in Jesus' death and resurrection. In Baptism, we die to what separates us from God and are raised to newness of life in Christ. Baptism points us back to the grace of God expressed in Jesus Christ, who died for us and who was raised for us. Baptism points us forward to that same Christ who will fulfill God's purpose in God's promised future.

W-2.3000: Scots Conf. 3.21-3.23; Heid.Cat. 4.069-4.074; 2 Helv.Conf. 5.185-5.192; West.Conf. 6.154-6.160; S.Cat. 7.094-7.095; L.Cat. 7.275-7.277, 7.286-7.287; Conf.1967 9.51

W-2.3001: Matt. 3:15; 28:19-20; Mark 10:38-40; Acts 2:38-47.

W-2.3002: Rom. 6:3-11; Col. 2:12.

W-2.3003
Covenant and the
Water of Baptism

In Baptism, the Holy Spirit binds the Church in covenant to its Creator and Lord. The water of Baptism symbolizes the waters of Creation, of the Flood, and of the Exodus from Egypt. Thus, the water of Baptism links us to the goodness of God's creation and to the grace of God's covenants with Noah and Israel. Prophets of Israel, amidst the failure of their own generation to honor God's covenant, called for justice to roll down like waters and righteousness like an everflowing stream. (Amos 5:24) They envisioned a fresh expression of God's grace and of creation's goodness—a new covenant accompanied by the sprinkling of cleansing water. In his ministry, Jesus offered the gift of living water. So, Baptism is the sign and seal of God's grace and covenant in Christ.

W-2.3004
Inclusion in the
Covenant of
Grace

As circumcision was the sign and symbol of inclusion in God's grace and covenant with Israel, so Baptism is the sign and symbol of inclusion in God's grace and covenant with the Church. As an identifying mark, Baptism signifies

a. the faithfulness of God,

b. the washing away of sin,

c. rebirth,

d. putting on the fresh garment of Christ,

e. being sealed by God's Spirit,

f. adoption into the covenant family of the Church,

g. resurrection and illumination in Christ.

W-2.3005
Union with Christ
and One Another

The body of Christ is one, and Baptism is the bond of unity in Christ. As they are united with Christ through faith, Baptism unites the people of God with each other and with the church of every time and place. Barriers of race, gender, status, and age are to be transcended. Barriers of nationality, history, and practice are to be overcome.

W-2.3006
Baptism: Grace,
Repentance,
Commissioning

Baptism enacts and seals what the Word proclaims: God's redeeming grace offered to all people. Baptism is God's gift of grace and also God's summons to respond to that grace. Baptism calls to repentance, to faithfulness, and to discipleship. Baptism gives the church its identity and commissions the church for ministry to the world.

W-2.3007
Sign and Seal
of God's
Faithfulness

God's faithfulness signified in Baptism is constant and sure, even when human faithfulness to God is not. Baptism is received

---

W-2.3003: Gen. 1:2; Jer. 31:31-34; Ezek. 36:25-27; John 4:7-15; 7:37, 38; 1 Cor.10:1, 2; 1 Pet. 3:20-21

W-2.3004: Gen. 17:7-14; John 3:5; Acts 2:39; 22:16; 1 Cor. 6:11, 12:12-13; 2 Cor. 1:22; Gal. 3:27; Eph. 1:13-14; 5:14; Col. 2:11-12; Tit. 3:5

W-2.3005: 1 Cor. 12:12-13; Gal. 3:27-28; Eph. 2:11-22; 4:4-6

W-2.3006: Matt. 28:18-20; Luke 3:3,8-14; Acts 2:38,41-47; cf. Isa. 44:3; John 4:7-15; 7:37-38; Rev. 7:17, 22:17

only once. The efficacy of Baptism is not tied to the moment when it is administered, for Baptism signifies the beginning of life in Christ, not its completion. God's grace works steadily, calling to repentance and newness of life. God's faithfulness needs no renewal. Human faithfulness to God needs repeated renewal. Baptism calls for decision at every subsequent stage of life's way, both for those whose Baptism attends their profession of faith and for those who are nurtured from childhood within the family of faith.

W-2.3008
"One Baptism":
Its Meanings

a.   Both believers and their children are included in God's covenant love. Children of believers are to be baptized without undue delay, but without undue haste. Baptism, whether administered to those who profess their faith or to those presented for Baptism as children, is one and the same Sacrament.

Children

b.   The Baptism of children witnesses to the truth that God's love claims people before they are able to respond in faith.

Adults

c.   The Baptism of those who enter the covenant upon their own profession of faith witnesses to the truth that God's gift of grace calls for fulfillment in a response of faithfulness.

W-2.3009
Remembering
One's Baptism

Baptism is received only once. There are many times in worship, however, when believers acknowledge the grace of God continually at work. As they participate in the celebration of another's Baptism, as they experience the sustaining nurture of the Lord's Supper, and as they reaffirm the commitments made at Baptism, they confess their ongoing need of God's grace and pledge anew their obedience to God's covenant in Christ.

W-2.3010
One Body, One
Baptism

As there is one body, there is one Baptism. (Eph. 4:4-6) The Presbyterian Church (U.S.A.) recognizes all Baptisms with water in the name of the Father, of the Son, and of the Holy Spirit administered by other Christian churches.

W-2.3011
Responsibility
for Baptism

a.   For reasons of order, Baptism shall be authorized by the session, administered by a minister of the Word and Sacrament, or commissioned lay pastor when invited by the session and authorized by the presbytery, and accompanied by the reading and proclaiming of the Word. (G-11.0103p; W-3.3602-.3608) Baptism is celebrated in a service of public worship. Extraordinary circumstances may call for the administration of Baptism apart from the worship of the whole congregation. In such cases care should be taken that

(1) the congregation be represented by one or more members of the session;

(2) a proper understanding of the meaning of the Sacrament be offered by the minister;

(3) the session be consulted when possible;

(4) the Baptism be reported by the officiating minister and recorded by the session.

By Chaplains
and Others

b.   A governing body may also authorize the celebration of the Sacrament of Baptism by chaplains or other ministers serving in hospitals, prisons, schools, or other institutions where the governing body has an authorized ministry or an institutional witness, by chaplains ministering to members of the armed forces and their families, and by ministers engaged in new church development under the jurisdiction of the governing body. In all such cases of Baptism, the minister of the Word and Sacrament shall take responsibility that the newly baptized person is enrolled as a member of a particular church. Such enrollment may be arranged in advance in consultation with the session of the church, or the governing body may provide that any such newly baptized member shall be enrolled in absentia as a member of a particular church designated by the governing body and under its jurisdiction or upon the roll held by the governing body until a new church is organized.

W-2.3012
Session
Responsibility

The session's responsibilities for Baptism are

a.   encouraging parents to present their children for Baptism, reminding them that children of believers are to be baptized without undue haste, but without undue delay, and authorizing the Baptism of those presented; (W-2.3014)

b.   admitting to Baptism children of believers, after appropriate instruction and discussion with the parent(s) or one(s) rightly exercising parental responsibility, acquainting them with the significance of what God is doing in this act, and with the special responsibilities on parents and congregations for nurturing the baptized person in the Christian life;

c.   admitting to Baptism, after appropriate instruction and examination, those not yet baptized who come making public their personal profession of faith;

d.   placing all baptized persons on the appropriate roll as members of the congregation;

e.   making certain that those baptized are nurtured in understanding the meaning of Baptism, of the Lord's Supper, and of their interrelation, and that they are surrounded by Christian encouragement and support. (G-10.0102b, d, e; G-10.0302; W-2.3011)

W-2.3013
Church
Responsibility

The congregation as a whole, on behalf of the Church universal, assumes responsibility for nurturing the baptized person in the Christian life. In exercising this ministry, the session may designate certain members of the congregation as representatives of the church charged with special responsibility for nurture. For any person who is being baptized, sponsor(s) may be appointed by the session in consultation with those desiring Baptism for themselves or for their children and given the specific role of nurturing the baptized person. (W-6.2001; W-6.2005)

W-2.3014
Parental
Responsibility

When a child is being presented for Baptism, ordinarily the parent(s) or one(s) rightly exercising parental responsibility shall be an active member of the congregation. Those presenting children for Baptism shall promise to provide nurture and guidance within the community of faith until the child is ready to make a personal profession of faith and assume the responsibility of active church membership. (W-4.2002; W-4.2003) The session may also consider a request for the baptism of a child from a Christian parent who is an active member of another congregation. If the session approves such a request, it shall consult with the governing body of the other congregation and shall notify them when the Sacrament has been administered.

W-2.4000

4.   The Lord's Supper

W-2.4001
Jesus and the
Supper

a.   The Lord's Supper is the sign and seal of eating and drinking in communion with the crucified and risen Lord. During his earthly ministry Jesus shared meals with his followers as a sign of community and acceptance and as an occasion for his own ministry. He celebrated Israel's feasts of covenant commemoration.

Last Supper

b.   In his last meal before his death, Jesus took and shared with his disciples the bread and wine, speaking of them as his body and blood, signs of the new covenant. He commended breaking bread and sharing a cup to remember and proclaim his death.

Resurrection

c.   On the day of his resurrection, the risen Jesus made himself known to his followers in the breaking of bread. He continued to show himself to believers, by blessing and breaking bread, by preparing, serving, and sharing common meals. (W-1.3033)

W-2.4002
Church in
the New
Testament

The Church in the New Testament devoted itself to the apostles' teaching, to fellowship, to prayers, and to the common meal. The apostle Paul delivered to the Church the tradition he had received from the risen Lord, who commanded that his followers share the bread and cup as a remembrance and a showing forth of

---

W-2.4000: Scots Conf. 3.21-3.23; Heid.Cat. 4.075-4.082; 2 Helv.Conf. 5.193-
          5.210; West.Conf. 6.161-6.168; S.Cat. 7.096-7.097; L.Cat. 7.278-
          7.287; Conf.1967 9.52

W-2.4001: Matt. 14:13-21; 15:32-39; Luke 5:27-32; 7:36-50; 10:38-42; and par-
          allels. John 2:13; 5:1; 7:2-37; 10:22-33; 12:1-3; 13:1-4 ff. and syn-
          optic parallels. Matt. 26:17-29; Mark 14:12-25; Luke 22:7-20, 24:41-
          43; John 21:13; Acts 1:4

W-2.4002: Acts 2:42, 46; 1 Corinthians 11:23-26; Matt. 8:11; 22:1; 1 Cor.
          10:16-17; Rev. 19:9; cf. Ps. 107:1-3; Isa. 25:6-8; 43:5-7

his death until he comes. The New Testament describes the meal as a participation in Christ and with one another in the expectation of the Kingdom and as a foretaste of the messianic banquet.

W-2.4003
Thanksgiving

In the Lord's Supper the Church, gathered for worship,

a. blesses God for all that God has done through creation, redemption, and sanctification;

b. gives thanks that God is working in the world and in the Church in spite of human sin;

c. gratefully anticipates the fulfillment of the Kingdom Christ proclaimed, and offers itself in obedient service to God's reign.

W-2.4004
Remembering

At the Lord's Table, the Church is

a. renewed and empowered by the memory of Christ's life, death, resurrection, and promise to return;

b. sustained by Christ's pledge of undying love and continuing presence with God's people;

c. sealed in God's covenant of grace through partaking of Christ's self-offering.

In remembering, believers receive and trust the love of Christ present to them and to the world; they manifest the reality of the covenant of grace in reconciling and being reconciled; and they proclaim the power of Christ's reign for the renewal of the world in justice and in peace.

W-2.4005
Invocation

As the people of God bless and thank God the Father and remember Jesus Christ the Son, they call upon the Holy Spirit

a. to lift them into Christ's presence;

b. to accept their offering of bread and wine;

c. to make breaking bread and sharing the cup a participation in the body and blood of Christ;

d. to bind them with Christ and with one another;

e. to unite them in communion with all the faithful in heaven and on earth;

f. to nourish them with Christ's body and blood that they may mature into the fullness of Christ;

g. to keep them faithful as Christ's body, representing Christ and doing God's work in the world.

W-2.4005: 1 Cor. 10:16.

**W-2.4006
Communion of
the Faithful**

Around the Table of the Lord, God's people are in communion with Christ and with all who belong to Christ. Reconciliation with Christ compels reconciliation with one another. All the baptized faithful are to be welcomed to the Table, and none shall be excluded because of race, sex, age, economic status, social class, handicapping condition, difference of culture or language, or any barrier created by human injustice. Coming to the Lord's Table the faithful are actively to seek reconciliation in every instance of conflict or division between them and their neighbors. Each time they gather at the Table the believing community

a. are united with the Church in every place, and the whole Church is present;

b. join with all the faithful in heaven and on earth in offering thanksgiving to the triune God;

c. renew the vows taken at Baptism;

and they commit themselves afresh to love and serve God, one another, and their neighbors in the world.

**W-2.4007
Foretaste of the
Kingdom Meal**

In this meal the Church celebrates the joyful feast of the people of God, and anticipates the great banquet and marriage supper of the Lamb. Brought by the Holy Spirit into Christ's presence, the Church eagerly expects and prays for the day when Christ shall come in glory and God be all in all. Nourished by this hope, the Church rises from the Table and is sent by the power of the Holy Spirit to participate in God's mission to the world, to proclaim the gospel, to exercise compassion, to work for justice and peace until Christ's Kingdom shall come at last.

**W-2.4008
Word and
Sacrament
Together**

In the life of the worshiping congregation, Word and Sacrament have an integral relationship. Whenever the Lord's Supper is observed, it shall be preceded by the reading and the proclamation of the Word. (W-1.1005)

**W-2.4009
Time, Place, and
Frequency**

The Lord's Supper is to be observed on the Lord's Day, in the regular place of worship, and in a manner suitable to the particular occasion and local congregation. It is appropriate to celebrate the Lord's Supper as often as each Lord's Day. It is to be celebrated regularly and frequently enough to be recognized as integral to the Service for the Lord's Day.

**W-2.4010
Special Occasions**

It is also appropriate to observe the Lord's Supper on other occasions of special significance in the life of the Christian

---

W-2.4006: Matt. 5:23-24; 18:15-18; 1 Cor. 11:18-22, 27-29; Gal. 3:28; Jas. 2:1-7

W-2.4007: Matt. 22:1-10; Luke 14:15-24; 1 Cor. 15:20-28; Eph. 1:23; Phil. 2:10, 11; Col. 3:1-4; 1 Thess. 4:16, 17; Rev. 19:9; Ps. 72:2-4, 12-14; Isa. 2:1-4; Mic. 4:1-4, 6:8; Matt. 5:21-26; 28:18-20; Luke 3:10-14; 4:18-21; Acts 1:3-8; Jas. 2:14-17; 1 Jn. 3:16-18

community, as long as the celebration of the Sacrament is open to the whole believing community. The Lord's Supper may be observed in connection with the visitation of the sick and those isolated from public worship as a means of extending the church's ministry to them. On all such occasions of the celebration of the Sacrament, the Word shall be read and proclaimed. Even though such a celebration may involve only a few members of the congregation, nevertheless it is not to be understood as a private ceremony or devotional exercise, but as an act of the whole church, which shall be represented not only by the minister or the one authorized by presbytery to administer the Sacrament, but also by one or more members of the congregation authorized by the session to represent the church. (W-2.4012; W-3.3609-.3618; W-3.6204)

W-2.4011
Who May
Receive

a.   The invitation to the Lord's Supper is extended to all who have been baptized, remembering that access to the Table is not a right conferred upon the worthy, but a privilege given to the undeserving who come in faith, repentance, and love. In preparing to receive Christ in this Sacrament, the believer is to confess sin and brokenness, to seek reconciliation with God and neighbor, and to trust in Jesus Christ for cleansing and renewal. Even one who doubts or whose trust is wavering may come to the Table in order to be assured of God's love and grace in Christ Jesus.

Baptized Children

b.   Baptized children who are being nurtured and instructed in the significance of the invitation to the Table and the meaning of their response are invited to receive the Lord's Supper, recognizing that their understanding of participation will vary according to their maturity. (W-4.2002)

W-2.4012
Responsibility

a.   The session is responsible for authorizing all observances of the Lord's Supper in the life of a particular church and shall ensure regular and frequent celebration of the Sacrament, in no case less than quarterly. Any other governing body of the church, also, may appoint times for the celebration of the Lord's Supper during their meetings. A governing body may also authorize the celebration of the Sacrament in connection with the public worship of some gathering of believers which is under its jurisdiction or in institutions where it has a missional witness or authorized ministry. A governing body may delegate the authority to approve the celebration of the Lord's Supper to an appropriate overseeing body in the institutions for which it has responsibility. (cf. W-3.6205)

Chaplains or
Others

b.   Chaplains or other ministers serving in hospitals, prisons, schools, or other institutions, and chaplains ministering to members of the armed forces and their families, may administer the Sacrament of the Lord's Supper when authorized to do so by the

---

W-2.4011: L.Cat. 7.281-7.282

governing body which has jurisdiction over the ministry exercised by the particular minister. The terms of the authority to administer the Sacrament of the Lord's Supper shall be stated in the minister's terms of call or endorsement.

Administered by Minister

    c.   For reasons of order the Sacrament of the Lord's Supper shall be administered by a minister of the Word and Sacrament or commissioned lay pastor when invited by the session and authorized by the presbytery. Missional concerns may lead to exceptions as determined and authorized by presbytery. (G-11.0103k, p, z; G-14.0801)

W-2.5000

5. Self-Offering

**W-2.5001
Response to Christ**

    The Christian life is an offering of one's self to God. In worship the people are presented with the costly self-offering of Jesus Christ, are claimed and set free by him, and are led to respond by offering to him their lives, their particular gifts and abilities, and their material goods.

**W-2.5002
Offering Spiritual Gifts**

    Worship should always offer opportunities to respond to Christ's call to become disciples by professing faith, by uniting with the church, and by taking up the mission of the people of God, as well as opportunities for disciples to renew the commitment of their lives to Jesus Christ and his mission in the world. As the Holy Spirit has graced each member with particular gifts for strengthening the body of Christ for mission, so worship should provide opportunities to recognize these gifts and to offer them to serve Christ in the church and in the world.

**W-2.5003
Offering Material Gifts and Goods**

    a.   The offering of material goods in worship is a corporate act of self-dedication in response to God. It expresses thanksgiving to God, the giver of life and all goods, the redeemer from sin and evil. It is an affirmation by Christ's disciples of

    (1)   their commitment to be stewards in all creation;

    (2)   their responsibility to share the Word with and to care for all people;

    (3)   their desire to share God's gifts with those to whom believers are bound in the Church universal;

    (4)   their common bond in the body of Christ.

W-2.5001: 2 Helv.Conf. 5.110-5.123; West.Conf. 6.088
W-2.5002: Rom. 12:4-8; 1 Cor. 12; Eph. 4:7-16
W-2.5003: Gen. 1:28 ff., 2:15; Lev. 23:22; Num. 18:21-29; Deut. 28:7-12; 2 Chron. 24:8-14; Mal. 3:8-10; Matt. 28:19; Acts 1:8; 2:44-45; 4:34-37; 1 Cor. 16:1, 2; 2 Cor. 8:1-15; 9:5-15; 1 Tim. 5:17, 18; Jas. 2:4; 3 Jn. 5-8; 2 Helv.Conf. 5.211

Disciplined
and Generous
Support

   b.   In the Old Testament the people of Israel were commanded to bring a tenth of their income to support the work of the house of God and those who served God in it. In the New Testament the apostles recognized that the work of the Church required disciplined support. Both in Israel and in the early Church the people were encouraged to give generously to meet the needs of the poor. God calls believers today to be disciplined and generous in giving support to the ministries of the church. (W-5.5004)

Received in
Worship

   c.   During public worship, at an appropriate time, and as an act of thanksgiving, the tithes and offerings of the people are gathered and received.

W-2.6000

6. Relating to Each Other and the World

W-2.6001
Community
Concerns

   Worship is an activity of the common life of the people of God in which the care of the members for each other and for the quality of their life and ministry together expresses the reality of God's power to create and sustain community in the midst of a sinful world. As God is concerned for the events in daily life, so members of the community in worship appropriately express concern for one another and for their ministry in the world.

Greetings

   a.   as they

   (1)   greet one another and are greeted by those who are leading them in worship;

   (2)   welcome visitors, note their presence, and extend Christian hospitality;

Reconciliation

   b.   as they

   (1)   take opportunity to seek and to offer forgiveness for hurts, misunderstandings, and broken relationships among themselves;

   (2)   respond to God's act of reconciliation by exchanging signs and words of reconciliation and of Christ's peace;

Preparation
for Prayer

   c.   as they

   (1)   prepare for intercessions by expressing concerns and requesting prayer on behalf of those with needs in the congregation, the church, and the world;

   (2)   offer thanksgiving for life and life's transitions, rejoicing with those who rejoice and mourning with those who mourn;

W-2.6000: 2 Helv.Conf. 5.135; West.Conf. 6:146-6.147; Conf.1967 9.35-9.38

Interpretation   d.   as they

                        (1)   apply God's Word to daily life;

                        (2)   interpret the mission and work of the church;

                        (3)   give witness to faith and service;

Mission   e.   as they

                        (1)   make and renew covenants;

                        (2)   commit themselves to and are commissioned for specific corporate and personal ministries of compassion, justice, peacemaking, reconciliation, and witness.

W-3.0000

CHAPTER III. THE ORDERING OF CHRISTIAN WORSHIP

W-3.1000

W-3.1001
Scripture and
History

1. Principles and Sources of Ordering

Those responsible for ordering Christian worship shall be faithful to the authority of the Holy Spirit speaking in and through Scripture. Beyond Scripture no single warrant for ordering worship exists, but the worship of the Church is informed and shaped by history, culture, and contemporary need. Thus the worship of the Presbyterian Church (U.S.A.) should be guided by the historic experience of the Church at worship through the ages, especially in the Reformed tradition. (W-1.4001)

W-3.1002
Form and
Freedom

a. The Church has always experienced a tension between form and freedom in worship. In the history of the Church, some have offered established forms for ordering worship in accordance with God's Word. Others, in the effort to be faithful to the Word, have resisted imposing any fixed forms upon the worshiping community. The Presbyterian Church (U.S.A.) acknowledges that all forms of worship are provisional and subject to reformation. In ordering worship the church is to seek openness to the creativity of the Holy Spirit, who guides the church toward worship which is orderly yet spontaneous, consistent with God's Word and open to the newness of God's future. (W-1.4001)

Guidance of
Session.

b. Manifestations of the Spirit in worship edify the whole church. When actions in worship are present only for personal expression, call attention to themselves, or are insensitive to the congregation at worship, they are not in order and call for the counsel and guidance of the session.

W-3.1003
Participation and
Leadership

The ordering of worship should also reflect the richness of the cultural diversity in which the church ministers, as well as the local circumstances and needs of its congregations. While the authority for ordering worship belongs to those so designated (G-6.0202; G-10.0102d; W-1.4000) and leadership in worship is assigned to those with gifts, training, and authorization (W-1.4003), the order for worship should provide for and encourage the participation of all.

W-3.1004
Children in
Worship

Children bring special gifts to worship and grow in the faith through their regular inclusion and participation in the worship of the congregation. Those responsible for planning and leading the

---

W-3.1000: Scots Conf. 3.20; West.Conf. 6.006
W-3.1002: 1 Cor. 12-14

participation of children in worship should consider the children's level of understanding and ability to respond, and should avoid both excessive formality and condescension. The session should ensure that regular programs of the church do not prevent children's full participation with the whole congregation in worship, in Word and Sacrament, on the Lord's Day. (W-3.3201; W-3.5202; W-6.2001; W-6.2006)

W-3.2000

W-3.2001
Days

W-3.2002
Church Year

W-3.2003
Other Seasons

2. Days and Seasons

God has appointed one day in seven to be kept holy, set aside as the occasion for the people of God to worship corporately. God has also commended daily worship by the people, whether gathered in assembly or at home. (W-1.3011-.3012; W-5.5001)

God has provided a rhythm of seasons which orders life and influences the church's worship. (Cf. W-1.3013) God's work of redemption in Jesus Christ offers the Church a central pattern for ordering worship in relationship to significant occasions in the life of Jesus and of the people of God. The Church thus has come to observe the following days and seasons:

a. Advent, a season to recollect the hope of the coming of Christ, and to look forward to the Lord's coming again;

b. Christmas, a celebration of the birth of Christ;

c. Epiphany, a day for commemorating God's self-manifestation to all people;

d. Lent, a season of spiritual discipline and preparation, beginning with Ash Wednesday, anticipating the celebration of the death and resurrection of Christ;

e. Holy Week, a time of remembrance and proclamation of the atoning suffering and death of Jesus Christ;

f. Easter, the day of the Lord's resurrection and the season of rejoicing which commemorates his ministry until his Ascension, and continues through

g. the Day of Pentecost, the celebration of the gift of the Holy Spirit to the Church.

The church also observes other days such as Baptism of the Lord, Transfiguration of the Lord, Trinity Sunday, All Saints Day, and Christ the King.

Human life in community reflects a variety of rhythms which also affect Christian worship. Among these are the annual cycles of

---

W-3.2002: 2 Helv.Conf. 5.226

civic, agricultural, school, and business life; special times of family remembrance and celebration; and the patterns of a variety of cultural expressions, commemorations, and events. The church in carrying out its mission also creates a cycle of activities, programs, and observances. While such events may be appropriately recognized in Christian worship, care shall be taken to ensure that they do not obscure the proclamation of the gospel on the Lord's Day.

W-3.3000	**3.**	**Service for the Lord's Day**
W-3.3100	**a.**	**Appropriate Actions**
W-3.3101 What Is Included:		In the Service for the Lord's Day:

Scripture   (1) The Scriptures shall be read and proclaimed (W-2.2001). Lessons should be read from both Testaments. (W-2.2002) Scripture shall be interpreted in a sermon or other form of exposition. (W-2.2007-.2008)

Prayer   (2) Prayer shall be offered. (W-2.1001) Prayers may be offered on behalf of the congregation, whose participation may be affirmed by their corporate response, "Amen." Prayer forms may encourage the participation of the worshipers through unison and responsive, bidding and spontaneous prayers. Times of silence may be provided for prayer and meditation. (W-2.1000)

Music   (3) Music may serve as presentation and interpretation of Scripture, as response to the gospel, and as prayer, through psalms and canticles, hymns and anthems, spirituals and spiritual songs. (W-2.1003-.1004; W-2.2008)

Baptism   (4) The Sacrament of Baptism shall be administered as people present children or themselves for incorporation into the church. (W-2.3000)

Lord's Supper   (5) The Sacrament of the Lord's Supper shall be celebrated regularly and frequently as determined by the session. (W-2.4000)

Tithes and Offerings   (6) The tithes and offerings of the people shall be gathered and received. (W-2.5000)

Special Times   (7) Times for gathering, greeting, and calling to worship; for sharing common concerns; and for blessing and sending forth should be provided at points in the service suitable to the life of the particular church. (W-2.6000)

Special Services   (8) Services of receiving new members; of ordaining, installing, and commissioning; of making and renewing covenants; and of recognizing and sharing life's transitions should be provided as called for in the life of the congregation. (W-2.5000-.6000; W-4.0000)

W-3.3200   **b. Ordering the Actions**

W-3.3201
Setting an Order
for Worship

In setting an order for worship on the Lord's Day, the pastor with the concurrence of the session shall provide opportunity for the people from youngest to oldest to participate in a worthy offering of praise to God and for them to hear and to respond to God's Word. (W-1.4004-.4007; W-3.1004)

W-3.3202
A Suggested
Order

The order offered here is a logical progression, is rooted in the Old and New Testaments, and reflects the tradition of the universal Church and our Reformed heritage. Other orders of worship may also serve the needs of a particular church and be orderly, faithful to Scripture, and true to historic principles. The order that follows is presented in terms of five major actions centered in the Word of God:

(1) gathering around the Word;

(2) proclaiming the Word;

(3) responding to the Word;

(4) the sealing of the Word;

(5) bearing and following the Word into the world.

W-3.3300   **(1) Gathering Around the Word**

W-3.3301
Gathering

(a) Worship begins as the people gather. One or more of the following actions are appropriate: People may greet one another; people may prepare in silent prayer or meditation; announcements of concern to the congregation may be made; or music may be offered.

(b) The people are called to worship God. Words of Scripture are spoken or sung to proclaim who God is and what God has done.

(c) A prayer or hymn of adoration and praise is offered.

(d) A prayer of confession of the reality of sin in personal and common life follows. In a declaration of pardon, the gospel is proclaimed and forgiveness is declared in the name of Jesus Christ. God's redemption and God's claim upon human life are remembered.

(e) The people give glory to God, and they may at this point share signs of reconciliation and the peace of Christ.

W-3.3400   **(2) Proclaiming the Word**

W-3.3401
Proclaiming

(a) In preparation for the reading, proclaiming, and hearing of God's Word, a prayer seeking the illumination of the Holy Spirit is appropriately offered.

(b) Scripture lessons suitable for the day are read by a minister, by a member of the congregation, or by the people responsively, antiphonally, or in unison. (W-2.2006)

(c) Psalms or anthems, and other musical forms or artistic expression which proclaim or interpret the Scripture lessons or their themes, may be included with the reading lessons.

(d) The Word shall be interpreted in a sermon preached by the minister or in other forms authorized by the session and by the pastor. (W-1.4004-.4006; W-2.2007-.2008) This proclamation concludes with a prayer, acclamation, or ascription of praise. It is appropriate also to call the people to discipleship. (W-2.2007; W-2.2009)

W-3.3500

(3) Responding to the Word

W-3.3501
Responding:
Affirmation

The response to the proclamation of the Word is expressed in an affirmation of faith and commitment. A common affirmation may be offered by the congregation through singing a hymn or other appropriate musical response, or through saying or singing a creed of the church. The choir may lead the congregation with an anthem or other musical form of affirmation. An opportunity for personal response may also be provided during this time.

W-3.3502
Affirming and
Reaffirming
Commitments

Response to the Word also involves acts of commitment and recognition. The Sacrament of Baptism may be observed. (W-3.3601-.3607) Baptized believers may be received as members of the particular church as they make public their profession of faith for the first time, or as they reaffirm that faith or transfer their church membership. (For the services of reception and commissioning see W-4.2000; W-4.3000; cf. G-5.0000; G-10.0102b.) It is also appropriate to offer opportunities for individuals or the gathered congregation to engage in reaffirming the commitments made at Baptism. (W-4.2005)

W-3.3503
Other Acts of
Commitment

Other acts of commitment which may appropriately be included as response to the Word are

(a) Christian marriage (W-4.9000),

(b) ordination and installation of church officers (W-4.4000; cf. G-14.0206-.0209; G-14.0405; G-14.0510),

(c) commissioning for service in and to the church in such roles as Christian educator, church school teacher, organizational officer, or group adviser (W-4.3000; cf. W-3.3701).

W-3.3504
Acts of
Recognition

It is appropriate as a response to the Word to recognize and give thanks for life and life's transitions,

(a) commemorating significant events in the lives of individuals and in the life of the community,

      (b)   celebrating reunions and bidding farewell,

      (c)   noting and remembering the lives of those who have died. (Cf. W-4.5000; W-4.7000; W-4.8000)

W-3.3505 Mission Concerns

Witness to faith and service and interpretation of the mission and programs of the church may be included in the service as a response to the Word. They should be presented in such a way as to reflect this response and may prepare for the people's prayers of intercession and supplication, as well as for their self-offering and gifts in support of the ministry of Christ and the church.

W-3.3506 Prayers

As the people respond to the Word, prayers of intercession are offered for

    (a)   the Church universal, its ministry and those who minister, that the world might believe;

    (b)   the world, those in distress or special need, and all in authority, that peace and justice might prevail;

    (c)   the nation, the state, local communities, and those who govern in them, that they may know and have strength to do what is right.

Prayers of supplication are offered for

    (d)   the local church, that it have the mind of Christ in facing special issues and needs;

    (e)   those who struggle with their faith, that they be given assurance;

    (f)   those in the midst of transitions in life, that they be guided and supported;

    (g)   those who face critical decisions, that they receive wisdom;

    (h)   those who are sick, grieving, lonely, and anxious, that they be comforted and healed;

    (i)   all members, that grace conform them to God's purpose. (W-2.1000)

Prayers of confession may be included at this time. (W-3.3301) When the service does not include the Lord's Supper, prayers of thanksgiving are offered and the prayers are concluded with the Lord's Prayer. (W-3.3613)

W-3.3507 Offerings

The tithes and offerings of God's people are gathered and received with prayer, spoken or sung. (W-2.5003) Signs of reconciliation and peace may be exchanged, if this was not done as a response to the Word of assurance of God's pardon. (W-3.3301) When the Lord's Supper is to be celebrated, gifts of bread and wine may be brought to the Table in thanksgiving for God's Word. (W-2.4003; W-3.3609)

W-3.3600   **(4) The Sealing of the Word: Sacraments**

W-3.3601
Sacraments as
Seals

The Sacraments of Baptism and the Lord's Supper are God's acts of sealing the promises of faith within the community of faith as the congregation worships, and include the responses of the faithful to the Word proclaimed and enacted in the Sacraments.

W-3.3602
Baptism

The Sacrament of Baptism (W-2.3000), the sign and seal of God's grace and our response, is the foundational recognition of Christian commitment. It is appropriately celebrated following the reading and the proclaiming of the Word, and shall include statements concerning the biblical meaning of Baptism, the responsibility to be assumed by those desiring Baptism for themselves or their children, and the nurture to be undertaken by the church.

W-3.3603
Commitments
and Vows

Those desiring the Sacrament of Baptism for their children or for themselves shall make vows that

    (a)   profess their faith in Jesus Christ as Lord and Savior,

    (b)   renounce evil and affirm their reliance on God's grace,

    (c)   declare their intention to participate actively and responsibly in the worship and mission of the church,

    (d)   declare their intention to provide for the Christian nurture of their child.

The congregation shall

    (e)   profess its faith, using the Apostles' Creed,

    (f)   voice its support of those baptized,

    (g)   express its willingness to take responsibility for the nurture of those baptized.

An elder may lead the congregation in these professions and affirmations. (W-2.2009; W-2.3011-.3014)

W-3.3604
The Prayer

The minister of the Word and Sacrament offers a baptismal prayer. This prayer

    (a)   expresses thanksgiving for God's covenant faithfulness,

    (b)   gives praise for God's reconciling acts,

    (c)   asks that the Holy Spirit
              attend and empower the Baptism,
              make the water a water of redemption and rebirth,
              equip the church for faithfulness.

W-3.3605
The Water

The water used for Baptism should be common to the location, and shall be applied to the person by pouring, sprinkling, or immersion. By whatever mode, the water should be applied visibly and generously.

W-3.3606
The Words of
Baptism

The minister shall use the name given the person to be baptized and shall baptize in the name of the triune God. The baptismal formula is: "_____, I baptize you in the name of the Father, and of the Son, and of the Holy Spirit."

W-3.3607
Other Actions

Care shall be taken that the central act of baptizing with water is not overshadowed. Other actions that are rooted deeply in the history of Baptism such as the laying on of hands in blessing, the praying for the anointing of the Holy Spirit, anointing with oil, and the presentation of the newly baptized to the congregation may also be included. When such actions are introduced, they should be explained carefully in order to avoid misinterpretation and misunderstanding.

W-3.3608
Welcoming

Declaration shall be made of the newly baptized person's membership in the Church of Jesus Christ. The welcome of the congregation is extended. Whenever the service is so ordered, the Lord's Supper may follow Baptism at the appropriate time in the service.

W-3.3609
Lord's Supper:
Preparing

The congregation should prepare themselves to celebrate the Sacrament of the Lord's Supper. (W-2.4006; W-2.4011; W-5.2001) If the Lord's Supper is celebrated less frequently than on each Lord's Day, public notice is to be given at least one week in advance. When the Lord's Supper is celebrated, the Table should be prepared and the elements provided to be placed on the Table before worship begins or during the gathering of the tithes and offerings.

W-3.3610
Bread

Bread common to the culture of the community should be provided to be broken by the one who presides. The use of the one bread expresses the unity of the body of Christ. Bread for the congregation may be broken from the same loaf or prepared in some manner suitable for distribution.

W-3.3611
Cup

A cup and pitcher may be provided for the one who presides to use in presenting the cup. The use of a common cup expresses the communal nature of the Sacrament and reflects the consistent New Testament reference to a single cup. Pouring into the cup signifies the shed blood of Christ poured out for the world. The manner of distribution used by the particular community of faith may involve the provision of one cup or a number of cups suitably prepared for the people. The session is to determine what form of the fruit of the vine is to be used. In making this decision the session should be informed by the biblical precedent, the history of the church, ecumenical usage, local custom, and concerns for health and the conscience of members of the congregation. Whenever wine is used in

---

W-3.3610: 1 Cor. 10:16-17

W-3.3611: Mark 14:23 ff. and parallels; 1 Cor. 10:16, 21; 11:25-28; Rom. 14:1-23; 1 Cor. 8:1-13; 10:14-33; 11:17-32

the Lord's Supper, unfermented grape juice should always be clearly identified and served also as an alternative for those who prefer it.

W-3.3612
Invitation

The minister or one presiding shall invite the people to the Lord's Table using suitable words from Scripture. (W-2.4011) If the words of institution (1 Cor. 11:23-26, or Gospel parallels) will not be spoken at the breaking of bread or included in the prayer of thanksgiving, they are to be said as part of the invitation.

W-3.3613
The Prayer

The one presiding is to lead the people in the prayer,

(a) thanking God for creation and providence, for covenant history, and for seasonal blessings, with an

acclamation of praise;

(b) remembering God's acts of salvation in Jesus Christ: his birth, life, death, resurrection, and promise of coming, and institution of the Supper (if not otherwise spoken), together with an

acclamation of faith;

(c) calling upon the Holy Spirit to draw the people into the presence of the risen Christ so that they

(1') may be fed,

(2') may be joined in the communion of saints to all God's people and to the risen Christ, and

(3') may be sent to serve as faithful disciples; followed by an

ascription of praise to the triune God,

and

(d) the Lord's Prayer.

W-3.3614
Breaking Bread

The one presiding is to take the bread and break it in the view of the people. If the words of institution have not previously been spoken as part of the invitation or in the communion prayer, 1 Cor. 11:23, 24 shall be used at this time.

W-3.3615
Presenting the
Cup

Having filled the cup, the one presiding is to present it in the view of the people. If the words of institution have not previously been spoken as part of the invitation or in the communion prayer, 1 Cor. 11:25, 26 shall be used at this time.

W-3.3616
Distributing
Bread and Cup

The elements are distributed in the manner most suitable to the particular occasion.

The Gathering

a. The people may gather about the Table to receive the bread and the cup; they may come to those serving to receive the elements; or those serving may distribute the elements to them where they are.

The Bread

b. The bread may be broken from that on the Table and placed in the people's hands; people may break off a portion from the broken loaf or other bread offered for distribution; or they may receive pieces of bread prepared for distribution.

The Cup

c. A common cup may be offered to all who wish to partake of it; several cups may be offered and shared; or individual cups may be prepared for distribution. Rather than drink from a common cup, communicants may dip the broken bread into the cup.

The Serving

d. The bread and the cup may be served by ordained officers of the church, or by other church members on invitation of the session or authorizing governing body.

e. The serving of the elements may be extended, by two or more ordained officers of the church, to those isolated from the community's worship, provided

> **(1) the elements are served following worship on the same calendar day, as a direct extension of the serving of the gathered congregation, to church members who have accepted the church's invitation to receive the Sacrament;**
>
> **(2) care is taken in the serving to ensure that the unity of Word and Sacrament is maintained, by the reading of Scripture and the offering of prayers; and**
>
> **(3) those serving have been instructed by the session or authorized governing body in the theological and pastoral foundations of this ministry and in the liturgical resources for it (W-6.3011).**

W-3.3617
Receiving the
Supper

While the bread and the cup are being shared,

> (a)   the people may sing psalms, hymns, spirituals, or other appropriate songs;
>
> (b)   the choir may sing anthems or other appropriate musical offerings;
>
> (c)   instrumental music suitable to the occasion may be played;
>
> (d)   appropriate passages of Scripture may be read; or
>
> (e)   people may pray in silence.

W-3.3618
Blessing After
Supper

When all have communed and the remaining elements have been placed on the Table, the one presiding leads the people in prayer, thanking God for the gift of Christ in the Sacrament, asking for God's grace to fulfill the pledges made by the people in the

Supper, and making supplication for the coming of the promised Kingdom. The congregation sings a psalm, canticle, hymn, spiritual, or spiritual song.

W-3.3619
Disposition of the
Elements

When the service is ended, the communion elements shall be removed from the Table and used or disposed of in a manner which is approved by the session, and which is consistent with the Reformed understanding of the Sacrament and the principles of good stewardship.

W-3.3700

(5) **Bearing and Following the Word Into the World**

W-3.3701
Acts of
Commitment and
Recognition

(a) Acts of commitment to discipleship, declaration of intent to seek Baptism, and reaffirmation of the vows taken at Baptism are appropriate responses to the Word received in Sacrament. (W-2.4005; W-2.4007) As the service comes to a close, other acts of commitment and recognition may be observed. People may make commitments to and be commissioned for specific corporate and personal acts of evangelism, compassion, justice, reconciliation, and peacemaking in the world. (W-4.3000)

When One
Leaves

(b) Those leaving the fellowship of a particular church

(1') to undertake these commissions; or

(2') to move to another place for purposes of education, national service, career change, family circumstance, or health

may be recognized with a farewell. This also may be an appropriate time to remember those of the congregation who have died.

W-3.3702
Going in the
Name of the
Triune God

The service concludes with a formal dismissal. This may include a charge to the people to go into the world in the name of Christ. It shall include words of blessing, using a trinitarian benediction or other words from Scripture, such as the apostolic benediction in 2 Cor. 13:13. Signs of reconciliation and peace may be exchanged as the people depart.

W-3.4000

4. **Service of Daily Prayer**

W-3.4001
Daily Prayer

a. The Service of Daily Prayer is a service of public worship observed regularly throughout the week. (W-1.3012; W-3.2001) This service may be offered in the morning, at midday, at the end of the day, in the evening, or at night, in keeping with the needs of the church and the community in which it ministers.

Word and Prayer

b. The service shall include the reading and hearing of the Word and prayer.

W-3.4002
Scripture

Scripture lessons are read, and time observed for reflection and meditation. An exposition of Scripture may be given. The Word may be expressed in music, drama, or dance. Psalms and canticles are especially appropriate to daily prayer because in using them worshipers both express and respond to the Word. (W-2.2000)

W-3.4003
Prayer

Prayers may be spoken, sung, enacted, and offered in silence. Daily prayer affords a unique opportunity for silence and meditation in community. Prayer in all its dimensions should be offered with special attention to the public and personal concerns of the community. (W-2.1000)

W-3.4004
Order

The Service of Daily Prayer should be ordered to move through

    (1)   praise,

    (2)   the reading and hearing of the Word,

    (3)   responding to the Word in meditation, prayer, and song,

    (4)   going forth in the name of Christ.

W-3.4005
Leadership

The service, authorized by the session, should be planned in consultation with the pastor, and may be led by appropriately prepared officers or other members of the church.

W-3.5000

5.   Other Regularly Scheduled Services of Worship

W-3.5100

a.   Sunday Services

W-3.5101
Other Sunday
Services

The primary service of worship on Sunday is the Service for the Lord's Day, scheduled at the time(s) when most members can participate. Other services may be regularly scheduled on Sunday, at times in the morning, afternoon, or evening. The time and nature of these services is to be determined by the session as it considers the needs of the congregation and the community. In planning these services, care should be taken to preserve the integrity of the Service for the Lord's Day.

W-3.5102
Elements

These services include the reading and hearing of the Word, prayer, and opportunities for self-offering and for relating to each other and the world. (W-2.1000-.2000; W-2.5000-.6000) They may place special emphasis upon prayer, congregational singing, the teaching of Scripture, and interpretation of the Word through the arts. Such services may include the preaching of the Word, or other forms of proclamation authorized by the pastor and the session. (W-1.4000; W-2.2000; W-3.3400) On those occasions the Sacraments may also be celebrated.

W-3.5103
Order

The order of each service should reflect the principles of worship in this directory as they relate to the particular occasion.

W-3.5200

b.   Church School

W-3.5201
Church School

When several classes of the church school assemble together for worship, there should be opportunity for prayer, singing, and reading and hearing the Word. There may be occasions when an offering of gifts is an appropriate expression of self-offering and of relating to the world.

W-3.5202
Elements and
Order

There should be regular opportunities for worship in each church school class. Such worship may be less formal and more spontaneous than in larger groups. Yet it should include prayer and song that grow out of the consideration of the Word. It may include acts and tokens of self-offering and commitment, which may lead

    (1) to requesting Baptism,

    (2) to participating in the Lord's Supper,

    (3) to affirming the vows taken at Baptism.

Worship in the church school is not to be a substitute for participation in the worship of the whole congregation on the Lord's Day. (W-3.1004; W-3.3201; W-6.2001)

W-3.5300   **c. Gatherings for Prayer**

W-3.5301
Prayer Meetings

In the life of a congregation people may gather for prayer in a number of settings. The session is responsible for the authorization of such gatherings. Regularly scheduled prayer meetings which are open to all may take several forms, including the midweek evening service, a morning, midday, or afternoon gathering, and prayer breakfasts and luncheons. Smaller groups may meet regularly as prayer circles, intercessory fellowships, or covenant groups. Special days and occasions in the life of the local community, the nation, and the ecumenical Church may draw people together for services of prayer.

W-3.5302
Elements

In these services the Word is read and heard, and may be proclaimed, taught, and discussed, or expressed in music and the other arts. Prayer is offered, and may be spoken, sung, enacted, or shared in silence. Opportunities may be given for the recognition and offering of gifts and for the commitment of life to Jesus Christ. Concern for one another may be shown in words and acts of welcome, reconciliation, and mutual ministry. Concern for the world may be enacted in prayer and ministries of compassion, justice, peacemaking, and witness.

W-3.5400   **d. Services for Wholeness**

W-3.5401
Healing Services

Healing was an integral part of the ministry of Jesus which the church has been called to continue as one dimension of its concern for the wholeness of people. Through services for wholeness, the church enacts in worship its ministry as a healing community.

W-3.5402
Authorization

Services for wholeness are to be authorized by the session, and shall be under the direction of the pastor. Such services may be observed as regularly scheduled services of worship, as occasional services, or as part of the Service for the Lord's Day. (W-3.3506)

These services should be open to all and not restricted to those desiring healing for themselves or for others of special concern to them. The services should be held in a place readily accessible to those who may be seeking healing.

W-3.5403
Forms of Prayer

The vital element of worship in the service for wholeness is prayer since this is essentially a time of waiting in faith upon God. Thanksgiving for God's promise of wholeness, intercessions, and supplications should be offered. Adequate time for silent prayer should be provided, as well as occasions for prayers spoken and sung. Enacted prayer in the form of the laying on of hands and anointing with oil is appropriate (James 5:14). The enactment of prayers involves the presiding minister of the Word and Sacrament together with representatives of the believing community.

W-3.5404
Word and
Sacrament

These prayers are a response to the Word read and proclaimed. Particular focus should be on announcing the gospel's promise of wholeness through Christ. The sealing of this promise in the Lord's Supper may be celebrated, and should follow the prayers and the laying on of hands. Occasion for offering one's life and gifts for ministry may be provided, as well as opportunities for reconciliation and renewed commitment to the service of Jesus Christ in the world.

W-3.5405
Source of Healing

When a service for wholeness includes anointing and the laying on of hands, these enacted prayers should be introduced carefully in order to avoid misinterpretation and misunderstanding. Healing is to be understood not as the result of the holiness, earnestness, or skill of those enacting the prayers, or of the faith of the ones seeking healing, but as the gift of God through the power of the Holy Spirit.

W-3.5500

e.   Services for Evangelism

W-3.5501
Invitations to
Discipleship

The invitation to respond to Jesus Christ should be offered frequently and regularly in the Service for the Lord's Day. (W-2.5002) It is appropriate for the session to authorize services for the particular purpose of evangelism, and to set such services at regular seasons. (W-3.2003; W-7.2000)

W-3.5502
Order

The central element of worship in services for evangelism is the proclamation of the Word, with a special emphasis on the redeeming grace of God in Christ, the claim Jesus Christ makes on human life, and his invitation to a life of discipleship empowered by the Holy Spirit. This proclamation involves

(1) the reading and hearing of Scripture,

(2) preaching and witness,

(3) the Word sung, enacted, and confessed.

W-3.5500: West.Conf. 6.055-6.058, 6.187-6.190

Surrounding this central act should be prayer,

    (4) in preparation for the services;

    (5) in the service itself
        as praise, thanksgiving, confession, intercession, and supplication;

    (6) following the service
        that the new disciples be supported in their commitment and vitally included in the life of the church.

W-3.5503
Commitment

The service shall move to a clear invitation to commitment or renewed commitment to Jesus Christ as Lord and Savior and to life in the covenant community which is Christ's body, the Church. Such commitment is a sign of grace and an act of self-offering which should issue in

    (1) new relationship to one another,

    (2) new awareness of one's gifts for ministry,

    (3) new involvement in the redemptive activity of Christ in the world.

W-3.5504
Responses to
New
Commitment

Those who respond to the invitation shall be offered nurture and instruction to support them in their commitment and to equip them for the life of discipleship. (G-5.0501) Those who are making their first commitment shall make public the profession of their faith during a Service for the Lord's Day, with those who have not been baptized receiving Baptism in that service. Those who are renewing a commitment shall be given opportunity for public acknowledgment of their reaffirmation during a Service for the Lord's Day. (W-3.3502; W-4.2000)

W-3.5600

f. Program and Mission Interpretation

W-3.5601
Services for
Mission
Emphasis

Interpretation of the program and mission of the church may occur in services of worship held for this purpose and regularly scheduled at appropriate seasons of the year. (W-3.2003) In these services, a primary focus is on the interpretation of the program or mission which has led the session to authorize the special service(s). Therefore a central emphasis of such worship is relating to the world and to each other. (W-2.6000)

W-3.5602
Elements

The Word should be read and heard. Prayers of thanksgiving, supplication, and intercession should be offered on behalf of the ministries interpreted in the service. Opportunities for offering of material gifts and for commitment of life may be appropriately included.

W-3.5700

g. Special Groups in the Local Congregation

W-3.5701
Special Groups

In every local congregation there are special groups, constituted by age, gender, or interest, which meet regularly. Worship should ordinarily occur in meetings of these groups and should reflect the principles of this directory. All of the elements of worship in Chapter Two are appropriate in these settings except celebration of the Sacraments, which are acts of worship authorized by the session, ordinarily for the participation of the entire congregation.

W-3.6000

6. Special Gatherings

W-3.6100

a. Governing Bodies

W-3.6101
Worship in
Governing Bodies

Governing bodies shall worship regularly and shall order that worship in accordance with the principles of this directory. Each governing body should establish a group charged with responsibility for and oversight of its worship. It may also adopt guidelines for the planning and conduct of worship at its meetings.

W-3.6102
Word and
Sacrament

In governing bodies above the session, provision is to be made for the regular reading, proclaiming, and hearing of the Word, and for the regular and frequent celebration of the Lord's Supper. (G-9.0301)

W-3.6103
Prayer

Every meeting of a governing body shall open and close with prayer (G-9.0301) and should provide for adequate occasions of prayer during the course of its deliberations. The prayers should express praise and thanksgiving, confession, intercession, and supplication in relation to proceedings of the governing body.

W-3.6200

b. Retreats, Camps, Conferences, and Special Gatherings

W-3.6201
Worship in
Conferences and
Retreats

Governing bodies have the responsibility for authorizing worship in special gatherings under their jurisdiction. Worship is an integral part of the life of retreats, camps, and conferences. That worship shall be guided by the principles of this directory and the guidelines established by the appropriate governing body.

W-3.6202
Order

The nature and focus of worship will vary with the type of gathering, its purpose, its participants, its location, the season, and the rhythm and order of its life. Worship may use the order of Daily Prayer (W-3.4000), be guided by the Service for the Lord's Day (W-3.3000), or adapt the form of other services described in this directory. (W-3.5000)

W-3.6203
Elements

The elements of worship appropriate for every gathering are prayer, the reading and hearing of Scripture, self-offering, and relating to each other and the world. (W-2.1000; W-2.2000; W-2.5000; W-2.6000) Different elements of worship may be emphasized in different settings, such as

(1) retreats for silent prayer or marriage enrichment,

(2) nature camps or mission caravans,

(3) youth leadership or music conferences.

Yet in every case, the Word shall be presented with integrity, and appropriate prayers should be offered. (W-2.1000-.2000)

W-3.6204
Lord's Supper
at Special
Gatherings

The Sacrament of the Lord's Supper is appropriate for any special gathering

(1) when it is authorized by the governing body responsible for the gathering or by the presbytery within whose bounds the event will take place,

(2) when a minister of the Word and Sacrament presides and other officers of the church are present,

(3) when it is observed in a service of worship following the preaching of the Word or other form of proclamation authorized by the governing body,

(4) when it is understood as participation in the life of the whole believing community rather than as a devotional exercise for a few. (W-2.4010-.4012)

The church bears strong witness to the unity of the body of Christ when Christians gather from a number of different churches or diverse ethnic or cultural groups, or in ecumenical assemblies for the celebration of the Lord's Supper. (W-2.4006)

W-3.6205
Ecumenical
Eucharist

Ministers of the Word and Sacrament invited to celebrate or participate in the celebration of the Lord's Supper in ecumenical settings have the authority to do so to the extent that the participation does not contradict the Reformed understanding of the Lord's Supper.

W-4.0000

CHAPTER IV. ORDERING WORSHIP
FOR SPECIAL PURPOSES

W-4.1000

W-4.1001
Services for
Special Occasions
and Purposes

1. Special Occasions and Recognitions

There are special occasions and transitions in the life of the congregation and the lives of its members which are appropriately recognized in worship. Many of these are ordinarily celebrated at particular points in the Service for the Lord's Day. Others may be celebrated in the Service for the Lord's Day or in other regularly scheduled services or in a service especially appointed for the occasion. No special recognitions should be included in the Service for the Lord's Day when they would diminish the importance of hearing the Word and celebrating the Sacraments in joyful expectation of encountering the risen Lord. (W-1.3011)

W-4.2000

W-4.2001
Baptism and
Membership

2. Services of Welcome and Reception

In Baptism a person is sealed by the Holy Spirit, given identity as a member of the church, welcomed to the Lord's Table, and set apart for a life of Christian service. (W-3.3602-.3608; W-3.5504) These aspects of Baptism are given further expression in worship through welcoming the baptized to the Lord's Table, confirming and commissioning, and receiving new members. (W-6.2001) These occasions are ordinarily observed in the Service for the Lord's Day in responding to the Word. (W-3.3502)

W-4.2002
Welcoming to the
Lord's Table.

It is the responsibility of the whole congregation, particularly exercised through the session, to nurture those who are baptized to respond to the invitation to the Lord's Supper. When a person is baptized as a child, the session shall equip and support the parent(s) or those exercising parental responsibility for their task of nurturing the child for receiving the Lord's Supper. (W-2.3012) When the child begins to express a desire to receive this Sacrament, the session should take note of this and provide an occasion for recognition and welcome.

W-4.2003
Confirming and
Commissioning

The church nurtures those baptized as children and calls them to make public their personal profession of faith and their acceptance of responsibility in the life of the church. When these persons are ready, they shall be examined by the session. (G-10.0102b) After the session has received them as active members they shall be presented to the congregation during a service of public worship. In that service the church shall confirm them in their baptismal identity. They shall reaffirm the vows taken at Baptism by

    a. professing their faith in Jesus Christ as Lord and Savior,

    b. renouncing evil and affirming their reliance on God's grace,

c.   declaring their intention to participate actively and responsibly in the worship and mission of the church.
(W-3.3603)

They are commissioned for full participation in the mission and
governance of the church, and are welcomed by the congregation.
(W-3.3502; W-3.3602-.3608; W-3.3701)

**W-4.2004
Reception of
Other Members**

The service for the reception of members into a congregation
by transfer of certificate or by reaffirmation of faith is an occasion to recall one's earlier Baptism, profession of faith, and commitment to discipleship. After examination and reception by the
session, these new members shall be recognized at a regularly
scheduled service of public worship. (W-3.3502) It is appropriate
for them to reaffirm the commitments made at Baptism, to make
public again their profession of faith in Jesus Christ as Lord and
Savior, and to express their intention to participate actively in the
worship and mission of the church. (W-3.3602) They are welcomed into the life of the congregation and are commissioned for
service as members.

**W-4.2005
Reaffirmation
by All**

On each occasion when people entering membership in a particular church make public their profession of faith, it is appropriate
for all baptized worshipers formally to reaffirm the commitments
made at Baptism.

**W-4.2006
Renewal and
Fresh
Commitment**

In the life of a believer there are times of special awakening,
renewal, and fresh commitment which call for public expression,
recognition, and celebration. People should be encouraged to share
with the minister(s) and with the session these decisive moments
and stirrings of the Holy Spirit. It may often be appropriate for people to make public this sense of deepened commitment in a service
of worship, and for the church to acknowledge it with prayer and
thanksgiving. (W-3.3502; W-3.3701)

**W-4.2007
Enacting
Welcome and
Recognition**

In all these services the welcoming, recognizing, commissioning, and acknowledging should be expressed in actions as well as
in words. Appropriate actions may include

a.   sharing the peace of Christ,

b.   offering hands in welcome,

c.   anointing,

d.   embracing,

and other acts of recognition and celebration common to the cul-
ture(s) of the participants.

W-4.3000

3.   Commissioning for Specific Acts of Discipleship

**W-4.3001
Recognizing
Discipleship**

In the life of the Christian community God calls people to particular acts of discipleship to use their personal gifts for service in

the Church and in the world. These specific acts may be strengthened and confirmed by formal recognition in worship.

W-4.3002
Forms of
Discipleship

Discipleship may be expressed

a. in the local church through service such as teacher in the church school, trustee, member of the choir, officer in a church organization, or adviser or helper with various church groups;

b. on behalf of the local church through its ministry in and to the community;

c. in the larger church as people serve in the ministries of presbytery, synod, and the General Assembly, and of ecumenical agencies and councils;

d. beyond the church cooperating with all who work for compassion and reconciliation. (W-7.3000-.4000)

W-4.3003
Recognition and
Commissioning

Recognition and commissioning of people called to such acts of discipleship may occur in the Service for the Lord's Day as a response to the proclamation of the Word (W-3.3500) or as a bearing and following of the Word into the world. (W-3.3700) Recognizing and commissioning for specific acts of discipleship may also occur in services of worship provided for this purpose or in other appropriate services. (W-3.5100; W-3.5300; W-3.5600)

W-4.4000

4. Ordination and Installation

W-4.4001
Ordination and
Installation

In ordination the church sets apart with prayer and the laying on of hands those who have been called through election by the church to serve as deacons, elders, and ministers of the Word and Sacrament. (W-2.1005) In installation the church sets apart with prayer those previously ordained to the office of deacon, elder, or minister of the Word and Sacrament, and called anew to service in that office.

W-4.4002
Setting of the
Service

The service of ordination and installation may take place during the Service for the Lord's Day as a response to the proclamation of the Word. (W-3.3503) Ordination and installation may also take place in a special service which focuses upon Jesus Christ and the mission and ministry of the church and which includes the proclamation of the Word.

W-4.4003
Form and Order

In the service of ordination and installation, the moderator shall state the nature and purpose of the occasion and ask the constitutional questions of the candidate(s). (G-14.0207 and G-14.0405) An elder shall ask the constitutional questions of the congregation. (G-14.0208 and G-14.0510) Following affirmative responses from the candidate(s) and the congregation, those to be ordained shall kneel, if able, for prayer and the laying on of hands. (G-14.0209, G-14.0405, and G-14.5010; W-2.1005)

Those previously ordained who are to be installed ordinarily shall stand, if able, for prayer. Following the prayer, the moderator shall make a declaration of the ordination or installation, and the one(s) ordained and installed shall receive welcome to office. (W-4.2007) A brief charge to the newly installed and to the congregation may be given. At the conclusion of the service, the newly ordained or installed minister(s) of the Word and Sacrament may make a brief statement and shall pronounce the benediction.

W-4.5000

W-4.5001
Recognition of
Transition

5.   Transitions in Ministry

When those especially commissioned for specific acts of discipleship; those ordained as deacons, elders, or ministers of the Word and Sacrament; or others serving in the church conclude a period of ministry, it is appropriate for the congregation and others associated with the ministry to recognize those persons' gifts and service.

W-4.5002
Form of
Recognition

This recognition may be given in the Service for the Lord's Day as a part of responding to the Word (W-3.3503) or of bearing and following the Word into the world (W-3.3701), or in another appointed service of worship. The service may include expressions of commendation and gratitude for the persons' ministry, and should include prayers of thanksgiving and intercession on their behalf as they make this transition in their ministry.

W-4.6000

W-4.6001
Censure and
Restoration

6.   Censure and Restoration

Forms for censure and for restoration are set forth in the Rules of Discipline in this *Book of Order.* (D-12.0102; D-12.0103; D-12.0104; D-12.0105; D-12.0202; D-12.0203) In using these forms, care should be taken that they be spoken and enacted in the spirit of pastoral concern and in the context of worship within the appropriate community.

W-4.7000

W-4.7001
Recognition of
Service

7.   Recognition of Service to the Community

Service given to the community beyond the particular mission of the church may be appropriately recognized as an expression of Christian discipleship with prayer and thanksgiving at a suitable time in an occasion of worship. Significant accomplishments in the lives of Christians or honors and other forms of recognition received by them may also be occasions for such celebration with the community of faith.

W-4.8000

8. Services of Acceptance and Reconciliation

W-4.8001
Brokenness and
Wholeness

Christians are forgiven sinners living in a sinful world, involved in brokenness which they suffer, involved in brokenness which they cause. Given this reality, a significant move toward wholeness is the recognition and acknowledgement of one's own responsibility in the brokenness and failure of a relationship

    a.   in friendship and in marriage,

    b.   in family and in church,

    c.   in workplace and in school,

    d.   in neighborhood, in community, and in the world.

W-4.8002
Services of
Acceptance and
Reconciliation

Beyond this the Christian community must recognize and acknowledge its involvement in sin, in broken structures, and in broken relationships. Opportunity is appropriately given in worship for special services of acknowledgement and recognition of failure in relationships, of grieving together over the loss of relationship, and of mutual forgiveness and reconciliation within the believing community. (W-2.6001; W-3.3301; W-3.5400; W-6.3007-.3008; W-6.3011; W-7.4004)

W-4.8003
Form of a Service

These services include

    a.   readings from Scripture which reveal the grace of God,

    b.   prayers of confession, intercession, and supplication,

    c.   declarations of forgiveness and freedom from guilt and shame,

    d.   expressions of praise and thanksgiving for forgiveness and reconciliation,

    e.   enactments of mutual commitment and reconciliation.

W-4.9000

9. Marriage

W-4.9001
Christian
Marriage

Marriage is a gift God has given to all humankind for the well-being of the entire human family. Marriage is a civil contract between a woman and a man. For Christians marriage is a covenant through which a man and a woman are called to live out together before God their lives of discipleship. In a service of Christian marriage a lifelong commitment is made by a woman and a man to each other, publicly witnessed and acknowledged by the community of faith.

W-4.9002
Preparing for
Marriage

    a.   In preparation for the marriage service, the minister shall provide for a discussion with the man and the woman concerning

---

W-4.8000: 2 Cor. 5:18-20; Jas. 5:16; West.Conf. 6.086; Conf.1967 9.07, 9.22
W-4.9000: 2 Helv.Conf. 5.245-5.251; West.Conf. 6.131-6.139

(1)   the nature of their Christian commitment, assuring that at least one is a professing Christian,

(2)   the legal requirements of the state,

(3)   the privileges and responsibilities of Christian marriage,

(4)   the nature and form of the marriage service,

(5)   the vows and commitments they will be asked to make,

(6)   the relationship of these commitments to their lives of discipleship,

(7)   the resources of the faith and the Christian community to assist them in fulfilling their marriage commitments.

This discussion is equally important in the case of a first marriage, a marriage after the death of a spouse, and a marriage following divorce.

If the Marriage Is Unwise

b.   If the minister is convinced after discussion with the couple that commitment, responsibility, maturity, or Christian understanding are so lacking that the marriage is unwise, the minister shall assure the couple of the church's continuing concern for them and not conduct the ceremony. In making this decision the minister may seek the counsel of the session.

**W-4.9003
Time and Place of the Service**

Christian marriage should be celebrated in the place where the community gathers for worship. As a service of Christian worship, the marriage service is under the direction of the minister and the supervision of the session. (W-1.4004-.4006) The marriage ordinarily takes place in a special service which focuses upon marriage as a gift of God and as an expression of the Christian life. Others may be invited to participate as leaders in the service at the discretion of the pastor. Celebration of the Lord's Supper at the marriage service requires the approval of the session, and care shall be taken that the invitation to the Table is extended to all baptized present. The marriage service may take place during the Service for the Lord's Day upon authorization by the session. It should be placed in the order as a response to the proclamation of the Word. It may then be followed by the Sacrament of the Lord's Supper. (W-2.4010; W-3.3503)

**W-4.9004
Form and Order of Service**

The service begins with scriptural sentences and a brief statement of purpose. The man and the woman shall declare their intention to enter into Christian marriage and shall exchange vows of love and faithfulness. The service includes appropriate passages of Scripture, which may be interpreted in various forms of proclamation. Prayers shall be offered for the couple, for the communities which support them in this new dimension of discipleship, and for all who seek to live in faithfulness. In the name of the triune God the minister shall declare publicly that the woman and the man are now joined in marriage. A charge may be given. Other actions common to the community and its cultures may appropriately be observed when these actions do not diminish the Christian understanding of marriage. The service concludes with a benediction.

W-4.9005
Music and
Appointments

Music suitable for the marriage service directs attention to God and expresses the faith of the church. (W-2.1004) The congregation may join in hymns and other musical forms of praise and prayer. Flowers, decorations, and other appointments should be appropriate to the place of worship, enhance the worshipers' consciousness of the reality of God, and reflect the integrity and simplicity of Christian life. (W-1.3034; W-1.4004-.4005; W-5.5006)

W-4.9006
Recognizing Civil
Marriage

A service of worship recognizing a civil marriage and confirming it in the community of faith may be appropriate when requested by the couple. The service will be similar to the marriage service except that the opening statement, the declaration of intention, the exchange of the vows by the husband and wife, and the public declaration by the minister reflect the fact that the woman and man are already married to one another according to the laws of the state.

W-4.10000

10. Services on the Occasion of Death

W-4.10001
Christians and
Death

The resurrection is a central doctrine of the Christian faith and shapes Christians' attitudes and responses to the event of death. Death brings loss, sorrow, and grief to all. In the face of death Christians affirm with tears and joy the hope of the gospel. Christians do not bear bereavement in isolation but are sustained by the power of the Spirit and the community of faith. The church offers a ministry of love and hope to all who grieve. (W-6.3006)

W-4.10002
Planning
Arrangements

Because it is difficult under emotional stress to plan wisely, the session should encourage members to discuss and plan in advance the arrangements which will be necessary at the time of death, including decisions about the Christian options of burial, cremation, or donation for medical purposes. These plans should provide for arrangements which are simple, which bear witness to resurrection hope, and in which the Christian community is central. The session is responsible for establishing general policies concerning the observance of services on the occasion of death. (W-1.4004)

W-4.10003
Setting of the
Service

The service on the occasion of death ordinarily should be held in the usual place of worship in order to join this service to the community's continuing life and witness to the resurrection. The service shall be under the direction of the pastor. Others may be

W-4.10000: 2 Helv.Conf. 5.235-5.236

invited to participate as leaders in the service at the discretion of the pastor. This service may be observed on any day. A request to observe such a service as a part of the Lord's Day service or to celebrate the Lord's Supper as a part of a service on the occasion of death requires the approval of the session.

**W-4.10004
Form and Order**

The service begins with scriptural sentences. It is appropriate for worshipers to sing hymns, psalms, spirituals, or spiritual songs which affirm God's power over death, a belief in the resurrection to life everlasting, and the assurance of the communion of the saints. Scripture shall be read; a sermon or other exposition of the Word may be proclaimed; an affirmation of faith may be made by the people. Aspects of the life of the one who has died may be recalled. Prayers shall be offered, giving thanks to God

(1) for life in Jesus Christ and the promise of the gospel,

(2) for the gift of the life of the one who has died,

(3) for the comfort of the Holy Spirit,

(4) for the community of faith;

making intercessions

(5) for family members and loved ones who grieve,

(6) for those who minister to and support the bereaved,

(7) for all who suffer loss;

lifting supplications

(8) for faith and grace for all who are present;

concluding with the Lord's Prayer.

The service ends by commending the one who has died to the care of the eternal God and sending the people forth with a benediction.

**W-4.10005
Alternatives and
Options**

This service may be observed before or after the committal of the body. In order that attention in the service be directed to God, when a casket is present it ordinarily is closed. It may be covered with a funeral pall. The service may include other actions common to the community of faith and its cultures when these actions do not detract from or diminish the Christian understanding of death and resurrection. The service shall be complete in itself, and any fraternal, civic, or military rites should be conducted separately. When there are important reasons not to hold the service in the usual place of worship, it may be held in another suitable place such as a home, a funeral home, a crematorium, or at graveside.

**W-4.10006
Service of
Committal**

Members and friends of the family of the one who has died should gather at the graveside or crematorium for a service of farewell, which is to be conducted with simplicity, dignity, and brevity. The service includes readings from Scripture, prayers, words of committal, and a blessing, reflecting the reality of death, entrusting the one who has died to the care of God, and bearing witness to faith in the resurrection from the dead.

W-5.0000

CHAPTER V. WORSHIP
AND PERSONAL DISCIPLESHIP

W-5.1000

1. Personal Worship, Discipleship, and the Community of Faith

W-5.1001
Personal and
Communal
Worship

Christians respond to God both in communal worship and service and in personal acts of worship and discipleship. The life of the Christian flows from the worship of the church, where identity as a believer is confirmed and where one is commissioned to a life of discipleship and of personal response to God. The believer's life of response and discipleship flows into the church's life of worship and service. (W-1.1006; W-2.1001)

W-5.1002
Worship and Life

Through worship people attend to the presence of God in their life. From a Christian's life in the world comes the need for worship; in worship one sees the world in light of God's grace; from worship come vision and power for living in the world.

W-5.1003
Worship and
Ministry

The Word of God proclaimed and received in worship calls each believer to faithful discipleship in the world. From such service the disciple turns to give thanks, to confess, to intercede, and to hear Christ's call anew. The rhythm of the life of the believer moves from worship to ministry, from ministry to worship.

W-5.1004
Worship and
Discipline

The life of a Christian is empowered by grace, is expressed in obedience, and is shaped by discipline. God has given as means of grace the elements of worship to be used by households and by individuals as well as by congregations. (W-2.0000) The session should encourage people to use the disciplines described in this directory as expressions of their obedience and discipleship and as means for living and growing in the grace of God. (W-5.2000-.5000)

W-5.2000

2. The Discipline of Daily Personal Worship

W-5.2001
Daily Personal
Worship

Daily personal worship is a discipline for attending to God and accepting God's grace. The daily challenge of discipleship requires the daily nurture of worship. Daily personal worship may occur in a gathered community of faith (W-1.1006; W-1.3012; W-3.4000), in households and families (W-5.7000), or in private. Scripture, prayer, self-offering, and commitments to service are elements of daily personal worship. Baptism and the Lord's Supper are by their nature communal, but preparing for and remembering these Sacraments are important in daily personal worship. An aspect of the discipline of daily personal worship is finding the times and places where one can focus on God's presence, hear God's Word, and respond to God's grace in prayer, self-offering, and commitment to service.

W-5.3000

3. Scripture in Personal Worship

W-5.3001
Scripture

Scripture is the record of God's self-revelation through which the Holy Spirit speaks to bear witness to Jesus Christ and to give authoritative direction for the life of faith. Personal worship centers upon Scripture as one reads and listens for God's Spirit to speak. (W-2.2000)

W-5.3002
Uses of Scripture

a. One may read Scripture for the guidance, support, comfort, encouragement, and challenge which the Word of God presents.

Study of Scripture

b. One may study the Scriptures to understand them in their literary forms and in their historical and cultural contexts in order to hear the Word of God more clearly and to obey more faithfully.

Meditate On

c. One may meditate upon the Word,

(1) committing passages of Scripture to memory,

(2) recalling and reflecting upon the revelation of God,

(3) analyzing and comparing biblical themes, images, and forms,

(4) finding touchpoints and exploring relationships between Scripture and life,

(5) entering imaginatively into the world and events portrayed in the Bible to participate in what God does and promises there,

(6) wrestling with the challenges and demands of the gospel,

(7) offering one's self afresh for life in response to God.

W-5.3003
Helps in Using
Scripture

It is often helpful to keep a record of one's insights and personal responses to reading, studying, and meditating upon the Word, or to share them with others. Writing paraphrases, summaries, and brief reflections, making creative responses, and keeping journals are all disciplines which assist in responding to the Word of God in Scripture. It is especially important in personal worship to read widely in Scripture. Using lectionaries and various translations and paraphrases is helpful in seeking to hear the full message of God's Word. (W-2.2004)

W-5.4000

4. Prayer in Personal Worship

W-5.4001
Prayer

Prayer is a conscious opening of the self to God, who initiates communion and communication with us. Prayer is receiving and responding, speaking and listening, waiting and acting in the presence of God. In prayer we respond to God in adoration, in thanksgiving, in confession, in supplication, in intercession, and in self-dedication. (W-2.1000)

W-5.4002
Expressing Prayer

Prayer in personal worship may be expressed in various ways.

One may engage in conscious conversation with God, putting into words one's joys and concerns, fears and hopes, needs and longings in life.

One may wait upon God in attentive and expectant silence.

One may meditate upon God's gifts, God's actions, God's Word, and God's character.

One may contemplate God, moving beyond words and thoughts to communion of one's spirit with the Spirit of God.

One may draw near to God in solitude.

One may pray in tongues as a personal and private discipline.

One may take on an individual discipline of enacted prayer through dance, physical exercise, music, or other expressive activity as a response to grace.

One may enact prayer as a public witness through keeping a vigil, through deeds of social responsibility or protest, or through symbolic acts of disciplined service.

One may take on the discipline of holding before God the people, transactions, and events of daily life in the world.

One may enter into prayer covenants or engage in the regular discipline of shared prayer.

The Christian is called to a life of constant prayer, of "prayer without ceasing." (Rom. 12:12; 1 Thess. 5:17)

W-5.4003
Helps in Prayer

In exercising the discipline of prayer in personal worship one may find help for shaping the form and content of one's prayers

a. in Scripture, especially the Lord's Prayer and other prayers, the psalms and other biblical songs;

b. in hymns, spirituals, and other songs;

c. in service books, prayer books, and worship aids;

d. in the heritages of prayer and devotion expressed in literature and visual arts.

Such resources may also help one see the occasions and subjects of prayer, as may the daily news and church program interpretation materials and guides to personal worship.

W-5.4002: Ps. 119, 130; Matt. 6:6; Luke 11:1-4; Rom. 8:26 f.; 1 Cor. 12-14

W-5.5000

W-5.5001
The Lord's Day

Disciplined
Observance of

5.　Other Disciplines in Personal Worship and Discipleship

a.　God has given means of grace beyond Scripture, Sacraments, and prayer.

b.　Christians have received the Lord's Day to be kept holy to the Lord. (W-1.3011, W-3.2001) It is the beginning of the believer's week and gives shape to the life of discipleship. Disciplined observance of this day includes preparation of one's self for

> (1)　participation in public worship,

> (2)　engagement in ministries of witness, service, and compassion,

> (3)　activities that contribute to spiritual re-creation and rest from daily occupation.

In observing this discipline, Christians whose work takes place on Sunday should set aside another day of the week for these observances.

W-5.5002
Seasons

The seasons of the Christian year provide a rhythm and content for personal worship and discipleship. (W-1.3013; W-3.2002) Special seasons, occasions, and transitions in one's own life also inform personal worship and discipleship.

W-5.5003
Disciplines of
Fasting and
Enacted Prayer

Christians observe special times and seasons for the disciplines of fasting, keeping vigil, and other forms of enacted prayer. It is also appropriate to observe these disciplines at any time, especially in preparation for specific acts of discipleship or as acts of penitence, reconciliation, peacemaking, social protest, and compassion.

W-5.5004
Christian Giving

Giving has always been a mark of Christian commitment and discipleship. The ways in which a believer uses God's gifts of material goods, personal abilities, and time should reflect a faithful response to God's self-giving in Jesus Christ and Christ's call to minister to and share with others in the world. Tithing is a primary expression of the Christian discipline of stewardship. (W-1.3030; W-2.5000)

W-5.5005
Stewardship of
Life

Those who follow the discipline of Christian stewardship will find themselves called to lives of simplicity, generosity, honesty, hospitality, compassion, receptivity, and concern for the earth and God's creatures. (W-7.5000)

W-5.5001: Heid.Cat. 4.103; West.Conf. 6.119; S.Cat. 7.061; L.Cat. 7.227
W-5.5004: 2 Helv.Conf. 5.227-5.231

W-5.6000   **6.   Christian Vocation**

W-5.6001
God's Call

God calls a people

    a.   to believe in Jesus Christ as Lord and Savior;

    b.   to follow Jesus Christ in obedient discipleship;

    c.   to use the gifts and abilities God has given, honoring and serving God

        (1) in personal life,

        (2) in household and families,

        (3) in daily occupations,

        (4) in community, nation, and the world.

W-5.6002
Our Response

A person responds to God's call to faith in Jesus Christ through Baptism and through life and worship in the community of faith.

Persons respond to God's call to discipleship through the ministries of God's people in and for the world.

Persons respond to God's call to honor and serve God in every aspect of human life

    a.   in their work and in their play,

    b.   in their thought and in their action,

    c.   in their private and in their public relationships.

W-5.6003
Worship and
Work

God hallows daily life, and daily life provides opportunity for holy living. As Christians honor and serve God in daily life, they worship God. For Christians, work and worship cannot be separated.

W-5.7000   **7.   Worship in Families and Households**

W-5.7001
Household
Worship

When Christians live together in a family or in a household they should observe times of worship together. When it is possible to worship together daily, households may engage in

    a.   table prayer, which may be accompanied by the use of Scripture and song;

    b.   morning and evening prayer;

    c.   Bible reading, study, reflection, and memorization;

    d.   singing psalms, hymns, spirituals, and other songs;

    e.   expressions of giving and sharing.

Given the complexity of schedules and the separations incurred in daily occupations, it is especially important to cultivate the discipline of regular household worship. When members of a household are not able to come together for worship, they may nevertheless observe a common time of personal worship with common readings and prayer concerns.

The parent(s) or the one(s) exercising parental responsibility should teach their children about Christian worship by example, by providing for household worship, and by discussion and instruction. Children join in household worship

a. praying and singing,

b. listening to and telling Bible stories,

c. reading and memorizing,

d. leading and sharing,

e. enacting and responding.

Children should be taught appropriate elements of worship used regularly in the Service for the Lord's Day. (W-2.3012-.3013; W-3.1004; W-3.3100; W-3.5202; W-6.2000)

Household worship should reflect those occasions of special recognition and celebration which occur in the life of the church and in the lives of those in the household. Birthdays, baptismal days, and other anniversaries are all appropriate occasions for special observance. It is also important in household worship to anticipate and remember the Lord's Day and the celebration of the Sacraments of Baptism and the Lord's Supper. Seasons of the Christian year provide direction and content for household worship, with the seasons of Advent and Lent and the celebration of Christmas and Easter being particularly appropriate to observe in worship in households. Worship in this setting will also recognize the cycle of seasons in nature and the rhythm of community, national, and world life, as well as those events and needs which remind believers of their call to live as disciples of Jesus Christ in the world. (W-2.3014; W-3.2000; W-3.3600)

W-6.0000

CHAPTER VI. WORSHIP AND MINISTRY
WITHIN THE COMMUNITY OF FAITH

W-6.1000

W-6.1001
Responding
to God in
Ministries

1. Mutual Ministries in the Church

In communal and personal worship God calls people to faith and discipleship. Those responding to this call offer themselves and the gifts which God has given them to be used in the life of the community of faith for ministries to the world and to one another. (W-1.1000; W-5.1000; G-3.0300; G-4.0200; G-4.0400)

W-6.1002
Mutual
Ministries
in the Church

Mutual ministries to one another in the church spring from and are nourished by the Word proclaimed and heard, by the Sacraments celebrated and received, and by prayer offered and shared in worship.

W-6.1003
Nurture and
Pastoral Care

Nurture and pastoral care are ways in which Christians minister to one another. The nurture of believers and their children in the Christian community is a process of bringing them to full maturity in Jesus Christ. Pastoral care is the support which Christians offer one another in daily living and at times of need and of crisis in personal and communal life. Often nurture involves pastoral care and pastoral care furthers Christian nurture.

W-6.2000

W-6.2001
Entering the
Community

2. Christian Nurture

The Christian community provides nurture for its members through all of life and life's transitions. The church offers nurture to those entering the community of faith,

    a.   preparing for Baptism,

    b.   including them in the life of the community,

    c.   welcoming them to participate in its worship and to come to the Lord's Table,

    d.   assisting them to claim their identity as believers in Jesus Christ,

    e.   equipping them to live as commissioned disciples in the world. (W-2.3012; W-2.3013; W-4.2002; W-4.2003)

W-6.2002
Assuming
Responsibility

The church offers nurture to people assuming responsibility in the world, assisting them

    a.   with self-discovery and world awareness,

    b.   with self-discipline and discipleship,

W-6.1003: Rom. 12:15; Gal. 6:2; Eph. 4:12b-16; 2 Helv.Conf. 5.233-5.234; West.Conf. 6.147

c.   with developing commitment to moral and ethical values,

d.   with making informed choices about education and occupations,

e.   with making wise commitments in personal relationships and marriage.

W-6.2003
Living Out
Vocation

As the church ministers to people who are discovering Christian vocation, so it offers nurture to those who are living out Christian vocation in public, active life. (W-5.6000) It guides and supports them in their discipleship

a.   as ministers to one another in the community of faith,

b.   as stewards of material resources, time, and talents,

c.   as members of families, especially in their own role of sharing the faith with others of their households,

d.   as responsible citizens,

e.   as servants of God for the world.

W-6.2004
Responding
to Change

The church provides nurture to guide and support people as they continue their discipleship in circumstances offering new limitations and new freedoms.

W-6.2005
Providers
of Nurture
in the Church

In the service of Baptism the congregation, trusting in the power of the Holy Spirit, and on behalf of the universal Church, pledges responsibility for Christian nurture. (W-2.3013; W-3.3603) The session and the elders are responsible for providing for the development and supervision of the educational program of the church, for instructing church officers, and for developing discipleship among members. (G-6.0304; G-10.0102e, f, h, j, l) The pastor nurtures the community through the ministries of Word and Sacrament, by praying with and for the congregation, through formal and informal teaching, and by example. (G-6.0106; G-6.0202) Some in the community of faith whose special gifts and training have prepared them for a ministry of education are called to the task of leadership in nurture. Teachers, advisers, and others appointed by the session guide, instruct, and equip those for whose education and nurture they are responsible. (W-3.3503) Parents or those exercising parental responsibility share the faith of the church with children. (W-4.3002; W-5.7000)

W-6.2006
Resources and
Occasions
for Nurture

The primary standard and resource for the nurture of the church is the Word of God in Scripture. The central occasion for nurture in the church is the Service for the Lord's Day, when the Word is proclaimed and the Sacraments are celebrated. All members of the community, from oldest to youngest, are encouraged to be present and to participate. Educational activities should not be scheduled which prevent regular participation in this service. (W-3.1004) An important and continuing context for Christian nurture is the home, where faith is shared through worship, teaching, and example. The church provides other occasions for nurture

a. in the classes of the church school,

b. in other groups and fellowships organized for education and nurture,

c. in groups and associations gathered for service and mission,

d. in committees, boards, and governing bodies,

e. in retreats, camps, and conferences.

The confessional documents of the church provide guidance in nurture. (G-2.0000) Shape and content for study and instruction are provided by the rich resources of the liturgical, cultural, and ethnic heritages of the church. Educational materials developed for various approaches to Christian nurture are appropriate for use as approved by the session. (G-10.0102f)

W-6.3000

W-6.3001
Pastoral Care

3. Pastoral Care

The Christian community offers pastoral care to its members in their personal and communal life. The church may provide different levels of this mutual ministry of care.

W-6.3002
Care by All
Christians

All Christians are called to care for one another in daily living, sharing joys and sorrows, supporting in times of stress and need, offering mutual forgiveness and reconciliation. This care is primarily offered as the community of faith worships together. It is also provided as people interact in community and as they come together in groups for nurture or to carry on ministries of the church. Elders, deacons, and pastors are called to special responsibility for this common pastoral care. (G-6.0202; G-6.0304; G-6.0402)

W-6.3003
Pastoral
Counseling

Some in the community of faith who have special gifts and appropriate training are called in the church to the particular ministry of pastoral counseling with individuals and with groups formed for this purpose.

W-6.3004
Referral

In certain circumstances the ministry of pastoral care may call for referral to specialized ministers or others qualified by credentials and faith-perspective to provide appropriate counseling or therapy.

W-6.3005
Care in
Illness

The church offers pastoral care to people in the special needs and crises of their lives. When people are ill, Christians respond with prayer, visits, and other acts which express love and support for those who are sick and for their households, their families, and their friends. When illness is critical or is prolonged, those offering pastoral care will give special attention to the needs and stresses experienced by everyone involved. Terminal illness calls for particular care which mediates trust in God, support in suffering, comfort for distress, and hope in the face of death.

W-6.3006
Care at
Death

When death comes, the church in its pastoral care immediately offers the ministry of presence, of shared loss and pain, of faith and hope in the power of the resurrection, and of ordinary acts of care and love. The church continues special pastoral care during the time of grieving and adjusting. (W-4.10000)

W-6.3007
Care in Loss

Other occasions of loss in life, such as

a.   the loss of power,

b.   the fading away of a once-important relationship,

c.   the departure of children from the home,

d.   the loss of meaningful employment, means of livelihood, or financial security,

e.   the ending of a marriage in separation or divorce, call for pastoral care which provides opportunities to grieve and offers practical help and support in the process of renewal and adjustment.

W-6.3008
Care in Broken Relationships

The church provides pastoral care which calls people to healing and seeks to support those caught up in the hurts, hostilities, and conflicts of daily living which lead to broken relationships in families and households, in the school and the workplace, in neighborhoods and communities, and in the church. (W-4.8000)

W-6.3009
Care in Sin and Forgiveness

The call to healing in pastoral care involves the recognition in each one's life of the reality of sin, which is the source of all human brokenness. The believing community announces the good news of God whose love gives people grace

a.   to confess their sin and complicity in brokenness,

b.   to repent, expressing sorrow and intention to change,

c.   to accept God's forgiveness and extend that forgiveness to another,

d.   to forgive the other and accept the other's forgiveness,

e.   to work toward reconciliation in brokenness,

f.   to trust the power of God to bring healing and peace. (W-4.8000)

Receiving confession and declaring God's forgiveness, calling for repentance and supporting in the struggle toward new life, encouraging people to forgive and receive forgiveness, and mediating reconciliation are appropriate acts of pastoral care.

W-6.3010
Care in the Transitions of Life

The church recognizes transitions which bring joy and sorrow in human life:

a.   children are born, grow up, become independent, find their aging parents becoming dependent upon them;

b.   people begin work, change jobs, retire;

c.   households are established, move to new locations, gain and lose members;

d.   people are empowered, restored, make new commitments.

The ministries of pastoral care support people in recognizing, accepting, and celebrating these and other such times of adjustment, assisting them in working toward a new role in life and affirming their identity through transition.

**W-6.3011
Resources of
Worship for
Pastoral Care**

The community of faith engages in the ministries of mutual care in its worship, and its members draw upon the resources of worship in giving pastoral care.

a. Scripture is central as a resource for support, comfort, and guidance. The proclamation of the Word in sermon and song may lead to recognizing need and may provide care. (W-2.2000; W-3.3400)

b. Prayers—silent, spoken, and sung—give thanks, intercede, make supplication, and acknowledge God's presence and power. Prayer enacted by the laying on of hands and anointing calls upon God to heal, empower, and sustain. (W-2.1000; W-3.3506; W-3.5400)

c. Offering the Sacraments in hospital or household celebrates the presence of Christ, and extends the community of faith beyond the sanctuary. (W-2.3000-.4000; W-3.3600)

d. The Lord's Prayer, psalms, doxologies, benedictions, and other familiar portions of a congregation's worship may extend the support and care of the community of faith to those whose special needs or circumstances have placed them in isolation and remind them of their place in that community.

e. Times of remembrance, concerns of the people, prayers of intercession, and other such occasions in corporate worship will bring into the worship of the community of faith those who are absent. (W-3.3500; W-3.3700)

**W-6.4000
Worship and
Ministry**

The worship of God in the Christian community is the foundation and context for the ministry of pastoral care as well as for the ministry of nurture in the faith.

W-7.0000

CHAPTER VII. WORSHIP AND THE MINISTRY
OF THE CHURCH IN THE WORLD

W-7.1000

W-7.1001
Worship and
Ministry

1. Worship and Mission

The church participates in God's mission to the world through its ministry and worship. Worship presents the reality of the divine rule which God has promised in Jesus Christ as the final renewal of creation. The worshiping community in its integrity before the Word and its unity in prayer and Sacraments is a sign of the presence of the reign of God. The church in its ministry bears witness to God's reign through the proclamation of the gospel, through works of compassion and reconciliation, and through the stewardship of creation and of life. Signs of God's reign are also manifest in the world wherever the Holy Spirit leads people to seek justice and to make peace. (G-3.0000)

W-7.1002
Worship and
Mission

God calls the church in worship to join the mission of Jesus Christ in service to the world. As it participates in that mission the church is called to worship God in Jesus Christ, who reigns over the world. (G-1.0200)

W-7.2000

W-7.2001
The Scope of
Evangelism

2. Proclamation and Evangelism

God sends the church in the power of the Holy Spirit

  a. to announce the good news that in Christ Jesus the world is reconciled to God,

  b. to tell all nations and peoples of Christ's call to repentance, faith, and obedience,

  c. to proclaim in deed and word that Jesus gave himself to set people free,

  d. to offer in Christ's name fullness of life now and forever,

  e. to call people everywhere to believe in and follow Jesus Christ as Lord and Savior,

  f. to invite them into the community of faith to worship and serve the triune God. (G-1.0200; G-3.0300)

W-7.2002
Contexts of
Evangelism

Worship is the primary context in which people regularly hear the proclamation of the gospel, are presented with God's promise, are given the opportunity to respond with faith and acts of commitment, and receive the nurture and support of the community. (W-2.2000; W-2.5001; W-3.3501-.3503; W-3.5500) In the life of

---

W-7.2001: 2 Cor. 5:19-20; West.Conf. 6.055-6.058, 6.187-6.190

the church, the transforming power of the Holy Spirit is manifest in mutual love and service, in self-giving and acceptance, drawing people from their separateness into the community of shared faith in Jesus Christ. As Christians daily live out their vocation in the world, they invite those they meet to come and share the life of the people of God and join in their worship.

W-7.3000

W-7.3001
A Ministry of
Compassion

3.   Compassion

God sends the church in the power of the Holy Spirit to exercise compassion in the world,

    a.   feeding the hungry,

    b.   comforting the grieving,

    c.   caring for the sick,

    d.   visiting the prisoners,

    e.   freeing the captives,

    f.   sheltering the homeless,

    g.   befriending the lonely.

W-7.3002
Compassion and
Worship

God's call to compassion is proclaimed in worship. Those called are equipped and strengthened for the ministry of compassion by the proclamation of the Word and by the celebration of the Sacraments. The call is accepted as the faithful respond in prayers of confession and intercession, in acts of self-offering, and in offering material goods to be shared in ministries of compassion. (W-2.1002; W-2.5000; W-3.3505-.3507) Those called are commissioned and sent by the church to do acts of compassion on Christ's behalf. (W-2.6000; W-3.3701; W-4.3000)

W-7.3003
Compassion and
Advocacy

Such acts of compassion, done corporately and individually, are the work of the church as the body of Christ. The church is called to minister to the immediate needs and hurts of people. The church is also called to engage those structures and systems which create or foster brokenness and distortion. Christians respond to these calls through acts of advocacy and compassion, through service in common ministries of the church, and through cooperation with agencies and organizations committed to these ends. (G-3.0300)

W-7.3004
Faithful
Compassion

Following the example of Jesus Christ, faithful disciples today express compassion

    a.   with respect for the dignity of those in need,

W-7.3001: Matt. 25:31-46; Luke 4:18-21; Rom. 12:6-8; Gal. 6:9-10; Jas. 1:27, 2:14-17
W-7.3004: Mark 1:32-38; Luke 6:12

b.   with openness to help even those judged undeserving,

c.   with willingness to risk their own comfort and safety,

d.   with readiness to receive as well as to give,

e.   with constant prayer in the midst of ministering, always in communion with the renewing power of the worshiping community. (G-3.0400)

W-7.4000

4.   Reconciliation: Justice and Peace

W-7.4001
Reconciliation in
Christ

God sends the church in the power of the Holy Spirit to share with Christ in establishing God's just, peaceable, and loving rule in the world. (G-3.0300) God's reconciliation in Jesus Christ is the ground of justice and peace. (Conf. 1967 9.45) The church in worship proclaims, receives, and enacts reconciliation in Jesus Christ and commits itself to strive for justice and peace in its own life and in the world.

W-7.4002
Doing Justice

Justice is the order God sets in human life for fair and honest dealing and for giving rights to those who have no power to claim rights for themselves. The biblical vision of doing justice calls for

a.   dealing honestly in personal and public business,

b.   exercising power for the common good,

c.   supporting people who seek the dignity, freedom, and respect that they have been denied,

d.   working for fair laws and just administration of the law,

e.   welcoming the stranger in the land,

f.   seeking to overcome the disparity between rich and poor,

g.   bearing witness against political oppression and exploitation,

h.   redressing wrongs against individuals, groups, and peoples in the church, in this nation, and in the whole world.

W-7.4003
Making Peace

There is no peace without justice. Wherever there is brokenness, violence, and injustice the people of God are called to peacemaking

---

W-7.4000: Conf.1967 9.43-9.47

W-7.4002: Ex. 22:21-27; Lev. 19:33, 34; Ps. 34, 82; Isa. 2:1-5; 32:1-8, 16, 17; Amos 5:6-15; Mic. 6:8; Matt. 23:23-24; Luke 4:16-21; West.Conf. 6.127-6.128; L.Cat. 7.246, 7.251, 7.252, 7.254, 7.255; Conf.1967 9.43-9.47

W-7.4003: Isa. 2:1-5; 32:16, 17; Mic. 6:8; Jas. 3:13-18; West.Conf. 6.128; L.Cat. 7.245, 7.246; Conf.1967 9.43-9.47, 9.53-9.56

a. in the Church universal fragmented and separated by histories and cultures, in denominations internally polarized by mutual distrust, and in congregations plagued by dissension and conflict;

b. in the world where nations place national security above all else, where the zealotry of religion, race, or ideology explodes in violence, and where the lust for getting and keeping economic or political power erupts in rioting or war;

c. in communities racked by crime and fear, in schools and workplaces marked by vicious competition and rebellion against order, and in households and families divided against themselves, scarred by violence and paralyzed by fear.

W-7.4004
Reconciliation
in Worship

The ministries of reconciliation, justice, and peace are initiated and nurtured in the church's worship of God. In the proclamation of God's Word people are given assurance of freedom from the guilt and fear which keep them from fulfilling these ministries. In Baptism and the Lord's Supper believers are united in Christ, are made one in the church through the Holy Spirit, and recognize one another across all boundaries and divisions as sisters and brothers in the faith. (W-2.3000-.4000) In prayer the faithful lift intercessions for all who experience brokenness, violence, and injustice; give thanks to God for reconciliation, peace, and justice in Jesus Christ; and commit themselves to be reconcilers seeking justice and pursuing peace. (W-2.1000; W-2.6000; W-3.3506; W-3.3700)

W-7.5000

5. Caring for Creation and Life

W-7.5001
God's Mandate

God calls the Church in the power of the Holy Spirit to participate in God's work of creation and preservation. God has given humankind awesome power and perilous responsibility to rule and tame the earth, to sustain and reshape it, to replenish and renew it.

W-7.5002
Worship and the
Use of Creation

In worship Christians rejoice and give thanks to God, who gives and sustains the created universe, the earth, all life, and all goods. They acknowledge God's command to be stewards. They confess their own failures in caring for creation and life. They rejoice in the promise of the redemption and renewal of the creation in Jesus Christ, proclaimed in the Word and sealed in the Sacraments. They commit themselves to live as God's stewards until the day when God will make all things new. (W-1.0000)

W-7.5001: Gen. 1:26-28; 2:15-20; Ps. 8

W-7.5003
Stewardship of
Creation

As stewards of God's creation who hold the earth in trust, the people of God are called to

    a.   use the earth's resources responsibly without plundering, polluting, or destroying,

    b.   develop technological methods and processes that work together with the earth's environment to preserve and enhance life,

    c.   produce and consume in ways that make available to all people what is sufficient for life,

    d.   work for responsible attitudes and practices in procreation and reproduction,

    e.   use and shape earth's goods to create beauty, order, health, and peace in ways that reflect God's love for all creatures.

In gratitude for the gifts of creation, the faithful bring material goods to God in worship as a means of expressing praise, as a symbol of their self-offering, and as a token of their commitment to share earth's goods. (W-2.5000; W-3.3507; W-5.5005-.5006; W-5.6000)

W-7.6000

6. The Church and the Reign of God

W-7.6001
The Church and
the Kingdom

The church in its worship and ministry is a sign of the reign of God, which is both a present reality and a promise of the future. The church's worship and service do not make the Kingdom of God come. In an age hostile to the reign of God, the church worships and serves, with confidence that God's rule has been established and with firm hope in the ultimate manifestation of the triumph of God.

W-7.6002
Confidence
and Hope

In the present age the church's ministries of evangelism and caring for creation, of compassion and reconciliation are signs of God's reign and offer hope in the midst of life-denying situations. That hope is not dependent on the success of the church's ministries or the effectiveness of its worship, but is sustained by the power of God present with the church as it ministers and worships.

W-7.7000

7. Worship as Praise

W-7.7001
Ascription
of Praise

In worship the church is transformed and renewed, equipped and sent to serve God's reign in the world. The church looks for the day

           when every knee shall bow,
       in heaven and on earth and under the earth
           and every tongue confess
           that Jesus Christ is Lord,
         to the glory of God the Father.   (Phil. 2:9-11)

Now to the One who is able to keep us from falling
and to present us without blemish
before the presence of God's glory with rejoicing,
to the only God, our Savior
through Jesus Christ our Lord,
be glory, majesty, dominion, and authority,
before all time, now, and forever.   (Jude 24)

Amen!
Blessing and glory and wisdom and thanksgiving
and honor and power and might
be to our God
for ever and ever!
Amen.   (Rev. 7:12)

The
RULES OF
DISCIPLINE

[TEXT]

[Approved 1996, Effective July 6, 1996.]

1995—RULES OF DISCIPLINE—1994

This guide is not part of the Constitution. It is provided by the Office of the General Assembly for the convenience of readers.

* notes that the provision did not exist in 1994 Rules of Discipline

*** notes that the provision is not included in the newly adopted Rules of Discipline.

1995	PARAGRAPH OR PROVISION	1994

CHAPTER I. PRINCIPLES OF CHURCH DISCIPLINE

Preamble

D- 1.0101	Church discipline defined	Preamble a
D- 1.0102	Discipline for building up	Preamble b
D- 1.0103	Obligation to seek conciliation	*

CHAPTER II. JUDICIAL PROCESS DEFINED

D- 2.0101	Judicial process as means of discipline	D- 1.0100
a	in re. irregularities/delinquencies	D- 1.0300 a
b	in re. offenses by persons	D- 1.0300 b
D- 2.0102	Governing bodies enumerated	D- 1.0400
D- 2.0201	Types of cases defined	D- 1.0500
D- 2.0202	Remedial	D- 1.0500 a
D- 2.0203	Disciplinary	D- 1.0500 b

CHAPTER III. JURISDICTION IN JUDICIAL PROCESS

D- 3.0101	Jurisdiction of governing bodies	D- 5.0100
a	Session and disciplinary cases	D- 5.0100 b
b	Presbytery and disciplinary cases	D- 5.0100 c
c	Remedial cases	D- 5.0100 a
d	When a church is dissolved	D- 5.0100 d
D- 3.0102	No further judicial action by government body	D- 4.0200 c
D- 3.0103	When a lower governing body fails to act	D- 5.0100 e
D- 3.0104	Jurisdiction over ministers being transferred	D- 5.0200
D- 3.0105	When an officer or member renounces jurisdiction	D- 5.0300

CHAPTER VII. TRIAL IN A REMEDIAL CASE

CHAPTER VIII. APPEAL IN A REMEDIAL CASE

CHAPTER IX. REQUEST FOR VINDICATION

CHAPTER X. DISCIPLINARY CASES

CHAPTER XI. TRIAL IN A DISCIPLINARY CASE

CHAPTER XII. CENSURE AND RESTORATION IN A DISCIPLINARY CASE

CHAPTER XIII. APPEAL IN A DISCIPLINARY CASE

D-13.0404 a–f	Decision of PJC	D-13.1300 a–d
D-13.0405	Effect of reversal on appeal in disciplinary case	D-13.1400 a,b

CHAPTER XIV. EVIDENCE IN REMEDIAL OR DISCIPLINARY CASES

D-14.0101		Evidence defined	D- 9.0100
			D- 9.0200
D-14.0201		Challenge ability of witness to testify	D- 9.0300 b
D-14.0202		Husband or wife	D- 9.0300 c
D-14.0203		Counselor	D- 9.0300 d
D-14.0204		Counsel for parties	D- 9.0300 e
D-14.0205		Credibility of witnesses	D- 9.0400
D-14.0301		Separate examination	D- 9.0700
D-14.0302		Examination of witnesses	D- 9.0800
***		Leading questions prohibited	D- 9.0900
	a	Oath	D- 9.1000 a
	b	Affirmation	D- 9.1000 b
D-14.0303		Record of testimony	D- 9.1100
D-14.0304		Testimony on Deposition	D- 9.1300 a
	a	Persons from another governing body	D- 9.1300 b
	b	Taking of testimony	D- 9.1300 c
	c	Offered as evidence	D- 9.1300 d
	d	Questions of admissibility	D- 9.1300 e
***		Reference to court reporter	D- 9.1300 f
D-14.0305		Member as witness	D- 9.1400
D-14.0401		Admissibility of records	D- 9.1200 a
D-14.0402		Admissibility of testimony	D- 9.1200 b
D-14.0501		Application for new trial	D- 9.1500 a
D-14.0502		Appellate body may receive such evidence	D- 9.1500 b

REVISIONS TO THE FORM OF GOVERNMENT

[Two sections were moved to the Form of Government from the Rules of Discipline because they are administrative matters, not disciplinary.]

G- 9.0407	Administrative Review		D- 1.0200
			D- 3.0100
		thru	D- 3.0500
G- 9.0303	Dissents and Protests		D- 2.0100
		thru	D- 2.0500

[A new section was added to the Form of Government.]

G- 9.0600	Mediation or Conciliation	*

D-1.0000   # CHAPTER I. PRINCIPLES OF CHURCH DISCIPLINE

PREAMBLE

D-1.0101
Church Discipline

Church discipline is the church's exercise of authority given by Christ, both in the direction of guidance, control, and nurture of its members and in the direction of constructive criticism of offenders. Thus, the purpose of discipline is to honor God by making clear the significance of membership in the body of Christ; to preserve the purity of the church by nourishing the individual within the life of the believing community; to correct or restrain wrongdoing in order to bring members to repentance and restoration; to restore the unity of the church by removing the causes of discord and division; and to secure the just, speedy, and economical determination of proceedings. In all respects, members are to be accorded procedural safeguards and due process, and it is the intention of these rules so to provide.

D-1.0102
Power Vested in
Christ's Church

The power that Jesus Christ has vested in his Church, a power manifested in the exercise of church discipline, is one for building up the body of Christ, not for destroying it, for redeeming, not for punishing. It should be exercised as a dispensation of mercy and not of wrath so that the great ends of the Church may be achieved, that all children of God may be presented faultless in the day of Christ.

D-1.0103
Conciliate and
Mediate

The traditional biblical obligation to conciliate, mediate, and adjust differences without strife is not diminished by these Rules of Discipline. Although the Rules of Discipline describe the way in which judicial process within the church, when necessary, shall be conducted, it is not their intent or purpose to encourage judicial process of any kind or to make it more expensive or difficult. The biblical duty of church people to "come to terms quickly with your accuser while you are on the way to court..." (Matthew 5:25) is not abated or diminished. It remains the duty of every church member to try (prayerfully and seriously) to bring about an adjustment or settlement of the quarrel, complaint, delinquency, or irregularity asserted, and to avoid formal proceedings under the Rules of Discipline unless, after prayerful deliberation, they are determined to be necessary to preserve the purity and purposes of the church.

D-2.0000

CHAPTER II. JUDICIAL PROCESS DEFINED

D-2.0100

D-2.0101
Church
Discipline

1. Judicial Process

Judicial process is the means by which church discipline is implemented within the context of pastoral care and oversight. It is the exercise of authority by the governing bodies of the church for

    a.   the prevention and correction of irregularities and delinquencies by governing bodies, the General Assembly Council, or an entity of the General Assembly (Remedial Cases, D-6.0000);

    b.   the prevention and correction of offenses by persons (Disciplinary Cases, D-10.0000).

D-2.0102
Governing
Bodies of
the Church

The governing bodies of the church for judicial process are the session, the presbytery, the synod, and the General Assembly. The session itself conducts trials. The presbytery, the synod, and the General Assembly conduct trials and hearings through permanent judicial commissions.

D-2.0103
Alternative
Forms of
Resolution

To meet the goals of D-1.0103, the investigating committee may initiate if it deems appropriate, and with the written consent of all parties involved, alternative forms of resolution conducted by professionally trained and certified mediators and arbitrators. The purpose of this process is to achieve justice and compassion for all parties involved through mediation and settlement.

No statements, written or oral, made at or in connection with this process, shall be themselves admissible in evidence at a subsequent investigation or trial.

D-2.0200

D-2.0201
Remedial or
Disciplinary

2. Types of Cases

Judicial process consists of two types of cases: remedial and disciplinary.

D-2.0202
Remedial

A remedial case is one in which an irregularity or a delinquency of a lower governing body, the General Assembly Council, or an entity of the General Assembly may be corrected by a higher governing body.

Irregularity

    a.   An irregularity is an erroneous decision or action.

Delinquency

    b.   A delinquency is an omission or failure to act.

D-2.0203
Disciplinary

A disciplinary case is one in which a church member or officer may be censured for an offense.

Church
Officers

    a.   Church officers are ministers of the Word and Sacrament, elders, and deacons.

Offense b. An offense is any act or omission by a member or officer of the church that is contrary to the Scriptures or the *Constitution of the Presbyterian Church (U.S.A.)*.

D-3.0000

CHAPTER III. JURISDICTION IN JUDICIAL PROCESS

D-3.0101
Jurisdiction

In judicial process, each of the governing bodies has jurisdiction as follows:

Session

a.   The session of a church has original jurisdiction in disciplinary cases involving members of that church.

Presbytery

b.   The presbytery has original jurisdiction in disciplinary cases involving minister members of that presbytery and commissioned lay pastors serving in congregations in the presbytery. (G-11.0502f)

Presbytery,
Synod, General
Assembly

c.   The presbytery, the synod, and the General Assembly have jurisdiction in remedial cases (D-6.0000) and in appeals (D-8.0000 and D-13.0000).

Church Is
Dissolved

d.   When a church is dissolved, the presbytery shall determine any case of discipline begun by the session and not concluded.

D-3.0102
No Further
Judicial Action

When a case, either remedial or disciplinary, has been transmitted to a permanent judicial commission, the electing governing body shall take no further judicial action on the case.

D-3.0103
Lower
Governing Body
Fails to Act

When a lower governing body fails to act in a particular remedial or disciplinary case for a period of ninety days after the filing of a complaint in a remedial case or charges in a disciplinary case, the higher governing body, on the request of any party, may assume jurisdiction in the case. It may either issue specific instructions to the lower governing body as to its disposition or conclude the matter itself.

D-3.0104
Jurisdiction over
Transferred
Ministers

A minister transferred from one presbytery to another presbytery shall be subject to the jurisdiction of the first until received by the second. A minister transferred by a presbytery to another denomination shall be subject to the jurisdiction of the presbytery until received by that denomination.

D-3.0105
When
Jurisdiction Ends

Jurisdiction in judicial process ends when a church officer or a member renounces the jurisdiction of the church. Should the accused in a disciplinary case renounce the jurisdiction of the church as provided in G-6.0501 and G-6.0503, the clerk or stated clerk shall report to the governing body both the renunciation and the status of the matter at that time.

D-4.0000   CHAPTER IV. REFERENCE

D-4.0100   1.   **Reference**

D-4.0101   A reference is a written request, made by a session or a per-
Definition   manent judicial commission of a presbytery or synod to the permanent judicial commission of the next higher governing body, for
trial and decision or a hearing on appeal in a remedial or disciplinary case not yet decided.

D-4.0102   A proper subject of reference involves matters or questions for
Proper Subject which it is desirable or necessary that a higher governing body decide the case.

D-4.0103   With its written request for reference to a higher governing
Duty of Lower   body, the lower governing body shall specify its reasons for the re-
Governing Body quest and transmit the whole record of proceedings in the case and
shall take no further action thereon. If the reference is accepted, all
proceedings, including the trial or hearing on appeal, shall thereafter be held in the higher governing body.

D-4.0200   2.   **Action on Reference**

D-4.0201   Upon receipt of a request for reference, the stated clerk of the
Duty of Higher higher governing body shall transmit the request to the permanent
Governing Body judicial commission for a decision whether or not to accept the case.

D-4.0202   If the permanent judicial commission decides to accept the
Acceptance   reference, it shall proceed to trial and decision or to a hearing on
appeal.

D-4.0203   The permanent judicial commission may refuse to accept the
Refusal   case for reference and return it to the lower governing body, stating
its reasons for refusal. The lower governing body shall then conduct the trial or hearing on appeal and proceed to a decision.

D-5.0000 · CHAPTER V. PERMANENT JUDICIAL COMMISSIONS

D-5.0100 · **1. Service on Permanent Judicial Commissions**

D-5.0101
Election

The General Assembly, each synod, and each presbytery shall elect a permanent judicial commission from the ministers and elders subject to its jurisdiction. Each commission shall be composed of ministers and elders in numbers as nearly equal as possible. When the commission consists of an odd number of members, the additional member may be either a minister or an elder. The General Assembly commission shall be composed of one member from each of its constituent synods. The synod commission shall be composed of no fewer than eleven members distributed equally, insofar as possible, among the constituent presbyteries. In those synods with fewer than eleven presbyteries, each presbytery shall have at least one member. The presbytery commission shall be composed of no fewer than seven members, with no more than one of its elder members from any one of its constituent churches.

D-5.0102
Term

The term of each member of a permanent judicial commission shall be six years, with the exception that membership on the Permanent Judicial Commission of the General Assembly shall end when that member transfers membership to a church or presbytery outside the synod from which nominated. In each odd-numbered year, the General Assembly shall elect members for a term of six years to fill the vacancies then occurring. Their terms of office will begin with the dissolution of the General Assembly at which they are elected.

D-5.0103
Classes

In synods and presbyteries, commissioners shall be elected in three classes, with no more than one half of the members to be in one class. When established for the first time, one class shall serve for two years, the second class for four years, and the third class for six years.

D-5.0104
Vacancy

Any vacancy due to resignation, death, or any other cause may be filled by the electing governing body, which may elect a person to fill the unexpired term at any meeting thereof.

D-5.0105
Eligibility

No person who has served on a permanent judicial commission for a full term of six years shall be eligible for reelection until four years have elapsed after the expired six-year term. No person shall serve on more than one permanent judicial commission at the same time. No person shall serve on the Permanent Judicial Commission of the General Assembly who is a member of any other entity elected by the General Assembly until that person shall have resigned such membership. The moderator, stated clerk, or any member of the staff of a governing body or the staff of any of its entities or councils shall not serve on its permanent judicial commission.

D-5.0106
Commission
Expenses

All necessary expenses of a permanent judicial commission shall be paid by the electing governing body.

D-5.0200

2. Meetings

D-5.0201
Officers

Each permanent judicial commission shall meet and elect from its members a moderator and a clerk.

D-5.0202
Bases of Power

In the cases transmitted to it, the permanent judicial commission shall have only the powers prescribed by and conduct its proceedings according to the *Constitution of the Presbyterian Church (U.S.A.).*

D-5.0203
Meetings

The meetings of the permanent judicial commission shall be held at such times and places as the electing governing body shall direct, or, if no directions are given, at such times and places as the commission shall determine.

D-5.0204
Quorum

The quorum of a permanent judicial commission shall be a majority of the members.

D-5.0205
Who Shall Not
Participate

When a church or lower governing body is a party to a case, members of a permanent judicial commission who are members of that church, or of that lower governing body, or of churches within that lower governing body shall not participate in the trial or appeal of that case.

D-5.0206
Lack of Quorum

If, through absence, disqualification, or disability, a sufficient number of the members of a permanent judicial commission are not present to constitute a quorum, the permanent judicial commission shall recess until a quorum can be obtained.

Inability to Reach
a Quorum

a.   The permanent judicial commission shall report its inability to reach a quorum to the stated clerk of the governing body that elected it.

Roster of Former
Members

b.   The stated clerk of the governing body shall keep a current roster of those members of the permanent judicial commission whose terms have expired within the past six years. The names shall be arranged alphabetically within classes beginning with the most recent class. Whenever the permanent judicial commission reports its inability to obtain a quorum, the stated clerk shall immediately select, by rotation from that roster, a sufficient number of former members of the permanent judicial commission to constitute a quorum. The stated clerk shall report the roster annually to the governing body.

Participant
Expenses

c.   If a permanent judicial commission is unable to try a case for lack of a quorum, the governing body shall reimburse the expenses reasonably incurred by those persons required to be present.

CHAPTER VI. REMEDIAL CASES

D-6.0000

D-6.0100

1. Initiating a Remedial Case and Stay of Enforcement

D-6.0101
Method of
Initiation

A remedial case is initiated by the filing of a complaint with the stated clerk of the governing body having jurisdiction.

D-6.0102
Definition of
Complaint

A complaint is a written statement alleging an irregularity in a particular decision or action, or alleging a delinquency. (D-2.0202) The filing of a complaint does not, by itself, stay enforcement of the decision or action.

D-6.0103
Stay of
Enforcement

The action or decision of a governing body, of its permanent judicial commission, or of a respondent named in D-6.0202b may be suspended by a stay of enforcement. A stay of enforcement is a written statement that requests the implementation of a decision or action be delayed until a complaint or appeal is finally determined.

Who May File

a. Any person or governing body qualified to file a complaint or appeal may stay enforcement by filing with the governing body, commission, or respondent whose action or decision is to be stayed, no later than thirty days after the decision or action, one of the following:

(1) a stay of enforcement signed by at least one third of the members recorded as present when the decision or action was made by the governing body; or

(2) a stay of enforcement signed by at least one third of the members of the permanent judicial commission who decided the case; or

(3) a stay of enforcement signed by at least three of the members of the permanent judicial commission having jurisdiction to hear the complaint or appeal on the decision or action, provided there has been submitted to such members of the permanent judicial commission either a copy of the complaint or notice of appeal, or the substance of the complaint or appeal to be filed, with the reasons therefor, and that such members certify that in their judgment probable grounds exist for finding the decision or action erroneous.

Copy Provided

b. A copy of the stay of enforcement must also be provided to the permanent judicial commission that will hear the complaint or appeal.

Effective Time

c. The stay of enforcement shall be effective until the time for filing a complaint or notice of appeal shall have expired or, if timely filed, until the decision of the permanent judicial commission having jurisdiction over the case, except as hereafter provided.

Objection to Stay
of Enforcement

d.　The respondent may, within thirty days of the filing of a stay of enforcement, file with the permanent judicial commission having jurisdiction over the case an objection to the stay of enforcement, whereupon no fewer than three members of such permanent judicial commission shall conduct a hearing on all of the issues relating to the stay of enforcement. The parties may be present or represented at such hearing. At such hearing, the stay of enforcement may be modified, terminated, or continued until the decision on the merits of the case by the permanent judicial commission.

D-6.0200

D-6.0201
Parties

2.　Filing a Complaint in a Remedial Case

In a remedial case the party or parties filing the complaint shall be known as the complainant or complainants and the party or parties against whom the complaint is made shall be known as the respondent or respondents.

D-6.0202
Who May File
Complaint

A complaint of an irregularity or a complaint of a delinquency may be filed by one or more persons or governing bodies subject to and submitting to the jurisdiction of a governing body.

Against
Presbytery,
Synod, or
Governing Body
at Same Level

a.　In the instance of a complaint against a presbytery, a synod, or by a governing body against another governing body at the same level, a complaint of an irregularity shall be filed within ninety days after the alleged irregularity has occurred; and a complaint of a delinquency shall be filed within ninety days after failure or refusal of respondent to cure the alleged delinquency at its next meeting, provided that a written request to do so has been made prior to said meeting. Those eligible to file such a complaint are

(1)　a minister or an elder enrolled as a member of a presbytery concerning an irregularity or a delinquency during that period of enrollment, against the presbytery, with the synod;

(2)　a commissioner to a synod, concerning an irregularity or a delinquency during that commissioner's period of enrollment, against the synod, with the General Assembly;

(3)　a session against the presbytery, with the synod;

(4)　a presbytery against the synod, with the General Assembly;

(5)　any governing body against any other governing body of the same level, with the governing body immediately higher than the governing body complained against and to which the latter governing body is subject.

(6)　a person who is an employee of a presbytery, a synod, or an entity of a presbytery or synod, claiming to have sustained injury or damage to person or property

by the governing body or entity, against the presbytery, with the synod, or against the synod, with the
General Assembly.

Against Session
or General
Assembly
Council or Entity

b.   In the instance of a complaint against a session, the General Assembly Council, or an entity of the General Assembly,
a complaint of an irregularity shall be filed within ninety days
after the alleged irregularity has occurred; and a complaint of
a delinquency shall be filed within ninety days after failure or
refusal of respondent to cure the alleged delinquency at its
next meeting, provided that a written request to do so has been
made prior to said meeting. Those eligible to file such a complaint are

(1) a member of a particular church against the session
of that church, with the presbytery;

(2) a session, a presbytery, or a synod against the General
Assembly Council or an entity of the General Assembly,
with the General Assembly;

(3) a person who is an employee of the General Assembly Council or an entity of the General Assembly, claiming to have sustained injury or damage to person or property by the General Assembly Council or an entity of the
General Assembly, with the General Assembly.

(4) a person who is an employee of a particular
church claiming to have sustained injury or damage
to person or property by the session or an entity of the
session against the session of the church, with the
presbytery.

D-6.0300

D-6.0301
Statements in
Complaint

3.   Pretrial Procedures

A complaint shall state the following:

a.   The name of the complainant and the name of the respondent.

b.   The particular irregularity including the date, place, and
circumstances thereof; or the particular delinquency including
the dates of the written request to cure the delinquency and of
the next meeting at which the respondent failed to do so.

c.   The reasons for complaint of the irregularity or delinquency.

d.   The interest or relationship of the complainant, showing
why that party has a right to file the complaint.

e.   The relief requested.

f.   That a copy of the complaint has been delivered to the respondent by certified delivery or personal service. The complainant shall file with the stated clerk of the higher governing

body a receipt signed by the addressee or an affidavit of personal service.

**D-6.0302
Committee of
Counsel**

When a governing body, the General Assembly Council, or an entity of the General Assembly becomes either a complainant or a respondent, it shall designate no more than three persons to be a committee of counsel. This committee shall represent that complainant or respondent in the case until final decision is reached in the highest governing body to which the case is appealed.

Provide by Rule

a. A governing body, the General Assembly Council, or an entity of the General Assembly may provide by rule for the appointment of a committee of counsel.

Shall Not Serve

b. The clerk of session, the stated clerk, or executive of presbytery or synod shall not serve on a committee of counsel of the governing body served.

**D-6.0303
Answer to
Complaint**

The committee of counsel of the respondent shall file with the stated clerk of the higher governing body a concise answer within thirty days after receipt of the complaint, and shall furnish a copy of the answer to the complainant. The answer shall admit those facts alleged in the complaint that are true, deny those allegations that are not true or are mistakenly stated, and present other facts that may explain the situation identified as an irregularity or delinquency. The answer may also raise any issues mentioned in D-6.0307.

**D-6.0304
Duty of
Respondent**

a. Within thirty days after the receipt of a complaint, the clerk of session or stated clerk of the respondent governing body or the respondent entity or council shall file with the stated clerk of the higher governing body of jurisdiction all the minutes and papers pertaining to the case and furnish a copy thereof to the complainant.

Additional Papers

b. Within ten days thereafter, the complainant may request in writing that the respondent file additional minutes or papers pertaining to the case which, if available, shall be filed without delay with the stated clerk of the higher governing body.

**D-6.0305
Procedure Prior to
Trial**

When the minutes and papers have been filed with the stated clerk of the higher governing body, the stated clerk shall transmit them at once to the permanent judicial commission of the governing body that shall, within ten days of their receipt, give notice to the parties that the case has been received, together with notice of an estimated date for trial.

**D-6.0306
Trial Briefs**

The permanent judicial commission may require either party in an original proceeding to file a trial brief outlining the evidence to be produced and the theory upon which the evidence is considered to be relevant.

D-6.0307
Examination of
Papers

Upon receiving the papers in a case, the moderator and the clerk of the permanent judicial commission of the body that will try the case shall promptly examine the papers to determine whether

a.   the governing body has jurisdiction;

b.   the complainant has standing to file the case;

c.   the complaint was timely filed; and

d.   the complaint states a claim upon which relief can be granted.

D-6.0308
Preliminary
Questions
Determined

The moderator and clerk shall report their findings to the parties and to the permanent judicial commission.

a.   If a challenge is made to the findings of the moderator and clerk, either by a party to the case or by a member of the permanent judicial commission, opportunity shall be provided to present evidence and argument on the finding in question.

b.   If a hearing is necessary to decide the finding in question, that hearing shall be scheduled at least thirty days prior to the trial on the complaint, unless the circumstances, including monetary considerations, render advisable the disposition of the preliminary questions immediately before the trial on the complaint.

c.   If the permanent judicial commission determines that any point listed in D-6.0307 has been answered in the negative, the permanent judicial commission shall dismiss the case.

D-6.0309
Pretrial
Conference

At any time after a case is received by a permanent judicial commission, the commission may provide by rule for the parties or their counsel, if any, to explore settlement possibilities; or, in a pretrial conference, to seek agreement on a statement of facts and disputed issues, to exchange documents and other evidence, and to take other action which might reasonably and impartially narrow the dispute and expedite its resolution.

D-7.0000 CHAPTER VII. TRIAL IN A REMEDIAL CASE

D-7.0100 1. **Conduct of Trial**

D-7.0101
Trial—Remedial

The trial of a remedial case shall be conducted by a permanent judicial commission.

D-7.0102
Conducted
Formally

The trial shall be conducted formally with full decorum in a neutral place suitable to the occasion.

D-7.0200 2. **Citations and Testimony**

D-7.0201
Citation of Parties
and Witnesses

Citations to appear at trial for parties or such witnesses as either party may request shall be signed by the moderator or clerk of the permanent judicial commission, who shall cause them to be served.

Members Cited

a. Only members of the Presbyterian Church (U.S.A.) may be cited to appear.

Others Requested

b. Other persons can only be requested to attend.

Witnesses from
Another
Governing Body

c. When it is necessary in the trial to summon witnesses who are under the jurisdiction of another governing body of the church, the clerk or stated clerk of the other governing body shall, on the application of the permanent judicial commission trying the case, issue a citation to the witnesses to appear at the place of trial and give evidence as may be required.

Expenses

d. Any witness shall be entitled to receive from the party calling the witness reimbursement for expenses incurred in attendance at the trial.

D-7.0202
Service of
Citation

A citation shall be delivered by personal service or by certified delivery. The moderator or clerk of the permanent judicial commission trying the case shall certify the fact and date of service or delivery.

D-7.0203
Second Citation

If a party or a witness who is a member of the Presbyterian Church (U.S.A.) fails to obey a citation, a second citation shall be issued accompanied by a notice that if the party or witness does not appear at the time appointed, unless excused for good cause, the party or witness shall be considered guilty of disobedience and contempt, and for such offense may be subject to disciplinary action.

D-7.0204
Refusal of
Witness to Testify

A member of the Presbyterian Church (U.S.A.) who, having been summoned as a witness and having appeared, refuses without good cause to testify, and, after warning, continues to refuse may be subject to disciplinary action.

D-7.0205
Deposition

Testimony by deposition may be taken and received in accordance with the provisions of D-14.0304.

D-7.0300

3.   Procedures in Trial

D-7.0301
Counsel

Each of the parties in a remedial case shall be entitled to appear and may be represented by counsel, provided, however, that no person shall act as counsel who is not a member of the Presbyterian Church (U.S.A.). No member of a permanent judicial commission shall appear as counsel before that commission while a member.

D-7.0302
Circulation of
Materials

No party to a remedial case or any other person shall circulate or cause to be circulated among the members of the permanent judicial commission any written, printed, or visual materials of any kind upon any matter pertaining to the case before the final disposition thereof. Notwithstanding this prohibition, the permanent judicial commission may request, or grant leave to file, additional materials.

D-7.0303
Control Conduct
of Trial

The permanent judicial commission shall have full authority and power to control the conduct of the trial and of all parties, witnesses, counsel, and the public, including removal of them, to the end that proper dignity and decorum shall be maintained.

Questions as to
Procedure

a.   Questions as to procedure or the admissibility of evidence arising in the course of a trial shall be decided by the moderator after the parties have had an opportunity to be heard. A party or a member of the permanent judicial commission may appeal from the decision of the moderator to the commission, which shall decide the question by majority vote.

Absences

b.   The absence of any member of the permanent judicial commission after a trial has commenced shall be recorded. That person shall not thereafter participate in that case.

D-7.0304
Loss of Quorum

Loss of a quorum shall result in a mistrial and the case shall be tried again from the beginning.

D-7.0400

4.   Trial

D-7.0401
Procedure in a
Remedial Case

The trial of a remedial case shall proceed as follows:

Announcement
by the Moderator

a.   The moderator shall read aloud sections D-1.0101 and D-1.0102, shall announce that the governing body is about to proceed to trial, and shall enjoin the members to recollect and regard their high character as judges of a governing body of the Church of Jesus Christ and the solemn duties they are about to undertake.

Eligibility of
Commission
Members

b.   The parties or their counsel may object and be heard on the organization and jurisdiction of the permanent judicial commission.

Disqualification

(1) A member of a permanent judicial commission is disqualified if the member is personally interested in the case, is related by blood or marriage to any party, has been

active for or against any party, or is ineligible under the provisions of D-5.0205.

Challenges
(2) Any member of a permanent judicial commission may be challenged by any party, and the validity of the challenge shall be determined by the remaining members of the permanent judicial commission.

Procedural Objections
c. The permanent judicial commission shall determine all preliminary objections, and any other objections affecting the order or regularity of the proceedings.

Amend Complaint
d. The complainant shall be permitted to amend the complaint at the time of the trial, provided that the amendment does not change the substance of the complaint or prejudice the respondent.

Opening Statements
e. The parties shall be given an opportunity to make opening statements.

Rules of Evidence
f. The rules of evidence in D-14.0000 shall be followed.

Evidence
g. Evidence as is deemed necessary or proper, if any, shall be presented on behalf of the complainant and the respondent.

Final Statements
h. The parties shall be given an opportunity to make final statements, the complainant having the right of opening and closing the argument.

D-7.0402 Decision
The permanent judicial commission shall then meet privately. All persons not members of the commission shall be excluded.

Deliberation
a. No complaint in a remedial case shall be sustained unless it has been proved by a preponderance of the evidence. Preponderance means such evidence as, when weighed with that opposed to it, has more convincing force and the greater probability of truth. After careful deliberation the commission shall vote on each irregularity or delinquency assigned in the complaint and record the vote in its minutes.

Decision
b. The permanent judicial commission shall then decide the case. If the complaint is sustained either in whole or in part, the commission shall either order such action as is appropriate or direct the lower governing body to conduct further proceedings in the matter.

Written Decision
c. A written decision shall be prepared while in session, and shall become the final decision when a copy of the written decision is signed by the moderator and clerk of the permanent judicial commission. A copy of the written decision shall immediately be delivered to the parties to the case by personal service or by certified delivery.

Filed Promptly
d. Within thirty days of the conclusion of the trial, the decision shall be filed with the stated clerk of the governing body that appointed the permanent judicial commission.

Further Publicity

e. The moderator or clerk of the permanent judicial commission shall disseminate the decision as the permanent judicial commission may direct.

D-7.0500

D-7.0501
Appeal Time

5. Provisions for Appeal

For each party, the time for filing an appeal shall run from the date the decision is delivered to, or refused by, that party.

D-7.0502
Appeals

An appeal may be initiated only by one or more of the original parties. Rules of appeal are found in D-8.0000.

D-7.0600

D-7.0601
Record of
Proceedings

6. Record of Proceedings

The clerk of the permanent judicial commission shall do the following:

Verbatim
Recording

a. Arrange in advance for the accurate verbatim recording of all testimony and oral proceedings.

Exhibits

b. Identify and maintain all exhibits offered in evidence (noting whether or not they were accepted as evidence) and keep a list of all exhibits;

Minutes

c. Record minutes of the proceedings, which shall include any actions or orders of the permanent judicial commission relating to the case with the vote thereon.

Record

d. Prepare the record of the case, which shall consist of

(1) the complaint and the answer thereto;

(2) all minutes and papers filed in the case;

(3) a certified transcript, if requested;

(4) all properly marked exhibits, records, documents, and other papers;

(5) the written decision; and

(6) any actions or orders of the permanent judicial commission relating to the case with the vote thereon.

Preservation

e. Within fourteen days after the decision becomes final, certify and transmit the record of the case to the stated clerk of the electing governing body, who shall preserve it for at least two years.

Transcript

f. Upon the request, and at the expense of any requesting party, cause to be prepared, as promptly as circumstances permit, a true and complete transcript of all the testimony and oral proceedings during the course of the trial. A copy of this transcript, when certified by the person making the same to be true and complete, shall be delivered to each party requesting the same upon satisfactory arrangement for payment, and one additional copy shall be made for inclusion in the record to be sent forward upon any appeal pursuant to D-8.0000.

D-7.0602
Additions to the
Record

No person may supplement or add to the record in a case except for good cause as determined by the moderator and clerk of the permanent judicial commission responsible for conducting the trial. No request to supplement the record shall be considered until received in writing by the stated clerk of the lower governing body, who shall transmit it to the moderator and clerk of the permanent judicial commission. A copy of the request shall be delivered to all parties and every party shall have ten days to respond in writing.

D-7.0700

D-7.0701
Reporting the
Decision

7. Duty of Stated Clerk

If the governing body is meeting when the decision is received from the clerk of the permanent judicial commission, the stated clerk shall report the decision immediately and enter the full decision upon the minutes of the governing body. If the governing body is not meeting, the stated clerk shall report the decision to the governing body at its first stated or adjourned meeting thereafter, or at a meeting called for that purpose, and enter the full decision upon the minutes of the governing body.

D-8.0000   CHAPTER VIII. APPEAL IN A REMEDIAL CASE

D-8.0100   **1.   Initiation of an Appeal**

D-8.0101   An appeal of a remedial case is the transfer to the next higher
Definition   governing body of a case in which a decision has been rendered in
                    a lower governing body, for the purpose of obtaining a review of
                    the proceedings and decision to correct, modify, set aside, or re-
                    verse the decision.

D-8.0102   An appeal may be initiated only by one or more of the origi-
Initiation of   nal parties in the case, and is accomplished by the filing of a writ-
Appeal   ten notice of appeal.

D-8.0103   The notice of appeal shall not suspend any further action im-
Effect of Appeal   plementing the decision being appealed unless a stay of enforce-
                    ment has been obtained in accordance with the provisions of
                    D-6.0103.

D-8.0104   On application, the permanent judicial commission of the
Withdrawal of   higher governing body may grant a petition for withdrawal of an
Appeal   appeal. The permanent judicial commission shall deny a petition if
                    its approval would defeat the ends of justice.

D-8.0105   The grounds for appeal are
Grounds for
Appeal   a.   irregularity in the proceedings;

                    b.   refusing a party reasonable opportunity to be heard or to
                    obtain or present evidence;

                    c.   receiving improper, or declining to receive proper, evi-
                    dence or testimony;

                    d.   hastening to a decision before the evidence or testimony is
                    fully received;

                    e.   manifestation of prejudice in the conduct of the case;

                    f.   injustice in the process or decision; and

                    g.   error in constitutional interpretation.

D-8.0200   **2.   Filings in Appeal Process**

D-8.0201   A written notice of appeal shall be filed within thirty days af-
Time for Filing   ter a copy of the judgment has been delivered by certified delivery
Written Notice of   or personal service to the party appealing.
Appeal
                        a.   The written notice of appeal shall be filed with the stated
                        clerk of the lower governing body which elected the permanent
                        judicial commission from whose judgment the appeal is taken.

                        b.   The party appealing shall provide a copy of the notice of
                        appeal to each of the other parties and to the stated clerk of the
                        governing body which will hear the appeal.

D-8.0202
Content of
Written Notice of
Appeal

The written notice of appeal shall state and include

a.   the name of the party or parties filing the appeal, called the appellant or appellants, and their counsel if any;

b.   the name of the other party or parties, called the appellee or appellees, and their counsel if any;

c.   the governing body from whose judgment the appeal is taken;

d.   the judgment or decision, and date and place thereof, from which the appeal is taken;

e.   a statement of the grounds for the appeal (D-8.0105); and

f.   a certification that a copy of the notice of appeal was provided by certified delivery or by personal service to each of the other parties and to the stated clerk of the governing body that will hear the appeal.

D-8.0203
Record on Appeal

The record on appeal shall be formed as follows:

List of Record

a.   Within thirty days after the receipt of a written notice of appeal, the stated clerk of the lower governing body shall list in writing to the parties all of the papers and other materials that constitute the record of the case. (D-7.0601d)

Additional
Records

b.   Within ten days thereafter, any party may file with the stated clerk of the lower governing body a written statement challenging the accuracy or completeness of the record of the case as listed by the stated clerk. The written challenge shall state specifically the item or items listed in D-7.0601d which are claimed to be omitted from the record of the case.

Filing of Record
on Appeal

c.   Within forty-five days after the receipt of a notice of appeal, the stated clerk of the lower governing body shall certify and file the record of the case, which may include authenticated copies of parts of the record, and shall include any written challenges disputing the completeness or accuracy of the record, with the stated clerk of the higher governing body.

Correction of the
Record

d.   If anything material to either party is omitted from the record by error or accident, or is misstated therein, the omission or misstatement may be corrected. The parties may stipulate to the correction, or the session or permanent judicial commission of the lower governing body may certify and transmit a supplemental record, or the permanent judicial commission of the higher governing body may direct that the omission or misstatement be corrected. All other questions as to the form and content of the record shall be presented to the permanent judicial commission of the higher governing body.

Notice of Date of
Reception

e.   The stated clerk of the higher governing body shall notify the parties of the date the record on appeal was received.

Copy Furnished
at Cost

f.   Upon written request, the stated clerk of the higher governing body shall furnish any party to the appeal, at cost to that party, a copy of the record on appeal.

Extension

g.   For good cause shown, the stated clerk of the higher governing body may extend the time limits in D-8.0203 for a reasonable period.

D-8.0204
Filing of
Appellant's Brief

Within thirty days after the date of the filing of the record on appeal, the appellant shall file with the stated clerk of the higher governing body a written brief containing specifications of the errors alleged and arguments, reasons, and citations of authorities in support of the appellant's contentions as to the alleged errors specified.

Copy to Other
Party

a.   The brief shall be accompanied by a certification that a copy has been furnished to the other party or parties.

Extension

b.   For good cause shown, the stated clerk of the higher governing body may extend this time limit for a reasonable period.

Failure to File
Brief

c.   Failure of appellant to file a brief within the time allowed, without good cause, shall be deemed by the permanent judicial commission an abandonment of the appeal.

D-8.0205
Filing of
Appellee's Brief

Within thirty days after the filing of appellant's brief, the appellee shall file with the stated clerk of the higher governing body a written brief responding thereto.

Copy to Other
Party

a.   The brief shall be accompanied by a certification that a copy has been furnished to the other party or parties.

Extension

b.   For good cause shown, the stated clerk of the higher governing body may extend this time limit for a reasonable period.

Failure to File
Brief

c.   Failure of appellee to file a brief within the time allowed, without good cause, shall constitute waiver of the rights to file a brief, to appear, and to be heard.

D-8.0206
Transmittal to
Permanent
Judicial
Commission

Upon receipt of the record and the briefs, or upon the expiration of the time for filing them, the stated clerk of the higher governing body shall transmit the record and briefs to the clerk of the permanent judicial commission.

D-8.0300

3.   **Prehearing Proceedings**

D-8.0301
Examination of
Papers

Upon receiving the papers in an appeal, the moderator and the clerk of the permanent judicial commission of the governing body that will hear the case shall promptly examine the papers to determine whether

a.   the governing body has jurisdiction;

b.   the appellant has standing to file the appeal;

c.   the appeal papers were properly and timely filed; and

d.   the appeal states one or more of the grounds for appeal set forth in D-8.0105.

D-8.0302 Preliminary Questions Determined

The moderator and clerk shall report their findings to the parties and to the permanent judicial commission.

a.   If a challenge is made to the findings of the moderator and clerk, either by a party to the case or by a member of the permanent judicial commission, opportunity shall be provided to present evidence and argument on the finding in question.

b.   If a hearing is necessary to decide the item in question, that hearing shall be scheduled at least thirty days prior to the hearing on the appeal unless the circumstances, including monetary considerations, render advisable the disposition of the preliminary questions immediately before the hearing on the appeal.

c.   If the permanent judicial commission determines that any point listed in D-8.0301 has been answered in the negative, the permanent judicial commission shall dismiss the appeal.

D-8.0400

4.   Hearing of Appeal

D-8.0401 Notice of Hearing

The moderator or clerk of the permanent judicial commission shall notify the parties of the date when they may appear in person or by counsel before the permanent judicial commission to present the appeal.

D-8.0402 Failure to Appear

Failure of a party to appear in person or by counsel shall constitute a waiver of participation in the hearing on appeal.

D-8.0403 Hearing:

At the hearing the permanent judicial commission shall

New Evidence

a.   determine whether to receive newly discovered evidence, under the provisions of D-14.0502, providing for the verbatim recording of such new evidence; and

Hearing

b.   give opportunity to be heard on the grounds of the appeal to those parties who have not waived that right, the appellant having the right of opening and closing the argument.

D-8.0404 Decision of Permanent Judicial Commission

After the hearing and after deliberation, the permanent judicial commission shall vote separately on each specification of error alleged. The vote shall be on the question, "Shall the specification of error be sustained?" The minutes shall record the numerical vote on each specification of error.

If No Errors Are Found

a.   If not one of the specifications of error is sustained, and no other error is found, the decision of the lower governing body shall be affirmed.

If Errors Are Found

b.   If one or more errors are found, the permanent judicial commission shall determine whether the decision of the lower governing body shall be affirmed, modified, set aside, reversed, or the case remanded for a new trial.

Written Decision

c.   A written decision shall be prepared while in session, and shall become the final decision when a copy of the written decision is signed by the moderator and clerk of the permanent judicial commission. A copy of the decision shall immediately be delivered to the parties to the case by personal service or by certified delivery.

Determination of Each Error

d.   The decision shall include the determination of errors specified, and state the remedy as provided in D-8.0101. The permanent judicial commission may prepare its decision in a manner that will dispose of all substantive questions without redundancy. It may include an explanation of its determination.

Filed Promptly

e.   Within thirty days of the conclusion of the hearing, the decision shall be filed with the stated clerk of the governing body that appointed the permanent judicial commission.

Further Publicity

f.   The moderator or clerk of the permanent judicial commission shall disseminate the decision as the permanent judicial commission may direct.

D-9.0000

CHAPTER IX. REQUEST FOR VINDICATION

D-9.0101
Request for
Vindication

A member of the Presbyterian Church (U.S.A.) who feels injured by rumor or gossip may request an inquiry for vindication by submitting to the clerk of session or stated clerk of the presbytery a clear narrative and statement of alleged facts.

Review by
Governing Body

a.   If a governing body, through its appropriate committee, finds it proper to grant the request, it shall proceed with an investigating committee as provided in D-10.0201.

Investigating
Committee

b.   The investigating committee shall conduct an inquiry to ascertain the facts and circumstances and report in writing to the governing body.

D-9.0102
Concludes Matter
Unless Charges
Filed

The report shall conclude the matter, unless the investigating committee reports that charges are being filed against the person requesting vindication. If charges are to be filed, the matter shall proceed with appropriate judicial process beginning with D-10.0402.

CHAPTER X. DISCIPLINARY CASES

D-10.0000

D-10.0100   **1. Procedure Preliminary to a Disciplinary Case**

D-10.0101
Initiation of
Preliminary
Procedures

Procedure preliminary to a disciplinary case is initiated by submitting to the clerk of session or the stated clerk of the presbytery having jurisdiction over the member (D-3.0101) a written statement of an alleged offense, together with any supporting information. The statement shall give a clear narrative and allege facts that, if proven true, would likely result in disciplinary action. Such allegations shall be referred to an investigating committee. (D-10.0201)

D-10.0102
Statement of
Offense

The written statement may be submitted by

Accusation

a.   a person under jurisdiction of a governing body of the Presbyterian Church (U.S.A.) making an accusation against another;

Governing Body

b.   a member of a governing body receiving information from any source that an offense may have occurred which should be investigated for the purpose of discipline; or

Self-Accusation

c.   a person under jurisdiction of a governing body of the Presbyterian Church (U.S.A.) coming forward in self-accusation.

D-10.0103
Referral to
Investigating
Committee

Upon receipt of a written statement of an alleged offense, the clerk of session or the stated clerk of presbytery, without undertaking further inquiry, shall then report to the governing body only that an offense has been alleged without naming the accused or the nature of the alleged offense, and refer the statement immediately to an investigating committee.

D-10.0104
Accusation from
Other Governing
Body

When a member is accused of an offense by a written statement presented to a governing body other than the one having jurisdiction over the member, it shall be the duty of the clerk of that session or the stated clerk of that presbytery to submit the written statement to the clerk of session or the stated clerk of the presbytery having jurisdiction over the member. The involved governing bodies shall proceed cooperatively with judicial process.

D-10.0105
Transfer
Prohibited

A session shall not grant a certificate of transfer to a member, nor shall a presbytery grant a certificate of transfer to a minister, while an inquiry or charges are pending. The reasons for not granting transfer may be communicated by the clerk of session or the stated clerk of the presbytery to the appropriate persons.

D-10.0200   **2. Investigation**

D-10.0201
Investigating
Committee

An inquiry shall be made by an investigating committee designated by the governing body having jurisdiction over the member
to determine whether charges should be filed.

Membership

a.   An investigating committee shall have no more than five
but no less than three members, and may include members
from another governing body, if appropriate, in accordance
with D-10.0104.

Appointment by
Rule

b.   A presbytery may provide by rule for appointment of an
investigating committee.

Expenses

c.   The expenses of an investigating committee shall normally be paid by the governing body having designated it. If,
however, the written statement results from information presented to a governing body other than the one having jurisdiction over a member, the governing body within whose bounds
the alleged offense occurred shall pay for the expenses of investigating within its bounds.

D-10.0202
Investigating
Committee
Responsibilities

The investigating committee shall

a.   provide the accused with a copy of the statement of alleged offense described in D-10.0101;

b.   make a thorough inquiry into the facts and circumstances
of the alleged offense;

c.   examine all relevant papers, documents, and records
available to it;

d.   ascertain all available witnesses and inquire of them;

e.   determine, in accordance with G-9.0102 and D-2.0203b,
whether there are probable grounds or cause to believe that an
offense was committed by the accused;

f.   decide whether the charge(s) filed—on the basis of the papers, documents, records, testimony, or other evidence—can
reasonably be proved, having due regard for the character,
availability, and credibility of the witnesses and evidence
available;

g.   initiate, if it deems appropriate, alternative forms of resolution, ordinarily after the investigation has been completed,
probable cause has been determined, but before the charges
have been filed. The purpose of alternative forms of resolution will be to determine if agreement can be reached between
all parties involved concerning any charges which may be
filed.

(1) Any mediation shall be completed within 120 days
unless a continuance is allowed by the session or permanent judicial commission.

(2) The investigating committee shall report any settlement agreement to the session or permanent judicial commission for its approval.

(3) All parties shall be provided an advocate throughout settlement negotiations.

(4) If a settlement satisfactory to all parties involved in the mediation is not reached, the investigating committee shall proceed to the filing of charges.

h.   report to the governing body having jurisdiction over the accused only whether or not it will file charges; and

Designate
Prosecuting
Committee

i.   if charges are to be filed, prepare and file them in accordance with the provisions of D-10.0401-.0404, and designate one or more persons (to be known as the prosecuting committee) from among its membership to prosecute the case.

D-10.0203
Rights of the
Person Accused

At the beginning of each and every conference with the person against whom an allegation has been made, the investigating committee shall inform the person of the right to remain silent, to be represented by counsel, and, if charges are later filed, to have counsel appointed if unable to secure counsel. (D-11.0301-.0302)

D-10.0300

3.   Communicate Determination

D-10.0301
Communicate
Determination

If the investigating committee initiates an alternative form of resolution, it shall notify the governing body through its clerk of session or stated clerk.

D-10.0302
If Charges Are to
Be Filed

If the investigating committee has decided to file charges, it shall promptly inform the accused in writing of the charges it will make, including a summary of the facts it expects to prove at trial to support those charges. It shall ask the accused if that person wishes to plead guilty to the charges to avoid full trial and indicate the censure it will recommend to the session or permanent judicial commission.

D-10.0303
Petition for
Review

If no charges are filed, the investigating committee shall file a written report of that fact alone with the clerk of session or stated clerk of the presbytery, and notify the person who submitted the written statement.

a.   Within 30 days of receipt of the report, that person may petition the session or the permanent judicial commission to review the decision of the investigating committee not to file charges. The petition shall allege those instances in which the investigating committee has not fulfilled the duties specified in D-10.0202.

b.   The investigating committee shall submit a written response to the facts alleged in the petition.

c.   The session or permanent judicial commission shall consider the petition and the response, giving attention to the duties specified in D-10.0202 and to the question of whether the principles of church discipline will be preserved by the decision of the investigating committee not to file charges. The decision of the session or permanent judicial commission upon the petition and response shall be rendered within ninety days.

d.   If it sustains the petition, a new investigating committee shall be appointed by the session or presbytery.

e.   If once again no charges are filed, the matter is concluded.

f.   If charges are filed, consideration shall be given to the possibility of reference. (D-4.0000)

D-10.0304
Disposition of
Records

If no charges are filed, the disposition of the investigating committee's records shall be in accordance with session or presbytery policy.

D-10.0400

4.   Charges

D-10.0401
Time Limit

Except in the instance where the offense alleged is sexual abuse of another person, no charges shall be filed later than three years from the time of the commission of the alleged offense, nor later than one year from the date the investigating committee was formed, whichever occurs first.

a.   For instances of sexual abuse of another person, the only time limit for filing charges shall be one year from the date the investigating committee was formed, regardless of the date on which an offense is alleged to have occurred.

b.   Sexual abuse of another person is any offense involving sexual conduct in relation to

(1) any person under the age of eighteen years or anyone over the age of eighteen years without the mental capacity to consent; or

(2) any person when the conduct includes force, threat, coercion, intimidation, or misuse of office or position.

c.   If an alternative form of resolution is initiated, the time limits herein provided shall be extended for the duration of the process.

D-10.0402
Prosecution of
Case

If charges are filed, the prosecuting committee shall prosecute the case and represent the church during any appeals. (D-10.0202h)

Parties

a.   All disciplinary cases shall be filed and prosecuted by a governing body through an investigating committee and a prosecuting committee in the name of the Presbyterian Church (U.S.A.). The prosecuting committee is the representative of the church and, as such, has all of the rights of the appropriate governing body in the case.

Only Two Parties	b. The only parties in a disciplinary case are the prosecuting governing body and the accused.
D-10.0403 Form of Charge	Each charge shall allege only one offense. (D-2.0203b)
Several Together	a. Several charges against the same person may be filed with the governing body at the same time.
Details of the Charge	b. Each charge shall be numbered and set forth the conduct that constituted the offense. Each charge shall state (as far as possible) the time, place, and circumstances of the commission of the alleged conduct. Each charge shall also be accompanied by a list of the names and addresses of the witnesses for the prosecution and a description of the records and documents to be cited for its support.
Tried Together	c. Several charges against the same person may, in the discretion of the session or permanent judicial commission, be tried together.
D-10.0404 Filing of Charge	Every charge shall be prepared in writing and filed with the clerk of session or stated clerk of the presbytery.
Session	a. Upon receipt of a charge, the clerk of a session shall present the charge to the session at its next meeting. The session shall determine whether it will try the case or refer it to the presbytery. (D-4.0000)
Presbytery	b. Upon receipt of a charge, the stated clerk of the presbytery shall immediately forward it to the moderator or clerk of the permanent judicial commission of that presbytery.
D-10.0405 Pretrial Conference	The session or permanent judicial commission, which is to try the case, shall hold a pretrial conference not later than thirty days after receipt of the charge(s).
Time and Place	a. The moderator and clerk of the session or of the permanent judicial commission shall notify the accused, the counsel for the accused, if any, and the prosecuting committee of the time and place of the pretrial conference, and shall furnish the accused with a copy of the charge(s).
Those Present	b. At the time set for the pretrial conference, the moderator and clerk of session or of the permanent judicial commission, the prosecuting committee, the accused, counsel for the accused, if any, and other appropriate persons at the discretion of the moderator and clerk shall ordinarily be present. The moderator shall

(1) read the charges to the accused;

(2) inform the accused of the right to counsel (D-11.0301);

(3) furnish the accused with the names and addresses of all the witnesses then known, and a description of the

records and documents that may be offered to support each charge;

(4) determine with the accused and the prosecuting committee those charges that are not in dispute and discuss alternatives to a full trial;

(5) schedule a trial to be held no sooner than thirty days following the pretrial conference, or, if all parties agree on those facts contained in the charges that are true and on a recommended degree of censure, schedule a censure hearing;

(6) order all parties to appear.

Nothing More   c.   Nothing more shall be done at that meeting.

D-10.0406
Witnesses
Disclosed

The accused shall provide a list of anticipated witnesses, including addresses, to the clerk of session or permanent judicial commission and the prosecuting committee at least twenty days prior to the trial date. The prosecuting committee and the accused shall each provide the session or permanent judicial commission and the other party with an updated list of witnesses no less than ten days prior to the trial date.

D-11.0000 CHAPTER XI. TRIAL IN A DISCIPLINARY CASE

D-11.0100 **1. Conduct of Trial**

D-11.0101
Trial—Disciplinary
The trial of a disciplinary case shall be conducted by a session or by a permanent judicial commission.

D-11.0102
Conducted
Formally
The trial shall be conducted formally with full decorum in a neutral place suitable to the occasion.

D-11.0200 **2. Citations and Testimony**

D-11.0201
Citation of Parties
and Witnesses
Citations to appear at trial for parties or such witnesses as either party may request shall be signed by the moderator or clerk of the session or permanent judicial commission.

Members Cited
a. Only members of the Presbyterian Church (U.S.A.) may be cited to appear.

Others Requested
b. Other persons can only be requested to attend.

Witnesses from
Another
Governing Body
c. When it is necessary in the trial to summon witnesses who are under the jurisdiction of another governing body of the church, the clerk or stated clerk of the other governing body shall, on the application of the session or permanent judicial commission trying the case, issue a citation to the witnesses to appear at the place of trial and give evidence as may be required.

Expenses
d. Any witness shall be entitled to receive from the party calling the witness reimbursement for expenses incurred in attendance at the trial.

D-11.0202
Service of
Citation
A citation shall be delivered by personal service or by certified delivery. The moderator or clerk of the session or permanent judicial commission trying the case shall certify the fact and date of service or delivery.

Second Citation
a. If a party or a witness who is a member of the Presbyterian Church (U.S.A.) fails to obey a citation, a second citation shall be issued accompanied by a notice that if the party or witness does not appear at the time appointed, unless excused for good cause shown, the party or witness shall be considered guilty of disobedience and contempt, and for such offense may be subject to disciplinary action.

Accused Does
Not Appear
b. If an accused in a disciplinary case does not appear after a second citation, the session or permanent judicial commission, after having appointed some person or persons to represent the accused as counsel, may proceed to trial and judgment in the absence of the accused.

D-11.0203
Refusal of
Witness to Testify
A member of the Presbyterian Church (U.S.A.) who, having been summoned as a witness and having appeared, refuses without

good cause to testify, and, after warning, continues to refuse may be subject to disciplinary action.

D-11.0204
Deposition

Testimony by deposition may be taken and received in accordance with the provisions of D-14.0304.

D-11.0300

3. Procedures in Trial

D-11.0301
Counsel

Each of the parties in a disciplinary case shall be entitled to appear and may be represented by counsel, provided, however, that no person shall act as counsel who is not a member of the Presbyterian Church (U.S.A.). No member of a permanent judicial commission shall appear as counsel before that commission while a member. Counsel need not be a paid representative or attorney-at-law.

D-11.0302
Unable to Secure
Counsel

If the accused in a disciplinary case is unable to secure counsel, the session or permanent judicial commission shall appoint counsel for the accused. Reasonable expenses for defense shall be authorized and reimbursed by the governing body in which the case originated.

D-11.0303
Circulation of
Materials

No party to a disciplinary case or any other person shall circulate or cause to be circulated among the members of the session or permanent judicial commission any written, printed, or visual materials of any kind upon any matter pertaining to the case before the final disposition thereof. Notwithstanding this prohibition, the session or permanent judicial commission may request, or grant leave to file, additional materials.

D-11.0304
Control Conduct
of Trial

The session or permanent judicial commission shall have full authority and power to control the conduct of the trial and of all parties, witnesses, counsel, and the public, including removal of them, to the end that proper dignity and decorum shall be maintained.

Questions as to
Procedure

a.   Questions as to procedure or the admissibility of evidence arising in the course of a trial shall be decided by the moderator after the parties have had an opportunity to be heard. A party or a member of the session or permanent judicial commission may appeal from the decision of the moderator to the session or commission, which shall decide the question by majority vote.

Absences

b.   The absence of any member of the session or permanent judicial commission after a trial has commenced shall be recorded. That person shall not thereafter participate in that case.

D-11.0305
Loss of Quorum

Loss of a quorum shall result in a mistrial and the case shall be tried again from the beginning.

D-11.0306
Closed
Proceedings

The proceedings shall ordinarily be conducted in open session; however, at the request of any party, or on its own initiative, the session or permanent judicial commission may determine at any stage of the proceedings, by a vote of two thirds of the members present, to exclude persons other than the parties and their counsel.

D-11.0400   **4. Trial**

D-11.0401
Presumption of
Innocence

The accused in a disciplinary case is presumed to be innocent until the contrary is proved, and unless guilt is established beyond a reasonable doubt, the accused is entitled to be found not guilty.

D-11.0402
Procedure in a
Disciplinary Case

The trial of a disciplinary case shall proceed as follows:

Announcement
by the Moderator

a. The moderator shall read aloud sections D-1.0101 and D-1.0102, shall announce that the governing body is about to proceed to trial, and shall enjoin the members to recollect and regard their high character as judges of a governing body of the Church of Jesus Christ and the solemn duties they are about to undertake.

Eligibility of
Commission
Members

b. The parties or their counsel may object and be heard on the organization and jurisdiction of the session or permanent judicial commission.

Disqualification

(1) A member of a session or permanent judicial commission is disqualified if the member is personally interested in the case, is related by blood or marriage to any party, has been active for or against any party, or is ineligible under the provisions of D-5.0205.

Challenges

(2) Any member of a session or permanent judicial commission may be challenged by any party, and the validity of the challenge shall be determined by the remaining members of the session or permanent judicial commission.

Preliminary
Objections

c. The session or permanent judicial commission shall determine all preliminary objections and any other objection affecting the order or regularity of the proceedings. It may dismiss the case or permit amendments to the charges in the furtherance of justice, provided that such amendments do not change the substance of the charges or prejudice the accused.

Plea

d. If the proceedings are found to be in order, and the charges are considered sufficient, the accused shall be called upon to plead 'guilty' or 'not guilty' to each charge. The plea shall be entered on the record. If the accused declines to answer or pleads 'not guilty,' a plea of 'not guilty' shall be entered on the record and the trial shall proceed. If the accused pleads 'guilty,' the governing body shall proceed in accordance with D-11.0403.

Opening
Statements

e. The parties shall be given an opportunity to make opening statements.

Rules of Evidence

f. The rules of evidence in D-14.0000 shall be followed.

Prosecution

g. The prosecuting committee shall present its evidence in support of the charges, subject to objection and cross-examination by the accused.

Defense

h. The accused shall have the opportunity to present evidence, subject to objection and cross-examination by the prosecuting committee.

Rebuttal

i. The prosecuting committee then may introduce additional evidence, but only to rebut evidence introduced on behalf of the accused. This additional evidence is subject to objection and cross-examination by the accused.

Final Statements

j. The parties shall be given an opportunity to make final statements. The prosecuting committee shall have the right of opening and closing the argument.

D-11.0403
Decision

The session or permanent judicial commission shall then meet privately. All persons not members of the session or permanent judicial commission shall be excluded.

Beyond a
Reasonable
Doubt

a. After careful deliberation, the session or permanent judicial commission shall vote on each charge separately and record the vote in its minutes. In order to find the accused guilty of a charge, the session or permanent judicial commission must find that the pertinent facts within that charge have been proven beyond a reasonable doubt. Proof beyond a reasonable doubt occurs when the comparison and consideration of all the evidence compels an abiding conviction that the material facts necessary to prove the charge are true.

Judgment of Guilt
by a Two-thirds
Vote

b. No judgment of guilt may be found on a charge unless at least two thirds of the members of the session or permanent judicial commission eligible to vote agree on the judgment.

Written Decision

c. A written decision stating the judgment on each charge and the determination of the degree of censure, if any, shall be prepared while in session. It shall become the final decision when signed by the moderator and clerk of the session or of the permanent judicial commission.

Announcement in
Open Meeting

d. When a session or permanent judicial commission has arrived at a decision, the moderator shall, in open meeting, announce the verdict for each charge separately.

Degree of
Censure

e. If the accused is found guilty or after the guilty plea, the session or permanent judicial commission may hear evidence as to the extent of the injury suffered, mitigation, rehabilitation, and redemption. This evidence may be offered by either party or the original accuser or that person's representative. The session or permanent judicial commission shall then meet privately to determine the degree of censure to be imposed. (D-12.0000) Following such determination and in an open meeting, the moderator of the session or permanent judicial commission shall then pronounce the censure.

Filed Promptly

f. The decision shall be filed promptly with the clerk or stated clerk of the governing body.

Notification of
Parties

g.   The clerk of session or clerk of the permanent judicial commission shall deliver a copy of the decision to each party named in the decision either by personal service or by certified delivery.

Further Publicity

h.   The moderator or clerk of session or of the permanent judicial commission shall disseminate the decision as the session or permanent judicial commission may direct.

D-11.0500

D-11.0501
Appeal Time

D-11.0502
Appeals

5.   Provisions for Appeal

The time for filing an appeal shall run from the date the decision is delivered to, or refused by, the person found guilty.

Only a person found guilty may initiate the first level of appeal. Either party may initiate an appeal of the appellate decision. Rules of appeal are found in D-13.0000.

D-11.0600

D-11.0601
Record of
Proceedings

Verbatim
Recording

Exhibits

Minutes

Record

6.   Record of Proceedings

The clerk of session or the clerk of the permanent judicial commission shall do the following:

a.   Arrange in advance for the accurate verbatim recording of all testimony and oral proceedings.

b.   Identify and maintain all exhibits offered in evidence (noting whether or not they were accepted as evidence) and keep a list of all exhibits.

c.   Record minutes of the proceedings, which shall include any actions or orders of the session or permanent judicial commission relating to the case with the vote thereon.

d.   Prepare the record of the case, which shall consist of

(1) the charges;

(2) a record of the plea entered by the accused on each charge;

(3) a certified transcript, if requested;

(4) all properly marked exhibits, records, documents, and other papers;

(5) the written decision, including the verdict for each charge and the degree of censure, if any, to be imposed by the governing body; and

(6) any actions or orders of the session or permanent judicial commission relating to the case, with the vote thereon.

Preservation of
the Record

e.   Preserve the original of all records in the following manner:

(1) The clerk of session shall, after the decision becomes final, retain the record of the case for at least two years.

(2) The clerk of the permanent judicial commission shall, within fourteen days after the decision becomes final, certify and transmit the record of the case to the stated clerk of the electing governing body, who shall preserve it for at least two years.

Transcript

f.   Upon the request, and at the expense of any requesting party, cause to be prepared, as promptly as circumstances permit, a true and complete transcript of all the testimony and oral proceedings during the course of the trial. A copy of this transcript, when certified by the person making the same to be true and complete, shall be delivered to each party requesting the same upon satisfactory arrangement for payment, and one additional copy shall be made for inclusion in the record to be sent forward upon any appeal pursuant to D-13.0000.

D-11.0602
Additions to the
Record

No person may supplement or add to the record in a case except for good cause as determined by the moderator and clerk of the session or of the permanent judicial commission responsible for conducting the trial. No request to supplement the record shall be considered until received in writing by the clerk of session or the stated clerk of the lower governing body who shall transmit it to the moderator of the session or moderator and clerk of the permanent judicial commission. A copy of the request shall be delivered to all parties and every party shall have ten days to respond in writing.

D-11.0700

7.   Duty of Stated Clerk

D-11.0701
Reporting the
Decision

If the presbytery is meeting when the decision is received from the clerk of the permanent judicial commission, the stated clerk shall read the decision to the presbytery immediately and enter the full decision upon the minutes of the presbytery. If the presbytery is not meeting, the stated clerk shall read the decision to the presbytery at its first stated or adjourned meeting thereafter, or at a meeting called for that purpose, and enter the full decision upon the minutes of the presbytery.

D-11.0800

8.   Enforcement

D-11.0801
Enforcement by
Governing Body

When a session has completed the trial and found the accused guilty and the decision has been pronounced, or when the stated clerk of a higher governing body has received the decision of its permanent judicial commission in which the accused was found guilty, the session or higher governing body shall proceed to enforce the decision. The person against whom the decision has been pronounced shall refrain from the exercise of office or from participating and voting in meetings, according to the situation, until an appeal has been decided or the time for appeal has expired, unless the session or the presbytery specifically grants a request to allow the person to continue in office pending an appeal.

D-12.0000

CHAPTER XII. CENSURE AND RESTORATION
IN A DISCIPLINARY CASE

D-12.0100

D-12.0101
Degrees of
Church Censure

D-12.0102
Rebuke

1. Censures

The degrees of church censure are rebuke, rebuke with supervised rehabilitation, temporary exclusion from exercise of ordained office or membership, and removal from ordained office or membership.

Rebuke is the lowest degree of censure for an offense and is completed when pronounced. (D-11.0403e) It consists of setting forth publicly the character of the offense, together with reproof, which shall be pronounced in the following or like form:

Whereas, you, (Name) _____,
have been found guilty of the offense(s) of _____
_____ (here insert the offense), and by such offense(s) you have acted contrary to (the Scriptures and/or the *Constitution of the Presbyterian Church (U.S.A.)*); now, therefore, the Presbytery (or Session) of _____
_____, in the name and authority of the Presbyterian Church (U.S.A.), expresses its condemnation of this offense, and rebukes you. You are enjoined to be more watchful and avoid such offense in the future. We urge you to use diligently the means of grace to the end that you may be more obedient to our Lord Jesus Christ.

Prayer

This formal rebuke shall be followed by intercessory prayer to Almighty God.

D-12.0103
Rebuke with
Supervised
Rehabilitation

Rebuke with supervised rehabilitation is the next to lowest degree of censure. It consists of setting forth the character of the offense, together with reproof and mandating a period of supervised rehabilitation imposed by the session or the permanent judicial commission (D-11.0403e). This censure shall be pronounced in the following or like form.

Whereas, you (Name) _____ have been found guilty in the offense(s) of _____
_____ and by such offense(s) you have acted contrary to the Scriptures and/or the *Constitution of the Presbyterian Church (U.S.A.)*; now, therefore, the Permanent Judicial Commission (or Session) of _____, in the name and authority of the Presbyterian Church (U.S.A.) expresses its condemnation of this offense, rebukes you, and orders you to complete a program of supervised rehabilitation supervised by_____ as described below:
_____.

You are enjoined to be more watchful and avoid such offense in the future. We urge you to use diligently the means of grace to the end so that you may be more obedient to our Lord Jesus Christ.

a.   The rebuke shall be followed by intercessory prayer to Almighty God.

b.   The session or permanent judicial commission shall formally communicate to the supervising entity and the person censured the goals of the rehabilitation and the specific authority conferred on the supervisor(s).

c.   The description of the rehabilitation program shall include a clear statement of how progress will be evaluated and how it will be determined when and if the supervised rehabilitation has been satisfactorily completed.

D-12.0104
Temporary
Exclusion

Temporary exclusion from the exercise of ordained office or membership is a higher degree of censure for a more aggravated offense and shall be for a definite period of time, or for a period defined by completion of supervised rehabilitation imposed by the session or the permanent judicial commission. (D-11.0403e) This censure shall be pronounced in the following or like form:

Whereas, you, (Name) _____, have been found guilty of the offense(s) of _____, (here insert the offense), and by such offense(s) you have acted contrary to (the Scriptures and/or the *Constitution of the Presbyterian Church (U.S.A.)*); now, therefore, the Presbytery (or Session) of _____, in the name and by the authority of the Presbyterian Church (U.S.A.), does now declare you temporarily excluded from _____ for a period of _____, or until completion of the following rehabilitation program supervised by _____, as described below:

_____

_____.

Prayer

a.   This formal declaration shall be followed by intercessory prayer to Almighty God.

Supervised
Rehabilitation

b.   If the period of temporary exclusion is defined by completion of supervised rehabilitation, the session or permanent judicial commission shall formally communicate to the supervising entity and the person found guilty the specific authority conferred on the supervisor.

Refrain from
Exercise of Office

c.   During the period of temporary exclusion from ordained office, the person found guilty shall refrain from the exercise of any function of ordained office.

Cannot Vote or
Hold Office

d.   During the period of temporary exclusion from membership, the person found guilty shall refrain from participating and voting in meetings and from holding or exercising any office.

Effect of
Temporary
Exclusion of a
Minister

e.   If a pastor is temporarily excluded from the exercise of the office of ordained minister, the presbytery may, if no appeal from the case is pending, declare the pastoral relationship dissolved.

Notice of
Temporary
Exclusion

f.   When the censure of temporary exclusion has been pronounced with respect to a minister, the stated clerk of the presbytery shall immediately send the information of the action taken to the Stated Clerk of the General Assembly, who shall make a quarterly report of all such information to every presbytery of the church.

Termination of
Censure of
Temporary
Exclusion

g.   A person under the censure of temporary exclusion shall apply in writing to the governing body, through the clerk of session or stated clerk, for restoration upon the expiration of the time of exclusion or completion of the supervised rehabilitation pronounced. The governing body that imposed the censure shall approve the restoration when the time of exclusion has expired or when the governing body is fully satisfied that the supervised rehabilitation pronounced has been completed.

Early Restoration

h.   A person under the censure of temporary exclusion from the exercise of ordained office or from membership may apply in writing to the governing body that imposed the censure (through its clerk) to be restored prior to the expiration of the time of exclusion or the completion of the supervised rehabilitation fixed in the censure. The governing body may approve such a restoration when it is fully satisfied that the action is justified.

D-12.0105
Removal from
Office or
Membership

Removal from office or membership is the highest degree of censure.

Removal from
Office

a.   Removal from office is the censure by which the ordination and election of the person found guilty are set aside, and the person is removed from all offices without removal from membership.

Removal from
Membership

b.   Removal from membership is the censure by which the membership of the person found guilty is terminated, the person is removed from all rolls, and the person's ordination and election to all offices are set aside.

This censure shall be pronounced in the following or like form:

Whereas, you, (Name) _____, have been found guilty of the offense(s) of _____ _____ (here insert the offense), and by such offense(s) you have acted contrary to (the Scriptures and/or the *Constitution of the Presbyterian Church (U.S.A.)*); now, therefore, the Presbytery (or Session) of _____, acting in the name and under the authority of the Presbyterian Church (U.S.A.), does hereby set aside and remove you from _____ (here state whether removal is from all ordained and elected offices or from membership, which includes removal from all offices).

Prayer

c.   This formal declaration shall be followed by intercessory prayer to Almighty God.

Consequences of Removal from Office

d.   If a minister is removed from office without removal from membership, the presbytery shall give the minister a certificate of membership to a Christian church of the minister's choice. If the minister is a pastor, the pastoral relationship is automatically dissolved by the censure.

Notice of Removal

e.   When the censure of removal has been pronounced with respect to a minister, the stated clerk of that presbytery shall immediately send the information of the action taken to the Stated Clerk of the General Assembly, who shall make a quarterly report of all such information to every presbytery of the church.

D-12.0200

2.   Restoration

D-12.0201 Decision of Governing Body

A person under the censure of removal from office or from membership may be restored by the governing body imposing the censure when the governing body is fully satisfied that the action is justified and the person makes a reaffirmation of faith for membership restoration or is reordained for restoration to office. The forms of the restoration are described in D-12.0202 and D-12.0203.

D-12.0202 Form of Restoration to Office after Removal

The restoration to office of a minister, elder, or deacon shall be announced by the moderator in the following or like form:

Form

a.   Whereas, you, (Name) _____, have manifested such repentance as satisfies the church, the Presbytery of _____ (or Session of this church) does now restore you to the office of _____ _____ and authorize you to perform the functions of that office in accordance with the *Constitution* of this church by this act of ordination.

Restored to Roll

b.   Thereafter, a full service of ordination shall take place and the name shall be restored to the appropriate roll. (G-14.0206 and G-14.0405)

D-12.0203
Form of
Restoration to
Membership after
Removal

The restoration to membership shall be announced by the moderator in a meeting of the governing body in the following or like form:

Form

a.   Whereas, you, (Name) _____, have manifested such repentance as satisfies the church, the Presbytery (or Session) of _____ does now restore you to full membership in the church by this act of reaffirmation.

Restored to Roll

b.   Thereafter, the act of reaffirmation shall take place and the name of the person shall be restored to the appropriate roll or a certificate of membership shall be issued to a Christian church of that person's choice.

Restored to
Office

c.   If the member is also to be restored to an ordained office, the procedure prescribed in D-12.0202 shall be followed.

D-13.0000

CHAPTER XIII. APPEAL IN A DISCIPLINARY CASE

D-13.0100

1. Initiation of Appeal

D-13.0101
Definition

An appeal of a disciplinary case is the transfer to the next higher governing body of a case in which a decision has been rendered in a lower governing body, for the purpose of obtaining a review of the proceedings and decision to correct, modify, set aside, or reverse the decision.

D-13.0102
Initiation of
Appeal

Only the person found guilty may initiate the first level of appeal by the filing of a written notice of appeal.

D-13.0103
Appeal of
Appellate
Decision

Either party may initiate an appeal of the appellate decision by the filing of a written notice of appeal.

D-13.0104
Effect of Appeal

The notice of appeal, if properly and timely filed, shall suspend further proceedings by lower governing bodies, except that, in the instance of temporary exclusion from exercise of ordained office or membership or removal from office or membership, the person against whom the judgment has been pronounced shall refrain from the exercise of office or from participating and voting in meetings until the appeal is finally decided.

D-13.0105
Withdrawal
of Appeal

On application, the permanent judicial commission of the higher governing body may grant a petition for withdrawal of an appeal. The permanent judicial commission shall deny a petition if its approval would defeat the ends of justice.

D-13.0106
Grounds for
Appeal

The grounds for appeal are

a.   irregularity in the proceedings;

b.   refusing a party reasonable opportunity to be heard or to obtain or present evidence;

c.   receiving improper, or declining to receive proper, evidence or testimony;

d.   hastening to a decision before the evidence or testimony is fully received;

e.   manifestation of prejudice in the conduct of the case;

f.   injustice in the process or decision;

g.   error in constitutional interpretation; and

h.   undue severity of censure.

D-13.0200

2.   Filings in Appeal Process

D-13.0201
Time for Filing
Written Notice
of Appeal

A written notice of appeal shall be filed within thirty days after a copy of the judgment has been delivered by certified delivery or personal service to the party appealing.

a.   The written notice of appeal shall be filed with the clerk of session or stated clerk of the governing body that elected the permanent judicial commission from whose judgment the appeal is taken.

b.   The party appealing shall provide to each of the other parties and the stated clerk of the governing body that will hear the appeal a copy of the notice of appeal.

D-13.0202
Content of
Written Notice
of Appeal

The written notice of appeal shall state and include

a.   the name of the party or parties filing the appeal, called the appellant or appellants;

b.   the name of the other party or parties, called the appellee or appellees;

c.   the governing body from whose judgment the appeal is taken;

d.   the judgment or decision, and date and place thereof, from which the appeal is taken;

e.   a statement of the grounds for appeal (D-13.0106); and

f.   a certification that a copy of the notice of appeal was provided by certified delivery or by personal service to each of the other parties and to the stated clerk of the governing body that will hear the appeal.

D-13.0203
Record on Appeal

The record on appeal shall be formed as follows:

List of Record

a.   Within thirty days after the receipt of a written notice of appeal, the clerk of session or stated clerk of the lower governing body shall list in writing to the parties all of the papers and other materials that constitute the record of the case. (D-11.0601d)

Additional
Records

b.   Within ten days thereafter, any party may file with the clerk of session or stated clerk of the governing body a written statement challenging the accuracy or completeness of the record of the case as listed by the clerk. The written challenge shall state specifically the item or items listed in D-11.0601d that are claimed to be omitted from the record of the case.

Filing of Record
on Appeal

c.   Within forty-five days after the receipt of a notice of appeal, the clerk of session or stated clerk of the lower governing body shall certify and file the record of the case, which may include authenticated copies of parts of the record, and shall include any written challenges disputing the completeness or accuracy of the record, with the stated clerk of the higher governing body.

Correction of the Record

d. If anything material to either party is omitted from the record by error or accident or is misstated therein, the omission or misstatement may be corrected. The parties may stipulate to the correction, or the session or permanent judicial commission of the lower governing body may certify and transmit a supplemental record, or the permanent judicial commission of the higher governing body may direct that the omission or misstatement be corrected. All other questions as to the form and content of the record shall be presented to the permanent judicial commission of the higher governing body.

Notice of Date of Reception

e. The stated clerk of the higher governing body shall notify the parties of the date the record on appeal was received.

Copy Furnished at Cost

f. Upon written request, the stated clerk of the higher governing body shall furnish any party to the appeal, at cost to that party, a copy of the record on appeal.

Extension

g. For good cause shown, the stated clerk of the higher governing body may extend the time limits in D-13.0203 for a reasonable period.

D-13.0204 Filing of Appellant's Brief

Within thirty days after the date of the filing of the record on appeal, the appellant shall file with the stated clerk of the higher governing body a written brief containing specifications of the errors alleged and arguments, reasons, and citations of authorities in support of the appellant's contentions as to the alleged errors specified.

Copy to Other Party

a. The brief shall be accompanied by a certification that a copy has been furnished to the other party or parties.

Extension

b. For good cause shown, the stated clerk of the higher governing body may extend this time limit for a reasonable period.

Failure to File Brief

c. Failure of appellant to file a brief within the time allowed, without good cause, shall be deemed by the permanent judicial commission an abandonment of the appeal.

D-13.0205 Filing of Appellee's Brief

Within thirty days after the filing of appellant's brief, the appellee shall file a written brief responding thereto.

Copy to Other Party

a. The brief shall be accompanied by a certification that a copy has been furnished to the other party or parties.

Extension

b. For good cause shown, the stated clerk of the higher governing body may extend this time limit for a reasonable period.

Failure to File Brief

c. Failure by appellee to file a brief, without good cause, shall constitute waiver of the rights to file a brief, to appear, and to be heard.

D-13.0206
Transmittal to
Permanent
Judicial
Committee

Upon receipt of the record and the briefs, or upon the expiration of the time for filing them, the stated clerk of the higher governing body shall transmit the record and briefs to the clerk of the permanent judicial commission.

D-13.0300

3. Prehearing Proceedings

D-13.0301
Examination
of Papers

Upon receiving the papers in an appeal, the moderator and the clerk of the permanent judicial commission of the governing body that will hear the case shall promptly examine the papers to determine whether

    a.   the governing body has jurisdiction;

    b.   the appellant has standing to file the appeal;

    c.   the appeal papers were properly and timely filed; and

    d.   the appeal states one or more of the grounds for appeal set forth in D-13.0106.

D-13.0302
Preliminary
Questions
Determined

The moderator and clerk shall report their findings to the parties and to the permanent judicial commission.

    a.   If a challenge is made to the findings of the moderator and clerk, either by a party to the case or by a member of the permanent judicial commission, opportunity shall be provided to present evidence and argument on the finding in question.

    b.   If a hearing is necessary to decide the item in question, that hearing shall be scheduled at least thirty days prior to the hearing on the appeal, unless the circumstances, including monetary considerations, render advisable the disposition of the preliminary questions immediately before the hearing on the appeal.

    c.   If the permanent judicial commission determines that any point listed in D-13.0301 has been answered in the negative, the permanent judicial commission shall dismiss the appeal.

D-13.0400

4. Hearing of Appeal

D-13.0401
Notice of Hearing

The moderator or clerk of the permanent judicial commission shall notify the parties of the date when they may appear in person or by counsel before the permanent judicial commission to present the appeal.

D-13.0402
Failure to Appear

Failure of a party to appear in person or by counsel shall constitute a waiver of participation in the hearing on appeal.

D-13.0403
Hearing:

New Evidence

At the hearing, the permanent judicial commission shall

    a.   determine whether to receive newly discovered evidence, under the provisions of D-14.0502, providing for the verbatim recording of such new evidence; and

Hearing

b. give opportunity to be heard on the grounds of the appeal to those parties who have not waived that right, the appellant having the right of opening and closing the argument.

D-13.0404
Decision of
Permanent
Judicial
Commission

After the hearing and after deliberation, the permanent judicial commission shall vote separately on each specification of error alleged. The vote shall be on the question, "Shall the specification of error be sustained?" The minutes shall record the numerical vote on each specification of error.

If No Errors
Found

a. If none of the specifications of error is sustained, and no other error is found, the decision of the lower governing body shall be affirmed.

If Errors Are
Found

b. If one or more errors are found, the permanent judicial commission shall determine whether the decision of the lower governing body shall be affirmed, set aside, reversed, modified, or the case remanded for a new trial.

Written Decision

c. A written decision shall be prepared while in session, and shall become the final decision when a copy of the written decision is signed by the clerk and moderator of the commission.

Determination of
Each Error

d. The decision shall include the determination of errors specified, and state the remedy as provided in D-13.0101. The permanent judicial commission may prepare its decision in a manner that will dispose of all substantive questions without redundancy. It may include an explanation of its determination.

Filed Promptly

e. The decision shall be filed promptly with the stated clerk of the governing body that appointed the permanent judicial commission and the parties to the case by personal service or by certified delivery.

Further Publicity

f. The moderator or clerk shall disseminate the decision as the commission may direct.

D-13.0405
Effect of Reversal
on Appeal in
Disciplinary Case

When a permanent judicial commission in an appeal in a disciplinary case reverses all findings of guilt, it is in effect an acquittal, and the person is automatically restored to office or membership in the church. Declaration to this effect shall be made in the lower governing body.

D-14.0000

CHAPTER XIV. EVIDENCE IN REMEDIAL OR DISCIPLINARY CASES

D-14.0100

D-14.0101
Evidence Defined

1. Evidence

Evidence, in addition to oral testimony of witnesses, may include records, writings, material objects, or other things presented to prove the existence or nonexistence of a fact. Evidence must be relevant to be received. No distinction should be made between direct and circumstantial evidence as to the degree of proof required.

D-14.0200

D-14.0201
Challenge

D-14.0202
Husband or Wife

D-14.0203
Counselor

D-14.0204
Counsel for
Parties

D-14.0205
Credibility of
Witnesses

2. Witnesses

Any party may challenge the ability of a witness to testify, and the session or permanent judicial commission shall determine the competence of the witness so challenged.

A husband or wife, otherwise competent to testify, may be a witness for or against the other, but neither shall be compelled to testify against the other.

A person duly appointed by a governing body to provide counseling services for persons within the jurisdiction of the governing body shall not testify before a session or permanent judicial commission, except that the restriction may be waived by the person about whom the testimony is sought.

The counsel for the parties involved in a case may not be compelled to testify about confidential matters, nor may they testify concerning any matters without the express permission of the party they represent.

Credibility means the degree of belief that may be given to the testimony of a witness. The session or permanent judicial commission may consider, in determining the credibility of a witness, any matter that bears upon the accuracy or truthfulness of the testimony of the witness.

D-14.0300

D-14.0301
Separate
Examination

D-14.0302
Examination of
Witnesses

3. Testimony

At the request of either party, no witness shall be present during the examination of another witness. This shall not limit the right of the accused or the committee of counsel of the respondent to be present and to have expert witnesses present.

Witnesses in either disciplinary or remedial cases shall be examined first by the party producing them, and then they may be cross-examined by the opposing party. Thereafter, any member of the session or permanent judicial commission may ask additional questions.

Oath

a. Prior to giving testimony, a witness shall make an oath by answering the following question in the affirmative:

"Do you solemnly swear that the evidence you will give in this matter shall be the truth, the whole truth, and nothing but the truth, so help you God?"

Affirmation

b. If a witness objects to making an oath, the witness shall answer the following question in the affirmative:

"Do you solemnly affirm that you will declare the truth, the whole truth, and nothing but the truth in the matter in which you are called to testify?"

D-14.0303 Record of Testimony

The testimony of each witness shall be accurately and fully recorded by a qualified reporter or other means.

D-14.0304 Testimony Taken on Deposition

Any session or permanent judicial commission before which a case may be pending shall have power to appoint, on the application of any party, one or more persons to take and record testimony in the form of a deposition.

Person from Another Governing Body

a. When necessary, the person or persons so appointed may be from within the geographical bounds of another governing body.

Taking of Testimony

b. Any person so appointed shall take the testimony offered by either party after notice has been given to all parties of the time and place where the witnesses are to be examined. All parties shall be entitled to be present and be permitted to cross-examine.

Offered as Evidence

c. This testimony, properly authenticated by the signature or signatures of the person or persons so appointed, shall be transmitted promptly to the clerk of the session or permanent judicial commission before which the case is pending and may be offered as evidence by any party.

Questions of Admissibility

d. All questions concerning the admissibility of statements made in deposition testimony shall be determined by the session or permanent judicial commission when the record of such testimony is offered as evidence.

D-14.0305 Member as Witness

A member of the session or permanent judicial commission before which the case is pending may testify, but thereafter shall not otherwise participate in the case.

D-14.0400

4. **Records as Evidence**

D-14.0401 Admissibility of Records

The authenticated written records of a governing body or permanent judicial commission shall be admissible in evidence in any proceeding.

D-14.0402
Admissibility of
Testimony

A record or transcript of testimony taken by one governing body or permanent judicial commission and regularly authenticated shall be admissible in any proceeding in another governing body.

D-14.0500

5. New Evidence

D-14.0501
Application for
New Trial

Prior to filing notice of appeal, but without extending the time for appeal, any person convicted of an offense, or any party against whom an order or decision has been entered in a remedial case, may apply for a new trial on the ground of newly discovered evidence. The session or permanent judicial commission—when satisfied that such evidence could reasonably have resulted in a different decision and which, in the exercise of reasonable diligence, could not have been produced at the time of trial—may grant such application.

D-14.0502
Consideration in
Appeal

If, subsequent to the filing by any party of a notice of appeal, new evidence is discovered, which in the exercise of reasonable diligence could not have been discovered prior to the filing of the notice of appeal, the permanent judicial commission receiving the appeal may, in its discretion, receive the newly discovered evidence and proceed to hear and determine the case. However, no newly discovered evidence may be admitted unless the party seeking to introduce it shall have made application, with copies to the adverse party, at least thirty days prior to the hearing. That application shall be accompanied by a summary of the evidence.

APPENDIX

FORMS FOR JUDICIAL PROCESS

(PLUS DISSENT AND PROTEST)

FORMS

FORMS FOR REGISTERING DISAGREEMENT

WITH GOVERNING BODY ACTIONS

FORM NO. 1
DISSENT, G-9.0303

I, _____, a member of or commissioner to _____
_____ (name of governing body), register my dissent from the
_____ (action or decision).

_____
(Signature)

[A dissent must be voiced prior to recess of the particular session at which the action is taken. The above form may be presented to the clerk or stated clerk or that person's assistant to confirm one's dissent. The name of the person dissenting shall be recorded.]

FORM NO. 2
PROTEST, G-9.0304

I, _____, a member of or commissioner to _____
_____ (name of governing body), wish to protest the _____
_____(irregularity or delinquency). The reasons for my protest are
_____.

_____
(Signature)

[Written notice of the protest shall be given at the particular session of the governing body during which it arose. The protest shall be filed with the clerk or stated clerk before adjournment.]

FORMS IN REMEDIAL CASES

FORM NO. 3
STAY OF ENFORCEMENT,
SIGNED BY ONE-THIRD OF GOVERNING BODY, D-6.0103a(1)

_____,
Complainant

v.

_____,
Respondent

    The persons whose signatures appear below constitute at least one third of the members of the _____ (insert name of governing body) recorded as present when the decision or action was made to _____ (insert the action sought to be stayed) and believe that the action was irregular.

    [This stay of enforcement shall be effective until the time for filing a complaint or appeal shall have expired or, if timely filed, until the decision of the permanent judicial commission having jurisdiction over the case. However, the respondent may file, within thirty days of the filing of a stay of enforcement, an objection to the stay of enforcement. As a result of a hearing as to whether the stay remains or is removed, the stay may be modified, terminated, or continued until the decision on the merits of the case by the permanent judicial commission.]

_____, date_____   _____, date_____

_____, date_____   _____, date_____

_____, date_____   _____, date_____

_____, date_____   _____, date_____

    I attest to the fact that the above named persons were recorded as present at the time of the decision or action. I have received the required number of signatures on this date.

_____   _____
Date   Signature of Stated Clerk or Clerk

    [Note: Use sufficient pages to record the number of signatures required, but each signature must be an original. Printed names or copies of pages of signatures will not meet the requirement.]

FORM NO. 4
STAY OF ENFORCEMENT,
SIGNED BY ONE-THIRD OF PJC DECIDING CASE, D-6.0103a(2)

_____,
Complainant, Appellant, Appellee

v.

_____,
Respondent, Appellant, Appellee

The following members of the permanent judicial commission of the _____ _____ (name of governing body), having participated in the announced decision of the above named case and believing that a stay of enforcement should be granted until the case is heard on appeal by a higher governing body, do hereby affix our signatures.

_____, date_____   _____, date_____

_____, date_____   _____, date_____

_____, date_____   _____, date_____

_____, date_____   _____, date_____

I have received the required number of signatures on this date.

_____   _____
Date   Signature of Stated Clerk or Clerk

[Note: Complainant/appellant may send a copy of the stay of enforcement to each individual member of the permanent judicial commission, requesting that each one who signs send the form directly to the clerk or stated clerk of the governing body whose action is to be stayed.]

FORM NO. 5
STAY OF ENFORCEMENT, SIGNED BY THREE MEMBERS OF PJC
RECEIVING COMPLAINT OR APPEAL, D-6.0103a(3)

_____,
Complainant, Appellant, Appellee

v.

_____,
Respondent, Appellant, Appellee

    The following members of the permanent judicial commission having jurisdiction to hear the complaint or appeal of the decision or action of the _____ (name of governing body, its permanent judicial commission, or a respondent named in D-6.0202b.{3}) on _____ (date) concerning _____ (insert subject matter of the decision or action), having received the complaint or notice of appeal, or the substance of the complaint or appeal, with the reasons therefor, certify that in their judgment probable grounds exist for finding the decision or action erroneous, do hereby grant a stay of enforcement.

_____, date_____   _____, date_____

_____, date_____   _____, date_____

_____, date_____   _____, date_____

_____, date_____   _____, date_____

I have received the required number of signatures on this date.

_____   _____

Date   Signature of Stated Clerk or Clerk

    [Note: Complainant/appellant may send a copy of the stay of enforcement to each individual member of the permanent judicial commission, requesting that each one who signs send the form directly to the clerk or stated clerk of the governing body whose action is to be stayed.]

FORM NO. 6
COMPLAINT, D-6.0301

_____,

Complainant(s)

v.

_____, (session, presbytery, synod, General Assembly Council,

Respondent   or entity of the General Assembly).

Statement of Complaint

I (We), _____ (name{s} of complainant{s}) complain(s) to the _____ (name of the next higher governing body or General Assembly) against _____ (name of governing body, GAC, or entity of GA) concerning _____ (an irregularity or a delinquency), in that at a meeting at _____ (place) on the _____ day of _____, 19____, said _____ (governing body or entity) did _____ (state the decision or action that was irregular or the delinquency complained of).

Complainant(s) believe(s) that the decision or action was irregular or the governing body failed to act as constitutionally required in the following particulars _____ _____ (reasons why the decision or action was irregular or the failure to act was a delinquency).

Complainant(s) has the right to complain because _____ (state the standing of complainant as set forth in D-6.0202a, b).

Complainant(s) request(s) that the _____ (name of governing body to which complaint is addressed) order the _____ (name of governing body complained against) to _____ (state the specific relief requested).

_____   _____

Date   Signature of Complainant(s)

[Reminder to complainant(s): **Form No. 7** must also be filed.]

FORM NO. 7
CERTIFICATION OF SERVICE OF COMPLAINT, D-6.0301f

I hereby certify that a copy of the above complaint was served upon _____ _____ (name of respondent governing body or entity complained against) by mailing it to _____ (clerk, stated clerk, General Assembly Council, or entity of GA) by _____ (certified or registered mail, return receipt requested, or by personal delivery) on the _____ day of _____, 19____.

_____   _____

Date   Signature of Complainant(s)

FORM NO. 8
RECEIPT OF COMPLAINT BY RESPONDENT, D-6.0301f

I, _____ (name of clerk or stated clerk or representative of the GAC or entity of the GA) of the _____ (name of governing body or GAC or entity of the GA) certify that I have received by _____ (personal delivery or service or certified or registered mail, return receipt requested) on _____, 19____, (date received) a copy of the complaint of _____ (name of complainant).

_____
Date

_____
Clerk or Stated Clerk or Representative

FORM NO. 9
ANSWER TO COMPLAINT, D-6.0303

_____,
Complainant(s)

v.

_____, (session, presbytery, synod, General Assembly Council,
Respondent   or entity of the General Assembly).

Answer

The _____ (committee of counsel of respondent) submits the following answer to the complaint of the _____ (irregularity or delinquency) alleged in the complaint of _____ (name of complainant(s)).

[The answer shall admit those facts alleged in the complaint that are true, deny those allegations that are not true or are mistakenly stated, and allege other facts that may explain the situation identified as an irregularity or delinquency. The answer may also raise any issues listed in D-6.0307.]

_____
Date

_____
Signature of Counsel of Respondent

[Reminder to respondent(s): **Form No. 10** must also be filed.]

FORM NO. 10
CERTIFICATION OF SERVICE OF ANSWER TO COMPLAINT, D-6.0303

I, _____ (name), certify that the enclosed is submitted as an answer to the complaint of _____ and that a copy has been furnished to the complainant(s) by _____ (certified or registered mail, return receipt requested, or by personal delivery) on the _____ day of _____, 19___.

_____
Date

_____
Signature of Complainant(s)

FORM NO. 11
CITATION TO A PARTY IN A REMEDIAL CASE, PRETRIAL CONFERENCE, D-6.0309

To: _____ (complainant or committee of counsel)

From: _____ (moderator or clerk of session or of
permanent judicial commission)

    You are cited to appear before the _____ (session or permanent judicial commission) of the _____ (name of governing body) meeting at the _____ (place) in _____ (city), on the _____ day of _____, 19___, at ____.m., for preliminary proceedings as described in Rules of Discipline, D-6.0309, concerning the complaint filed by or against you with the _____ (clerk of session or stated clerk of presbytery, synod, or GA) on the _____ day of _____, 19___.

_____
Date

                            _____
Moderator or Clerk of Session or
Moderator or Clerk of
Permanent Judicial Commission

FORM NO. 12
CITATION TO A PARTY IN A REMEDIAL CASE D-7.0201, .0202

To: _____ (complainant or committee of counsel)

From: _____ (moderator or clerk of session or of
permanent judicial commission)

    You are cited to appear before the _____ (session or permanent judicial commission) of the _____ (name of governing body) meeting at the _____ (place) in _____ (city), on the _____ day of _____, 19___, at ____.m., to prosecute the complaint filed by you or defend against the complaint filed against you with the _____ (clerk of session or stated clerk of presbytery, synod, or GA) on the _____ day of _____, 19___, so that the matter may be fully heard and decided.

_____
Date

                            _____
Moderator or Clerk of Session or
Moderator or Clerk of
Permanent Judicial Commission

FORM NO. 13
CITATION TO WITNESS, REMEDIAL CASE, D-7.0201a, .0202

To: _____ (name)

From: _____ (moderator or clerk of the
permanent judicial commission)

    Upon the request of _____ (name{s} of complainant{s} or respondent governing body or entity), you are cited to appear before the permanent judicial commission of _____ (name of governing body) meeting at the _____ (place) in _____ (city), on the _____ day of _____, 19___ at _____.m., to give testimony in the remedial case _____ (name of case).

_____
Date

_____
Moderator or Clerk of
Permanent Judicial Commission

FORM NO. 14
SECOND CITATION TO WITNESS, REMEDIAL CASE, D-7.0203

To: _____ (name)

From: _____ (moderator or clerk of the
permanent judicial commission)

    (The citation shall be the same as that in Form No. 13 except for necessary changes in date and place, and, in addition, shall contain the following paragraph):

    This being your second citation, you are informed according to D-7.0203 that if you fail to appear at the time and place named before the permanent judicial commission of the _____ (governing body), unless excused for cause, you may be subject to disciplinary action.

_____
Date

_____
Moderator or Clerk of
Permanent Judicial Commission

FORM NO. 15
ORDER TO SERVE CITATION, REMEDIAL CASE, D-7.0202

To: _____ (name)

From: _____ (moderator or clerk of
session or moderator or clerk of PJC)

    You are directed to serve the attached citation on _____ (name) by personally delivering it to the person cited. Certification of service shall be made to the clerk of the permanent judicial commission.

_____   _____
Date   Moderator or Clerk of PJC

FORM NO. 16
CERTIFICATE OF SERVICE OF CITATION, REMEDIAL CASE, D-7.0202

To: _____ (clerk)

From: _____ (person serving citation)

    I certify that I have served a citation on _____ (name) by personally delivering the citation on the _____ day of _____, 19___, (or I certify that I was unable to locate and serve the citation on _____ [name]).

_____   _____
Date   Signature

FORM NO. 17
REQUEST THAT A PERSON NOT A
MEMBER OF THE PRESBYTERIAN CHURCH (U.S.A.)
SERVE AS A WITNESS, REMEDIAL CASE, D-7.0201b

To: _____ (name of witness)

From: _____ (name of permanent judicial commission)

Upon the request of _____ (name{s} of complainant{s} or respondent governing body or entity), you are hereby requested to be present and to give testimony before the permanent judicial commission of the _____ (name of governing body) meeting at _____ (place) in _____ (city), on the _____ day of _____, 19___, at _____.m., in regard to the remedial case _____ _____ (name of case).

_____
Date

_____
Moderator or Clerk of
Permanent Judicial Commission

FORM NO. 18
REQUEST FOR TAKING TESTIMONY BY DEPOSITION,
REMEDIAL CASE, D-7.0205, 14.0304

To: _____ (permanent judicial commission)

From: _____ (name of complainant{s} or respondent)

I, _____, request that the testimony of _____ _____ (name of witness) in the trial of _____ (name of case) be taken by deposition because _____ _____ (list reasons).

I certify that a copy of this request has been provided to the _____ _____ (complainant or respondent).

_____
Date

_____
Signature

FORM NO. 19
NOTICE OF APPEAL, REMEDIAL CASE
D-8.0100, .0201, .0202

To: _____ (stated clerk of governing body from
whose judgment appeal is made)

From: _____ (appellant)

RE:

_____
Appellant (Complainant or Respondent)

v.

_____
Appellee (Respondent or Complainant)

    Notice is given of appeal to the _____ (synod or General
Assembly) from the decision rendered by the permanent judicial commission of _____
_____ (name of presbytery) on the _____ day of _____, 19___, at _____
_____ (place).

    (Provide all the information required by D-8.0202.)

_____   _____
Date   Signature of Appellant

[Reminder to appellant(s): **Form No. 20** must also be filed.]

FORM NO. 20
CERTIFICATION OF SERVICE OF NOTICE OF APPEAL,
REMEDIAL CASE, D-8.0202f

    I certify that a copy of the Notice of Appeal has been furnished to _____
_____ (stated clerk of higher governing body whose permanent judicial commission
will hear appeal) and to _____ (other parties and their counsel) by
_____ (certified or registered mail, return receipt requested, or by personal
delivery) on the _____ day of _____, 19_____.

_____   _____
Date   Signature of Appellant

FORM NO. 21
FORM OF BRIEF OF APPELLANT AND APPELLEE,
REMEDIAL CASE, D-8.0204, .0205

_____
Appellant (Complainant or Respondent)

v.

_____
Appellee (Respondent or Complainant)

Specification of Error

[Allegations of errors committed by lower governing body or permanent judicial commission. See D-8.0105 for grounds for appeal. Appellee should cite the specifications of error as listed in the appellant's brief.]

Statement of Facts

[Give a clear and concise narrative account of facts of the case leading up to appeal.]

Argument

[State argument to each specification of error, with an appropriate heading indicating the portions of the argument applicable to each specification. Reasons and citations of authorities in support of the contentions should be included.]

Conclusion

[State the relief or correction requested, if appellant. State the disposition of the appeal requested, if appellee.]

Appendix

[If applicable, copies of any decision by the lower governing body should be attached. Appropriate portions of governing body minutes, if referred to in the brief, should also be attached.]

_____   _____
Date   Signature of Appellant

[Reminder to appellant(s) and appellee(s): **Form No. 22** must also be filed.]

FORM NO. 22
CERTIFICATION OF SERVICE OF BRIEF,
REMEDIAL CASE, D-8.0204a, .0205a

I, _____ (name), certify that a copy of the brief of _____ (appellant, appellee) was served upon _____ _____ (other parties and their counsel) by _____ (certified or registered mail, return receipt requested, or by personal delivery) on the _____ day of _____, 19___.

_____   _____
Date   Signature of Appellant or Appellee

FORMS FOR VINDICATION
FORM NO. 23
REQUEST FOR VINDICATION, D-9.0101

To: _____ (clerk of session, stated clerk of presbytery)

From: _____ (name of person seeking vindication)

    I, _____ (name), feel that I have been injured by _____ (rumor or gossip) alleging that I have committed the offense of _____ _____. I request that the _____ (session or presbytery) designate an investigating committee to make inquiry and ascertain the facts and circumstances concerning the alleged offense.

    [Provide a narrative and a statement of alleged facts. What does the rumor or gossip allege as the conduct constituting an offense and what facts do you allege in response? Provide other pertinent information.]

_____
Date

_____
Signature

FORM NO. 24
REVIEW OF REQUEST FOR VINDICATION, D-9.0101a

To:_____ (clerk of session or stated clerk of presbytery)

From:_____ (committee on ministry or other appropriate committee)

    Having reviewed the request for vindication filed by _____ _____ (name), the _____ (name of committee), authorized to make a determination whether an investigating committee should be appointed, determined on _____ (date) that an investigating committee _____ _____(should or should not) be appointed to proceed as provided in D-10.0201.

    The _____ (clerk of session or stated clerk of presbytery) should provide for the appointment of such an investigating committee according to the provisions of D-10.0201.

_____
Date

_____
Signature

FORM NO. 25
REPORT OF INVESTIGATING COMMITTEE, VINDICATION PROCESS, D-9.0101b

To:_____ (clerk of session or
                                  stated clerk of presbytery,
                                  or person seeking vindication)

From:_____ (member of investigating committee)

It is the conclusion of the investigating committee formed on _____ (date of formation, D-10.0401) to investigate rumors and gossip concerning _____ (name of person) that _____ (no charges will be filed OR charges will be filed).

[The facts and circumstances from which the rumor or gossip arose should be reported.]

[If the investigating committee determines that charges are to be filed in the matter, appropriate judicial process, beginning at D-10.0402, shall be followed.]

_____
Date

_____
Signature

FORMS IN DISCIPLINARY CASES

FORM NO. 26
ACCUSATION BY INDIVIDUAL AS STATEMENT OF OFFENSE, D-10.0102a

To: _____ (clerk of session or
                                  stated clerk of presbytery)

From:_____ (name of person or
                                  persons making accusation)

I, _____, under the jurisdiction of the _____ (name of session of congregation or presbytery), accuse _____ (name of person accused) of committing the offense of _____ contrary to Holy Scripture and the *Constitution of the Presbyterian Church (U.S.A.)* and I submit the following information in support of said accusation:

The said _____ (name of accused) did, on or about _____ (date), _____ (insert a narrative and alleged facts believed to support the accusation).

_____
Date

_____
Signature of Accuser

FORM NO. 27
ACCUSATION BY A MEMBER OF A GOVERNING BODY
AS STATEMENT OF OFFENSE, D-10.0102b

To: _____ (clerk of session or
stated clerk of presbytery)

From: _____ (name of person or persons making accusation)

    I, _____, a member of the _____
_____ (name of session of congregation or presbytery), accuse
_____ (name of person accused) of committing the offense of
_____ contrary to Holy Scripture and the *Constitution of the Presbyterian Church (U.S.A.)* and I submit the following information in support of said accusation:

    The said _____ (name of accused) did, on or about
_____ (date), _____ (insert a narrative
and alleged facts believed to support the accusation).

_____   _____
Date   Signature of Accuser

FORM NO. 28
SELF-ACCUSATION BY A MEMBER AS STATEMENT OF OFFENSE, D-10.0102c

To: _____ (clerk of session or stated clerk
of presbytery)

From: _____ (name of person making self-accusation)

    I, being under the jurisdiction of the _____ (session of
congregation, presbytery), state that I am guilty of the offense of _____
_____ contrary to Holy Scripture and the *Constitution of the Presbyterian Church (U.S.A.).* I submit the following information in support of my self-accusation:

    I, _____, did on _____ (date)
_____ (insert a
narrative of information to substantiate self-accusation).

_____   _____
Date   Signature

FORM NO. 29
CONCLUSION OF INVESTIGATION, D-10.0202g, .0300

To:_____ (clerk of session or
stated clerk of presbytery,
person who submitted written statement,
or person against whom allegations were made)

From:_____ (member of investigating committee)

It is the conclusion of the investigating committee formed on _____(date of formation, D-10.0401) to investigate allegations against _____ (name of person) that _____(no charges will be filed OR charges will be filed).

[Such actions, specified in section D-10.0300, which follow the decision to file or not file charges must be taken by the investigating committee.]

FORM NO. 30
RECEIPT OF REPORT OF INVESTIGATING COMMITTEE, D-10.0300

This is to acknowledge receipt of the report of the Investigating Committee of the _____ _____ (name of governing body) formed on _____, 19___. The report, received on _____, 19___, states that _____ (no charges are to be filed OR charges are being filed) in relation to the matter referred to it.

_____   _____
Date   (Clerk or Stated Clerk)

FORM NO. 31
PETITION FOR REVIEW OF DECISION NOT TO FILE CHARGES, D-10.0303a

To:_____ (clerk of session or stated clerk of presbytery)

From:_____ (person making original statement of offense)

    I, _____, having received, on _____ (date), the communication from the investigating committee that no charges are to be filed in relation to the written statement of offense I provided to the _____ (clerk of session or stated clerk) of _____ (name of congregation or presbytery), do hereby petition the _____ (session or permanent judicial commission) to review the decision of the investigating committee not to file charges.

    [Give a narrative which explains what you believe to have been the errors committed by the investigating committee in reaching its decision not to file charges.]

    [This petition, along with the answer of the investigating committee, will be reviewed by the session or permanent judicial commission of presbytery. The review may result in either a confirmation of the decision of the investigating committee or in a new investigation.]

_____

Date

_____

Signature

FORM NO. 32
ANSWER OF INVESTIGATING COMMITTEE
TO PETITION FOR REVIEW, D-10.0303b

To:_____ (clerk of session or
                                  stated clerk of presbytery)

From:_____ (investigating committee)

    The investigating committee appointed to investigate the written statement of offense submitted by _____ (name) against _____ (name) submits the following response to the facts alleged by _____ (name) in (his/her) petition for review of the decision not to file charges:

    [Responses to each alleged fact.]

_____

Date

_____

Signature, Member of Investigating Committee

FORM NO. 33
CONCLUSION OF REVIEW BY PERMANENT JUDICIAL COMMISSION, D-10.0303

To:_____ (clerk of session or
stated clerk of presbytery,
person who submitted written statement,
or person against whom allegations were made)

From:_____ (moderator or clerk of session
or moderator or clerk of PJC)

It is the conclusion of the _____ (session or
permanent judicial commission) that the decision of the investigating committee not to file charges
against _____ (name of person) was based upon an
_____ (appropriate OR inappropriate) investigation. The petition of
_____ (name of petitioner) is _____
(not sustained OR sustained).

[If the petition is sustained, a new investigating committee shall be appointed
{D-10.0303d}. If the petition is not sustained, the matter is concluded.]

_____
Date

                                        _____
                                        Moderator or Clerk of Session or
                                        Moderator or Clerk of PJC

[Note: In order to prevent the need to reference any eventual trial (D-4.0000), it may be a
good idea for the session or PJC to provide by an internal rule for the moderator of the session or PJC to appoint two or three members to conduct the review of the petition and answer. Those members would not participate in a trial if one eventually were to take place.]

FORM NO. 34
CHARGES, D-10.0403, .0404

The Presbyterian Church (U.S.A.) charges you, _____
(name of member of church or presbytery), with the following offense(s):

["An offense is any act or omission by a member or officer of the church that is contrary to the Scriptures or the *Constitution of the Presbyterian Church (U.S.A.).*]

    1. On or about the _____ (date), you, _____ (name), did commit the offense of _____ in that you _____
_____.

[Each charge shall be numbered and set forth the conduct that constituted the offense. Each charge shall state (as far as possible) the time, place, and circumstances of the commission of the alleged conduct. Each charge shall also be accompanied by a list of the names and addresses of the witnesses for the prosecution and a description of the records and documents to be cited for its support.]

Witnesses (list names and addresses) in support of charge:

Records and documents (list and describe each) in support of charge:

_____
Date

_____
Signature, Investigating Committee

FORM NO. 35
CITATION TO PERSON ACCUSED, PRETRIAL CONFERENCE D-10.0405a

To: _____ (name of accused)

From: _____ (moderator or clerk of session or
                                                  moderator or clerk of PJC)

    You are hereby cited to appear before the _____ (session, permanent judicial commission) of _____ (name of church or presbytery), meeting at the _____ (place) in _____ (city), on the _____ day of _____, 19___, at _____.m., for preliminary proceedings as described in Rules of Discipline, D-10.0405 in the case of the Presbyterian Church (U.S.A.) through _____ (name of session or presbytery) v. _____ _____(name of accused). A copy of the charge(s) is attached.

_____
Date

_____
Moderator or Clerk of Session or
Moderator or Clerk of
Permanent Judicial Commission

FORM NO. 36
CITATION TO PROSECUTING COMMITTEE, PRETRIAL CONFERENCE D-10.0405a

To: _____ (name of prosecuting committee)

From: _____ (moderator or clerk of session or
moderator or clerk of PJC)

You are hereby cited to appear before the _____ (session,
permanent judicial commission) of the _____ (name of church or
presbytery), meeting at the _____ (place) in _____
(city), on the _____ day of _____, 19___, at _____.m., for preliminary proceedings as described in Rules of Discipline, D-10.0405, in the case of the Presbyterian Church (U.S.A.) through
_____ (name of session or presbytery) v. _____
_____(name of accused). A copy of the charge(s) is attached.

_____   _____
Date   Moderator or Clerk of Session or
                                           Moderator or Clerk of PJC

FORM NO. 37
CITATION TO PERSON ACCUSED, D-11.0201a, .0202

To: _____ (name)

From: _____ (moderator or clerk of session
or moderator or clerk of PJC)

You, _____(name), are cited to appear before the
_____ (session or permanent judicial commission) of the
_____ (name of church or presbytery), meeting at the _____
(place) in _____ (city), on the _____ day of _____, 19___, at _____.m., to
answer the charges filed against you by the Presbyterian Church (U.S.A.) through _____
_____(name of session or presbytery). A copy of the charge(s) is attached.

_____   _____
Date   Moderator or Clerk of Session or
                                           Moderator or Clerk of PJC

FORM NO. 38
SECOND CITATION TO PERSON ACCUSED, D-11.0202a, b

To: _____ (name)

From: _____ (moderator or clerk of session or
moderator or clerk of PJC)

(The citation shall be in the same form as that in Form No. 37 except for necessary changes in date and place, and, in addition, should contain the following paragraph):

This being your second citation, you are informed, according to D-11.0202b, that if you fail to appear at the time and place above named, unless excused for cause, the _____ _____ (session or permanent judicial commission), after having appointed some person or persons to represent you as counsel, may proceed to take testimony in your case, as if you were present. In addition, you may be found guilty of disobedience and contempt for which you may be subject to disciplinary action (D-11.0202a).

_____
Date

_____
Moderator or Clerk of Session or
Moderator or Clerk of PJC

FORM NO. 39
CITATION TO PROSECUTING COMMITTEE D-11.0201a, .0202

To: _____ (special disciplinary committee)

From: _____ (moderator or clerk of session or
moderator or clerk of PJC)

You are cited to appear before the _____ (session or permanent judicial commission) of the _____ (name of church or presbytery), meeting at the _____ (place) in _____ (city), on the _____ day of _____, 19__, at ____.m., to prosecute the charge(s) against _____ _____ (name) filed by you with the _____(clerk of session or stated clerk of presbytery) on the _____ day of _____, 19____, so that the matter may be fully heard and decided.

_____
Date

_____
Moderator or Clerk of Session or
Moderator of Clerk of PJC

FORM NO. 40
CITATION TO WITNESS, DISCIPLINARY CASE, D-11.0201a, .0202

To: _____ (name)

From: _____ (moderator or clerk of session or
moderator or clerk of PJC)

    You are cited to appear before the _____ (session or permanent judicial commission) of _____ (name of church or presbytery), meeting at the _____ (place) in _____ (city), on the _____ day of _____, 19___, at ____.m., to give testimony in regard to the charges filed against _____ by the Presbyterian Church (U.S.A.) through _____(name of session or presbytery).

_____
Date

                _____
                Moderator or Clerk of Session or
                Moderator or Clerk of PJC

FORM NO. 41
SECOND CITATION TO WITNESS, DISCIPLINARY CASE, D-11.0202a

To: _____ (name)

From: _____ (moderator or clerk of session or
moderator or clerk of PJC)

    (The citation shall be in the same form as that in Form No. 40 except for necessary changes in date and place, and, in addition, shall contain the following paragraph):

    This being your second citation, you are informed, according to D-11.0202a, that if you fail to appear at the time and place named before the _____ (session, permanent judicial commission) of the _____ (name of church or presbytery), unless excused for cause, you may be subject to disciplinary action.

_____
Date

                _____
                Moderator or Clerk of Session or
                Moderator or Clerk of PJC

FORM NO. 42
ORDER TO SERVE CITATION, DISCIPLINARY CASE, D-11.0202

To: _____ (name)

From: _____ (moderator or clerk of session or
moderator or clerk of PJC)

    You are directed to serve the attached citation on _____ (name) by personally delivering it to the person cited. Certification of service shall be made to the clerk of the _____ (session, permanent judicial commission).

_____
Date

_____
Moderator or Clerk of Session or
Moderator or Clerk of PJC

FORM NO. 43
CERTIFICATE OF SERVICE OF CITATION, DISCIPLINARY CASE, D-11.0202

To: _____ (clerk)

From: _____ (person serving citation)

    I certify that I have served a citation on _____ (name) by personally delivering the citation on the _____ day of _____, 19___, (or I certify that I was unable to locate and serve the citation) on _____ (name).

_____
Date

_____
Signature

A-23

FORM NO. 44
REQUEST THAT A PERSON NOT A MEMBER OF
THE PRESBYTERIAN CHURCH (U.S.A.)
SERVE AS A WITNESS, DISCIPLINARY CASE, D-11.0201b

To: _____ (name)

From: _____ (moderator or clerk of session or
moderator or clerk of PJC)

    You are requested to be present and to give testimony before the _____
_____ (session or permanent judicial commission) of the _____
(name of church or presbytery), meeting at _____ (place) in _____
(city), on the _____ day of _____, 19___, at _____.m., in regard to charge(s) against
_____ filed by the Presbyterian Church (U.S.A.) through
_____(name of session or presbytery).

_____
Date

                                 _____
                                 Moderator or Clerk of Session or
                                 Moderator or Clerk of PJC

FORM NO. 45
REQUEST FOR TAKING TESTIMONY BY DEPOSITION,
DISCIPLINARY CASE, D-11.0204, 14.0304

To: _____ (name of session or permanent judicial commission)

From: _____ (name of complainants{s} or respondent)

    I, _____, request that the testimony of
_____(name of witness) in the trial of
_____ (name of case) be taken by deposition because
_____ (list reasons).

    I certify that a copy of this request has been provided to the _____
_____(complainant or respondent).

_____
Date

                                 _____
                                 Signature

FORM NO. 46
NOTICE OF APPEAL, DISCIPLINARY CASE D-13.0100, .0201, .0202

To: _____ (clerk of session or stated clerk of governing body from whose judgment appeal is made)

From: _____ (appellant)

RE:

_____
Appellant (Person Found Guilty or Governing Body {D-13.0103})

v.

_____
Appellee (Governing Body or Person Found Guilty)

    Notice is given of appeal to the _____ (presbytery, synod, or General Assembly) from the decision rendered by _____ (session or permanent judicial commission) on the _____ day of _____, 19___, at _____ (place).

[Provide all the information required by D-13.0202.]

_____   _____
Date   Signature of Appellant

[Reminder to appellant(s): **Form No. 47** must also be filed.]

FORM NO. 47
CERTIFICATION OF SERVICE OF NOTICE OF APPEAL, DISCIPLINARY CASE, D-13.0202f

    I certify that a copy of the Notice of Appeal has been furnished to _____ _____ (stated clerk of higher governing body whose permanent judicial commission will hear appeal) and to _____ (other parties and their counsel) by _____ (certified or registered mail, return receipt requested, or by personal delivery) on the _____ day of _____, 19____.

_____   _____
Date   Signature of Appellant

FORM NO. 48
FORM OF BRIEF OF APPELLANT AND APPELLEE,
DISCIPLINARY CASE, D-13.0204, .0205

Appellant

v.

Appellee

Specification of Error

[Allegations of errors committed by lower governing body or permanent judicial commission. See D-13.0106 for grounds for appeal. Appellee should cite the specifications of error as listed in the appellant's brief.]

Statement of Facts

[Give a clear and concise narrative account of facts of the case leading up to appeal.]

Argument

[State argument to each specification of error, with an appropriate heading indicating the portions of the argument applicable to each specification. Reasons and citations of authorities in support of the contentions should be included.]

Conclusion

[State the relief or correction requested, if appellant. State the disposition of the appeal requested, if appellee.]

Appendix

[If applicable, copies of any decision by the lower governing body should be attached. Appropriate portions of governing body minutes, if referred to in the brief, should also be attached.]

Date

Signature of Appellant

[Reminder to appellant(s) and appellee(s): **Form No. 49** must also be filed.]

FORM NO. 49
CERTIFICATION OF SERVICE OF BRIEF,
DISCIPLINARY CASE, D-13.0204a, .0205a

I, _____ (name), certify that a copy of the brief of
_____ (appellant, appellee) was served upon _____
_____ (other parties and their counsel) by _____
(certified or registered mail, return receipt requested, or by personal delivery) on the _____ day of
_____, 19___.

_____   _____
Date   Signature of Appellant

FORMS FOR REFERENCE
FORM NO. 50
REFERENCE, D-4.0000

To: _____ (permanent judicial commission
                                      of next higher governing body)

From: _____ (session or permanent judicial commission)

The _____ (session, permanent judicial commission) of
the _____ (church, presbytery, synod) requests the Permanent
Judicial Commission of the _____ (name of higher governing body) to
assume jurisdiction for a _____ (trial and decision or hearing on appeal) in
the case of:

_____
Complainant
        v.
_____
Respondent
        OR
_____
Presbyterian Church (U.S.A.)
        v.
_____
Defendant

The case is referred for the following reasons (explain why it is desirable for the high governing body to handle case):

                                                _____
                                                Moderator
_____   _____
Date   Clerk

DECISION OF PERMANENT JUDICIAL COMMISSION
ON REFERENCE, D-4.0200

To: _____ (session or permanent judicial commission)

From: _____ (permanent judicial commission
of next higher governing body)

It is the determination of the permanent judicial commission of _____
(presbytery, synod, or GA) that the request of the _____ (session
or permanent judicial commission) that the _____ (disciplinary or
remedial) matter be handled by this body be _____ (approved or disapproved).

The Permanent Judicial Commission of _____(name of governing
body) _____ (assumes OR declines) original jurisdiction in the case of
_____.

[State reasons for refusal, (D-4.0203).]

[If the permanent judicial commission of the higher governing body refuses to accept
jurisdiction, the lower governing body shall conduct the trial or hearing on appeal and
proceed to a decision.]

_____
Date

_____
Moderator or Clerk of PJC

INDEX

The references in this index are to the section numbers.

Minister of the Word and Sacrament: (*Continued*)

Pastor: (*Continued*)
    And the Directory for Worship: (*Continued*)
        Lord's Supper:
            Administered by minister .... W- 2.4012 c
                                                             W- 3.3612
                                      through W- 3.3618
            And the Word .... W- 2.4008
            On special occasions .... W- 2.4010
        Marriage:
            If considered unwise .... W- 4.9002 b
            Preparation for .... W- 4.9002 a
            Service .... W- 4.9000
        Particular responsibilities .... W- 1.4005 a
        Proclaiming the Word .... W- 3.3401
        Service for the Lord's Day .... W- 3.3000
        Setting an order of worship .... W- 2.0000
    Call (See "Pastor, Election of")
    Compensation, annual review of .... G- 7.0302 a
                                                                G-10.0102 n
                                                               G-14.0506 e
    Congregational meeting to call .... G- 7.0303
                                                                G- 7.0304 a(2)
                                                               G-14.0502 a
    Designated .... G-14.0501 a,g
    Directs the work of associate .... G-14.0501 f
    Dissolution of relationship:
        Dissolved only by presbytery G-14.0601
        May be initiated by congregation G-14.0603
        May be initiated by pastor G-14.0602
    Election of (See under "Pastor, Election of")
    Expenses to church governing bodies, how paid .... G- 9.0303
    Former pastor's pastoral services G-14.0606
    Has power to convene session .... G-10.0103 a
    Moderator of congregational meeting .... G- 7.0306
    Must convene session when requested by two members of session G-10.0201
    Organizing pastor may be called as pastor G-14.0513
                                                                G-14.0501 a
    Pastor emerita and emeritus G-14.0605
    When churches unite .... G-11.0103 h
    Worship and (See under "And the Directory for Worship", above)
Pastor, Election of:
    By ballot vote of congregation .... G-14.0503 b
    Committee on ministry must be consulted .... G-14.0502 a
    Emerita, Emeritus G-14.0605
    Form of call .... G-14.0506 b
    Installation service G-14.0510
    Method of voting .... G-14.0503 b
    Moderator of congregational meeting .... G-14.0503 a
    Nominating committee to be elected .... G-14.0502 a
    Organizing pastor may be elected G-14.0513
                                                                G-14.0501 a
    Procedure .... G-14.0503 b
    Procedure when minority refuses to concur G-14.0505
    Prosecution of call G-14.0507
    Public notice of at least ten days .... G-14.0502 a

ARTICLES OF AGREEMENT

PREAMBLE

The Articles of Agreement embody the contractual commitments of the Presbyterian Church in the United States and The United Presbyterian Church in the United States of America concerning the means by which the confessional documents, members, officers, judicatories, courts, agencies, institutions and property of those churches shall be and become the confessional documents, members, officers, judicatories, courts, agencies, institutions and property of the Presbyterian Church (U.S.A.). The Articles of Agreement record the details of the reunion. Their contents demonstrate the continuity of the reunited church with each of its antecedents. The reunited church will be in all ecclesiastical, judicial, legal and other respects the continuing entity of the Presbyterian Church in the United States and The United Presbyterian Church in the United States of America.

Once the two churches have approved the plan in accordance with their separate Constitutions and the reunion has been effected, the single reunited church will come into being and the separate existences of the two churches will terminate. The two parties to the original agreement will no longer be in existence as separate churches and hence the agreement cannot thereafter be altered. By the act of reunion, the separate interests of the two parties reflected in the agreement are united in one reunited church that could not represent the concerns of either predecessor body if some change in the Agreement were proposed.

Immediately upon the formation of the reunited church, its new Constitution (G-1.0500)[1] will be operative. It, rather than the Articles of Agreement, is the basic document of the single church and is subject to amendment in accordance with its provisions.

---

[1]The following abbreviations are used throughout:

G - Form of Government

D - Rules of Discipline

S - Directory for the Service of God [After 1988 this book is called the Directory for Worship.]

ARTICLE 1. CONTINUITY OF THE PRESBYTERIAN CHURCH (U.S.A.) WITH THE PRESBYTERIAN CHURCH IN THE UNITED STATES AND THE UNITED PRESBYTERIAN CHURCH IN THE UNITED STATES OF AMERICA

1.1   These Articles of Agreement are intended to, and they do, provide for the union of the Presbyterian Church in the United States and The United Presbyterian Church in the United States of America to form one church which shall be known as the Presbyterian Church (U.S.A.). Whenever it becomes necessary to identify the Presbyterian Church in the United States or The United Presbyterian Church in the United States of America after union, the Presbyterian Church (U.S.A.) is, and shall be, the successor of each and the successor shall have that identity. The history of the Presbyterian Church (U.S.A.) is, and shall embody, the history of the Presbyterian Church in the United States and The United Presbyterian Church in the United States of America. These Articles shall be interpreted consistently with the foregoing. The Presbyterian Church in the United States, The United Presbyterian Church in the United States of America, and the Presbyterian Church (U.S.A.) affirm that it is the intention of each that the Presbyterian Church (U.S.A.), from the time of reunion, shall comprise and be one single ecclesiastical entity which is the continuing church resulting from the reunion of the Presbyterian Church in the United States and The United Presbyterian Church in the United States of America.

1.2   Each and every member of the Presbyterian Church in the United States and of The United Presbyterian Church in the United States of America shall be a member of the Presbyterian Church (U.S.A.).

1.3   Each and every ordained officer, whether minister, ruling elder or deacon, of the Presbyterian Church in the United States and of The United Presbyterian Church in the United States of America shall be the comparable ordained officer of the Presbyterian Church (U.S.A.), minister of the Word, elder or deacon.

1.4   Each and every congregation of the Presbyterian Church in the United States and of The United Presbyterian Church in the United States of America shall be a congregation of the Presbyterian Church (U.S.A.).

1.5   Each and every pastoral relationship between a pastor, co-pastor, associate or assistant pastor and a congregation in the Presbyterian Church in the United States and The United Presbyterian Church in the United States of America shall continue in the Presbyterian Church (U.S.A.). Any existing relationship as lay preacher or commissioned church worker shall be undisturbed by the formation of the Presbyterian Church (U.S.A.), but only for so long as the individual holding such relationship continues that relationship to the same particular church.

1.6   Each and every Session, Presbytery and Synod of the Presbyterian Church in the United States and of The United Presbyterian Church in the United States of America shall be the comparable governing body of the Presbyterian Church (U.S.A.).

1.7   The General Assembly of the Presbyterian Church (U.S.A.) shall be the highest governing body of that church and the successor to the General Assembly of the Presbyterian Church in the United States and to the General Assembly of The United Presbyterian Church in the United States of America.

1.8 Each and every board, agency, institution and committee of the Presbyterian Church in the United States or of The United Presbyterian Church in the United States of America, or under joint control of the two churches, shall have the same relationship to the appropriate governing body of the Presbyterian Church (U.S.A.) as it now has to a judicatory of the Presbyterian Church in the United States or of The United Presbyterian Church in the United States of America.

1.9 Each and every policy statement adopted by or issued at the direction of the General Assembly of the Presbyterian Church in the United States or of the General Assembly of The United Presbyterian Church in the United States of America shall have the same force and effect in the Presbyterian Church (U.S.A.) as in the church which adopted or issued it until rescinded, altered or supplanted by action of the General Assembly of the Presbyterian Church (U.S.A.).

ARTICLE 2. TRUSTEES AND CORPORATE STRUCTURES

2.1 Each and every trustee and corporate structure of the congregations, judicatories, boards, agencies and institutions of the Presbyterian Church in the United States and of The United Presbyterian Church in the United States of America, together with all property, real and personal, held by them shall be the trustees and corporate structures of the congregations, governing bodies, boards, agencies and institutions of the Presbyterian Church (U.S.A.). Such legal procedures shall be undertaken without delay as may be necessary and expedient to assure that such trustees and corporate structures together with all property, real and personal, held by them are clearly identified as trustees, corporate structures and property of the Presbyterian Church (U.S.A.).

2.2 The continuity and integrity of all funds held in trust by such trustees or corporations shall be maintained, and the intention of the settlor or testator as set out in the trust instrument shall be strictly complied with. Wherever necessary, steps shall be taken to demonstrate that the appropriate entity of the Presbyterian Church (U.S.A.) has succeeded to the beneficiary named in such trust instrument.

ARTICLE 3. CONFESSIONAL DOCUMENTS

3.1 The confessional documents of the two preceding churches shall be the confessional documents of the reunited church. The interim stated clerks of the Presbyterian Church (U.S.A.) shall prepare the official text of the confessional documents as defined in G-1.0501.

3.2 The General Assembly of the reunited Presbyterian Church shall at an early meeting appoint a committee representing diversities of points of view and of groups within the reunited church to prepare a Brief Statement of the Reformed Faith for possible inclusion in the Book of Confessions as provided in G-18.0201.

3.3 Until the Brief Statement of the Reformed Faith has been incorporated into the Book of Confessions, the Presbyterian Church (U.S.A.) accepts *A Brief Statement of Belief* adopted by the 102nd General Assembly of the Presbyterian Church in the United States in 1962, as a summary of the Reformed understanding of historic Christian doctrine set forth in Scripture and contained in the Confessions of the Presbyterian Church (U.S.A.). During that interval, *A Brief Statement of Belief* shall be utilized with the Confessions of the church in the instruction of church members and officers, in the orientation and examination of ordinands prior to ordination, and of ministers seeking membership in Presbyteries by transfer from other Presbyteries or other churches.

ARTICLE 4. THE OFFICE OF THE GENERAL ASSEMBLY

4.1   The work of the Office of the General Assembly immediately following reunion shall be provided for as follows:

The offices of the two highest governing bodies of the uniting churches shall be continued for a period of one year after the effective date of the reunion in order to assure the orderly transfer of records and functions to an office of the new highest governing body. During such transition period the stated clerk of the Presbyterian Church in the United States and the stated clerk of The United Presbyterian Church in the United States of America shall be titled interim stated clerks of the General Assembly and shall function in consultation with the General Assembly Council. The interim stated clerks shall, following consultation with the General Assembly Council, one year after the effective date of the union, recommend the assignments to and an organizational structure for the Office of the General Assembly.

4.2   Not later than nine months after the effective date of the union, the General Assembly Council shall select a Special Committee on Nominations for Stated Clerk. This committee shall be nine in number and representative of all the geographical areas of the reunited church. None of its members shall be considered eligible for nomination for the office of stated clerk. The committee shall consider at once the availability and qualifications of all persons whose names may be presented to it by individuals or governing bodies within the reunited church and shall seek out on its own initiative persons who, in its judgment, should be considered for the office. This committee shall be prepared to present directly to a committee of the next General Assembly the names of not more than three persons whom the Special Committee considers suitable for nomination.

That General Assembly shall establish a General Assembly Committee on Nominations for Stated Clerk to which the Special Committee mentioned in the preceding paragraph shall report with its recommendations. It is understood that the General Assembly Committee need not be limited in its choice to those whose names are suggested by the Special Committee. After full consideration and consultation with the Special Committee, the General Assembly Committee shall select not more than two candidates, whose names shall be presented to the General Assembly not later than forty-eight hours prior to its adjournment. If there is only one nominee and no further nominations from the floor, election may be by acclamation. If there are two or more candidates, the election shall be in the same manner as for the moderator. The candidate receiving a majority of the votes cast shall be declared elected.

ARTICLE 5. TRANSITIONAL COMPOSITION AND WORK OF THE GENERAL ASSEMBLY COUNCIL AND AGENCIES

5.1 During the period immediately following reunion, the General Assembly Council shall consist of the Moderator of the General Assembly, the Moderators of the two immediately preceding General Assemblies of each church, and forty-eight members elected by the General Assembly as provided in 5.2 below. In addition to the voting members, the stated clerk of the General Assembly, and such staff persons as the General Assembly on the recommendation of the General Assembly Council may from time to time designate, shall be corresponding members, with the right to speak but not to vote.

5.2 The first General Assembly of the Presbyterian Church (U.S.A.) shall elect forty-eight members of the General Assembly Council. Twenty-four shall be nominated by the last General Assembly of the Presbyterian Church in the United States, twenty-one from the membership of the General Assembly Mission Board and three from the Committee on Assembly Operations upon recommendation of those bodies. Twenty-four shall be nominated by the last General Assembly of The United Presbyterian Church in the United States of America from the membership of the General Assembly Mission Council upon recommendation of this body. Among those elected there shall be at least one resident of each of the Synods of the Church. Among those elected there shall also be persons from the divisions, agencies and councils of the General Assemblies of the reuniting churches including the Councils on Church and Race, the Council on Women and the Church, and the Committee on Women's Concerns. One half of those elected shall be ministers of the Word, one half laypersons. Care shall be taken to comply with the provisions of G-9.0104 and G-9.0105. The members so elected shall serve for five years without change except that vacancies occasioned by resignation or death may be filled through election by the General Assembly upon nomination of its Nominating Committee. At the end of the five years, the General Assembly Council shall assign its members to three classes of equal size, expiring at the end of one additional year, two additional years, and three additional years. Thereafter, members shall be elected in accordance with G-13.0202.

5.3 During the first five years after reunion, the General Assembly Council shall elect its own moderator and vice-moderator and shall designate its own staff, subject to confirmation by the General Assembly. The stated clerk of the General Assembly shall be its recording secretary.

5.4 The General Assembly Council shall have the responsibilities enumerated in G-13.0201, and in addition shall provide the necessary coordination, management and consolidation of the functions, divisions, agencies, councils, commissions and institutions of the General Assemblies of the reuniting churches. Upon adjournment of the first General Assembly of the Presbyterian Church (U.S.A.), the General Assembly Mission Council of The United Presbyterian Church in the United States of America will cease to exist. The General Assembly Mission Board of the Presbyterian Church in the United States (consisting of the members remaining after election of the General Assembly Council) and the Program Agency, the Support Agency, and the Vocation Agency of The United Presbyterian Church in the United States of America will continue to administer the programs, previously conducted by each of them, for five years unless earlier terminated by action of the General Assembly. During this period the elected membership of the agencies above shall continue to serve without change except that vacancies occasioned by resignation or death may be filled through election by the General Assembly upon nomination of its Nominating Committee.

The General Assembly Council shall develop and propose to subsequent General Assemblies a design for the work of the General Assembly which will effectively relate the functions, divisions, agencies, councils, commissions and institutions of the General Assemblies of the reuniting churches not otherwise provided for in these Articles of Agreement, except an agency for pensions which is hereinafter provided for in Article 11. Agencies whose functions will be served by other bodies or in other ways in the reunited church will not be continued.

5.5   The General Assembly Council shall carefully review the continuing mission directions and priorities approved by both General Assemblies prior to reuniting, and prepare means to harmonize the programmatic work of its agencies.

The General Assembly Council shall ensure the continuance of an organized approach in the areas of world mission, evangelism, education, church renewal, church extension and social-economic justice within the context of the unity of Christ's Church throughout the world.

The General Assembly Council shall take particular care to design agencies and to commit major resources, both human and financial, to put into action with other churches and agencies, in this land and other nations, ministries that serve the purpose of the Presbyterian Church (U.S.A.) to confront men and women, structures and principalities, with the claims of Jesus Christ.

5.6   The General Assembly Council in its development of a design for the work of the General Assembly shall also ensure the continuance of the advocacy and monitoring functions of the existing Councils on Church and Race (both denominations), Committee on Women's Concerns (Presbyterian Church in the United States) and Council on Women and the Church (The United Presbyterian Church in the United States of America). Until such time as the design for work of the General Assembly is completed and these functions are ensured, the existing structures and functions of these bodies shall be maintained.

5.7   As the various boards, agencies, councils and offices of the General Assemblies of the reuniting churches continue to function within the life of the reunited church, or as new agencies are created at the time of reunion, and especially as consideration is given to the location or locations of General Assembly offices and agencies, care and sensitivity shall be shown employed personnel. The General Assembly Council shall ensure continuity of employment at comparable levels insofar as possible. As staff vacancies occur, they shall be filled in accordance with the churchwide plan for equal employment opportunity (G-13.0201b) and the principle of full participation (G-4.0403). The General Assembly Council shall provide for an equitable termination policy.

ARTICLE 6. LOCATION OF THE GENERAL ASSEMBLY'S AGENCIES

6.1   The General Assembly Council shall immediately appoint a representative committee to examine with professional consultants the values of establishing a single location or multiple locations for the General Assembly's agencies. The committee shall propose a possible location or locations. The committee shall suggest a timetable for the move, if relocation is involved.

ARTICLE 7. SPECIAL COMMITTEE ON PRESBYTERY AND SYNOD BOUNDARIES

7.1   A Special Committee on Presbytery and Synod Boundaries shall be formed to work with the governing bodies where Presbyteries and Synods of the existing churches overlap and for other Presbyteries and Synods as necessary. Its work will be done on behalf of the General Assembly and its recommendations made for the General Assembly's action. (G-13.0103, l and m)

7.2   This Special Committee, composed of one person from each Synod of the reuniting churches, shall be elected by the uniting General Assembly through the regular nominating procedures of the existing churches. The committee shall elect its own moderator when it is convened by the interim stated clerks immediately upon adjournment of the uniting General Assembly.

7.3   The Special Committee shall set in motion a procedure whereby overlapping Presbyteries and Synods, through negotiation, shall consult in developing a mutually acceptable plan for Presbytery and Synod boundaries which shall become effective within five years following reunion. The governing bodies of affected Presbyteries and Synods shall be encouraged to initiate boundary adjustment by means of overture to the General Assembly. Recognizing that in several areas of the country some Presbyteries and Synods have overlapped and existed side by side for years, care must be taken, in the spirit of fair representation reflected in G-9.0104, that the responsibilities and privileges of governing now enjoyed by members of each Presbytery be honored and enhanced. The Special Committee shall develop guidelines for the governing bodies to use in their negotiations and, when each plan is approved by the governing bodies concerned and the Special Committee, shall forward the plan to the General Assembly recommending approval.

7.4   On the principle that a geographically related area makes possible greater fellowship and ease in the conduct of the business of a governing body, it shall be the further goal of the Special Committee that the resulting governing bodies shall be of sufficient strength and geographical proximity to enhance the total mission of the church. Care must be taken to protect the rights and privileges of members of each of the uniting governing bodies so that they may exercise the responsibilities of leadership in the newly formed governing body.

7.5   The Special Committee shall report annually to the General Assembly on the progress the governing bodies are making. If realignments are not mutually developed within the five years following reunion to the satisfaction of all parties concerned, application for continuance of the process may be made to the General Assembly. If granted, the efforts shall be reviewed by each General Assembly with the expectation that full geographical consolidation shall be accomplished no later than ten years following the uniting General Assembly.

7.6   In cases involving Presbyteries based on racial ethnic or language considerations, or Presbyteries whose membership consists predominately of racial ethnic persons, plans for realignment shall be completed within ten years or, if that is not accomplished, upon application for continuance of the process, which may be granted by the General Assembly, within fifteen years after the uniting General Assembly.

7.7   At such time as all problems of overlapping boundaries and related problems of other Presbyteries and Synods shall have received General Assembly action, the Special Committee shall be dissolved and future issues of boundaries shall be handled under the provisions of G-13.0103 l and m.

ARTICLE 8. RACIAL ETHNIC REPRESENTATION, PARTICIPATION AND ORGANIZATIONS

8.1   The Presbyterian Church (U.S.A.) shall provide for a Committee on Representation for each governing body above the Session. Its membership shall consist of equal numbers of men and women. A majority of the members shall be selected from the racial ethnic groups within the governing body and the total membership shall include persons from each of the following categories:

    a.   majority male membership

    b.   majority female membership

    c.   racial ethnic male membership

    d.   racial ethnic female membership

    e.   youth male and female membership

Its main function shall be to guide the governing bodies with respect to their membership and to that of their committees, boards, agencies and other units, in implementation of the principles of participation and inclusiveness, to ensure effective representation in the decision making of the church.

8.2   Governing bodies of the church shall be responsible for implementing the church's commitment to inclusiveness and participation which provides for the full expression of the rich diversity within its membership. All governing bodies shall work to become more open and inclusive and to correct past patterns of discrimination on the basis of racial ethnic background.

Racial ethnic members in the United States (Presbyterians of African, Hispanic and Asian descent and Native Americans) shall be guaranteed full participation and access to representation in the decision-making of the church, and shall be able to form caucuses.

Participation and representation of racial ethnic membership shall be assured by the Committees on Representation (8.1).

8.3 Consistent with the principles of diversity and inclusiveness as set forth in 8.2, the General Assembly Council shall consult with and receive input from the racial caucuses of the church, and shall make provision for the expenses necessary to such consultations. The purposes of such consultations shall include:

> determining the priorities for assisting racial ethnic churches and ministries,
>
> developing a denominational strategy for racial ethnic church development,
>
> finding ways to assure the funding and operational needs of schools and other institutions which historically have served Black Americans and other racial ethnic groups.

8.4 Racial ethnic educational institutions have been the primary source from which racial ethnic church leadership has developed. Consistent with the dire need for racial ethnic church leadership, the General Assembly Council shall propose to the General Assembly ways whereby the General Assembly shall be able to fulfill its responsibility for education through colleges and secondary schools and for meeting the operational and developmental needs of those Presbyterian schools that historically have served Black Americans and those serving other racial ethnic groups.

ARTICLE 9. WOMEN'S REPRESENTATION, PARTICIPATION AND ORGANIZATIONS

9.1 The Committees on Representation required by G-9.0105 for each governing body above the Session shall guide those bodies, with respect to their membership and that of their committees, boards, agencies and other units, in implementing the principles of participation and inclusiveness, to insure the fair representation of women, both of the majority race and of racial ethnic groups, in the decision making of the church.

9.2 The General Assembly Council in consultation with elected representatives from each recognized women's group of both churches shall make provision for the continuation of the women's programs and organizations of the two churches at all levels, until such time as programs are formulated as described in 9.3.

9.3 A group of representatives elected by each recognized women's group from the two churches shall meet to develop programs and organizations, these proposals to be approved by the constituent groups. Such approval shall be reported to the General Assembly Council by the Executive Committees of each of the women's groups. The group shall report to the General Assembly annually and is expected to complete its work in six years.

ARTICLE 10. INSTITUTIONS OF THEOLOGICAL EDUCATION

10.1 The reunited church has continuing responsibility for its institutions of theological education. These institutions are charged to prepare women and men for ordained ministries and other vocations of professional church leadership and to provide strong theological resource centers for the leadership of the whole church.

10.2 Theological institutions of the Presbyterian Church in the United States:

Austin Presbyterian Theological Seminary,
Austin, Texas,
Columbia Theological Seminary,
Decatur, Georgia,
Louisville Presbyterian Theological Seminary,
Louisville, Kentucky,[2]
Presbyterian School of Christian Education,
Richmond, Virginia,
Union Theological Seminary in Virginia,
Richmond, Virginia,

and of The United Presbyterian Church in the United States of America:

Dubuque Theological Seminary,
Dubuque, Iowa,
Johnson C. Smith Seminary, of the Interdenominational
Theological Center, Atlanta, Georgia,
Louisville Presbyterian Theological Seminary,
Louisville, Kentucky,[3]
McCormick Theological Seminary,
Chicago, Illinois,
Pittsburgh Theological Seminary,
Pittsburgh, Pennsylvania,
Princeton Theological Seminary,
Princeton, New Jersey,
San Francisco Theological Seminary,
San Anselmo, California,

shall continue into the reunited church with their present boards, charters and plans of governance.

10.3 The present pattern of financial support of these institutions by the courts or judicatories to which they are related at the time of the reunion shall continue in the united church. Levels of financial support to the theological institutions from Synods

---

[2]This seminary is operated jointly with The United Presbyterian Church in the United States of America.
[3]This seminary is operated jointly with the Presbyterian Church in the United States.

and the General Assembly shall continue so that each receives a similar percentage of the total amount allocated by the governing bodies in the year prior to reunion.

10.4 A Special Committee on Theological Institutions shall be established at the first General Assembly of the reunited church as a committee of the General Assembly. The Special Committee shall consist of twenty-two members. Eleven members shall be elected from the church at large by the General Assembly (following the procedures for nominating and electing special committees of the General Assembly). The boards of the eleven institutions named above each shall elect one representative from the institution to serve on the committee. The Special Committee shall be convened by the Moderator of the first General Assembly or the Moderator's designee, and shall elect its own moderator. It shall be funded from the budget of the General Assembly Council and assisted by its staff.

10.5 The Special Committee shall review the relationships between theological institutions and the governing bodies of the reunited church and study the system of funding theological education by the governing bodies. Plans shall be made for the continuation of and financial support for all the present institutions, with particular attention to be given to the developmental needs of Johnson C. Smith Seminary, which uniquely serves the constituency of Black Presbyterians. The Special Committee shall report to the General Assembly annually. At or before the sixth General Assembly of the reunited church, it shall make a final report with recommendations concerning the way theological institutions are to be funded through the governing bodies.

10.6 The Council of Theological Seminaries of The United Presbyterian Church in the United States of America and the Committee on Theological Education of the Presbyterian Church in the United States shall continue with their present functions and membership. Where vacancies occur, they shall be filled by the procedure appropriate for the category of membership. The Council and the Committee shall work cooperatively on the common concerns of the theological institutions until the General Assembly has acted upon the recommendations of the Special Committee on Theological Institutions.

ARTICLE 11. PENSION, ANNUITY, INSURANCE, BENEFIT, ASSISTANCE AND RELIEF PROGRAMS

11.1 Following the consummation of the union between the Presbyterian Church in the United States and The United Presbyterian Church in the United States of America, the Board of Annuities and Relief of the Presbyterian Church in the United States and the Board of Pensions of The United Presbyterian Church in the United States of America shall continue to function under their charters as separate corporations until their responsibilities are assumed by the corporate body provided for in 11.3. During the continued existence of these corporations as separate bodies, the membership of their Boards of Directors as constituted at the time of the reunion of the two churches shall be frozen, except that the General Assembly of the reunited church may elect new Directors in the event any vacancies occur. There shall be no interruption in the fulfillment of contractual commitments or other procedures in effect at the time of reunion.

11.2 Following the final vote by the two General Assemblies for reunion of the two churches, the Board of Annuities and Relief of the Presbyterian Church in the

United States and the Board of Pensions of The United Presbyterian Church in the United States of America shall, as expeditiously as possible, develop and recommend to the General Assembly of the reunited church:

    a.   new unified plans and programs to replace the present pension and benefit plans and the assistance and relief programs of the Presbyterian Church in the United States and The United Presbyterian Church in the United States of America; and

    b.   a program for the equitable application of the present Annuity, Relief and Insurance Funds of the Board of Annuities and Relief and the present Pension, Endowment, Assistance, Homes and Equipment and Specific Trust Funds of the Board of Pensions that assures adherence to the purposes for which such funds were set aside.

11.3 When the new unified plans and programs are approved by the General Assembly of the reunited church, they shall be administered by a legally responsible corporate body established under a civil charter and having no responsibilities other than to administer these plans and programs and to assume the responsibilities of the former Board of Annuities and Relief of the Presbyterian Church in the United States and the former Board of Pensions of The United Presbyterian Church in the United States of America. The members of the board of this corporate body shall be elected by the General Assembly of the reunited church.

Following approval by the General Assembly of the reunited church of the program for equitable application of the existing funds, said funds shall be placed under the administration of the corporate body provided for in the immediately preceding paragraph as soon as the necessary legal requirements are fulfilled.

11.4 Until the new unified plans and programs become effective, the existing plans and programs of the two denominations will be continued without amendment. All members will continue in the plan to which they belonged immediately prior to the reunion except that newly ordained ministers, new lay employees and those changing service among churches or employing organizations may participate in either plan, provided the individual and the employing organization agree on one plan and pay the requisite dues under the plan selected.

The new unified plans and programs shall make appropriate provision for all members of the present plans and programs who are ministers or lay employees of the reunited church. After the new pension and benefit plans are operating, no new members shall be enrolled in any of the previously existing plans and no dues related to salaries received after the effective date of the new plans shall be collected under any of the previously existing plans.

Each of the annuity and pension funds shall be administered on an actuarially sound basis for the sole and exclusive use of its members, active and retired, and their survivors, with a view to the final distribution of all assets occurring simultaneously with the fulfillment of all contractual commitments consistent with all legal requirements.

ARTICLE 12. ECUMENICAL RELATIONSHIPS

12.1 The General Assembly of the reunited church shall determine its ecumenical relationships, provided that the reunited church shall initially continue in relationship to those bodies to which either of the uniting churches had been related prior to reunion.

ARTICLE 13. PROCEDURES FOR DISMISSAL OF A CONGREGATION WITH ITS PROPERTY

13.1 The provisions of this article are intended to apply only to the reunion of the Presbyterian Church in the United States and The United Presbyterian Church in the United States of America to form the Presbyterian Church (U.S.A.) and shall not alter, abridge or nullify in any way the principles as to the ownership of property in either antecedent church or in the reunited church as established by ecclesiastical and civil law.

13.2 Following the consummation of union, no congregation shall be dismissed for a period of eighteen months except with the permission of the General Assembly. Members, officers, or ministers who do not desire to be a part of the union may, at any time, unite with other denominations and particular churches as set forth in G-10.0102r, G-10.0302b(1), G-11.0103n.

13.3 After one year from the consummation of union, a congregation formerly a part of the Presbyterian Church in the United States may be dismissed when the following conditions have been met:

  a. That the Session of the church shall call a congregational meeting for the purpose of discussing the question, "Shall the (Name)_____ _____ Presbyterian Church (U.S.A.) request dismissal to another Reformed body of its choice?" Due notice of such meeting shall be given orally from the pulpit of the church at regular church services on two successive Sundays, the first of which shall be at least ten days prior to the meeting. The required quorum shall be as follows:

    If the number of members is one hundred or less, one fourth of the members; or

    If the number of members is more than one hundred, twenty-five members or one tenth of the members, whichever is greater.

  b. That the Presbytery of jurisdiction shall appoint a special committee to meet with the congregation at the congregational meeting. Presbytery's committee shall have the privilege of the floor with the right to speak.

  c. That no type of vote for any purpose shall be taken at the meeting.

  d. That the Session call a special congregational meeting, to be held no sooner than six months and no later than twelve months from the date of the congregational meeting held for consideration of dismissal.

e. That due notice of such meeting shall be mailed to all members of the church at least thirty days prior to the meeting, and given orally from the pulpit of the church at regular church services on two successive Sundays, the first of which shall be at least ten days prior to the meeting. The Presbytery committee shall be present at the meeting and have the privilege of the floor with the right to speak.

The form of the call to the meeting shall be as follows:

A special meeting of the congregation of the __(Name)_____
_____ Presbyterian Church
(U.S.A.) is called for _____ (a.m. or p.m.) on the _____
day of _____, 19___, at _____ ,
to consider and decide whether it shall or shall not request to be dismissed to another Reformed body. Provisions and authority for this special meeting are found in the Articles of Agreement, Article 13, entered into by the Presbyterian Church in the United States and The United Presbyterian Church in the United States of America as a part of the plan of reunion in which both churches became one church, the Presbyterian Church (U.S.A.).

A quorum for this purpose shall be no less than one third of the active confirmed members in good and regular standing. It is urged that a decision on so important a matter be made by a group large enough to reflect the true mind of the whole congregation.

After discussion, a secret ballot will be taken on the categorical question: Shall the _____ Presbyterian Church (U.S.A.) request dismissal to, _____ another Reformed body?

Request dismissal _____ Do not request dismissal _____

If two thirds of those present and voting vote to request dismissal, this particular church will be dismissed under the special provisions of Article 13 of the Articles of Agreement, and will retain all of its property, subject to any existing liens and encumbrances, but will surrender its membership as a congregation in the Presbyterian Church (U.S.A.).

f. That within ten days any person of the unsuccessful side may contest the regularity of the call for, or the conduct of, or the vote taken in, the congregational meeting by a written notice to the Presbytery of jurisdiction. The Presbytery shall then review the questions at issue and, if the contest is sustained, it shall direct the calling of a new congregational meeting.

g. That if the contest is filed by those persons voting for dismissal from the Presbyterian Church (U.S.A.) and the contest is not sustained by the Presbytery, such church shall continue to be a member church of the Presbyterian Church (U.S.A.). If the contest is filed by those voting against dismissal, and is not sustained by Presbytery, such church shall be dismissed to another Reformed body and shall be permitted to retain all of its property subject to any liens and encumbrances.

h. That the jurisdiction of the Presbytery shall be final in any contest brought under this Article.

13.4 Any petition for dismissal with property filed later than eight years from the consummation of union shall be handled under the appropriate provisions for such a request in the Form of Government.

ARTICLE 14. PROCEDURES FOR IMPLEMENTING REUNION

14.1 When the General Assemblies of the two reuniting churches shall have approved the Plan for Reunion by a favorable vote on Formal Question 1, the Presbyteries of both churches shall consider the matter at a meeting held during February of the following calendar year. Formal Question 1 is:

> Resolved: that the General Assembly approve and recommend to the Presbyteries full organic union with the General Assembly of The United Presbyterian Church in the United States of America (with the General Assembly of the Presbyterian Church in the United States) under the proposed Plan for Reunion consisting of the Constitution of the Presbyterian Church (U.S.A.) as defined therein (G-1.0500) and the Articles of Agreement, together with all other documents and procedures incident thereto, all of which are attached to this resolution or by necessary implication are incident thereto, and by this reference are incorporated as a part hereof.

14.2 Each Presbytery shall report its action on Formal Question 2 below to the stated clerk of the General Assembly to which it belongs prior to the end of February. The report of the vote shall be on a ballot provided by the stated clerk of the General Assembly. Union Presbyteries shall report their votes to both General Assembly stated clerks. Formal Question 2 is:

> Resolved: that the Presbytery of _____ give its advice and consent (give its approval) to full organic union with the General Assembly of The United Presbyterian Church in the United States of America (with the General Assembly of the Presbyterian Church in the United States) under the proposed Plan for Reunion consisting of the Constitution of the Presbyterian Church (U.S.A.) as defined therein (G-1.0500) and the Articles of Agreement, together with all other documents and procedures incident thereto, all of which are attached to this resolution or by necessary implication are incident thereto, and by this reference are incorporated as a part hereof.

14.3 When the General Assemblies of the two uniting churches, following approval of Formal Question 2 by the requisite number of Presbyteries of the two uniting churches, shall both approve Formal Question 3:

> Resolved: that the General Assembly finally approve full organic union with the General Assembly of The United Presbyterian Church in the United States of America (with the General Assembly of the Presbyterian Church in the United States) under the proposed Plan for Reunion consisting of the Constitution of the Presbyterian Church (U.S.A.) as defined therein (G-1.0500) and the Articles of Agreement, together with all other documents and procedures incident thereto, all of which are attached to this resolution or by necessary implication are incident thereto, and by this reference are incorporated as a part hereof.

then the commissioners of each General Assembly shall gather in a common place of meeting to convene as the General Assembly of the Presbyterian Church (U.S.A.). All the commissioners of the General Assemblies of the reuniting churches shall be commissioners of the General Assembly of the reunited church, which shall be empowered to act upon all business properly docketed by both General Assemblies of the uniting churches, as well as the business which may come before it according to the requirements of the Form of Government of the Plan for Reunion.

14.4 The two stated clerks of the General Assemblies of the uniting churches, who shall be interim stated clerks of the General Assembly of the reunited church as set forth in Article 4.1 of the Articles of Agreement of the Plan for Reunion, shall prepare and establish a plan for the designation and membership of the necessary General Assembly committees and for recommending to the General Assembly of the reunited church the referral of business properly before the General Assembly.

14.5 The first act of the General Assembly shall be to convene in worship of Almighty God and for the celebration of the Lord's Supper. The election of a moderator shall be an early item on the docket of the first meeting of the General Assembly which shall follow the celebration of the Lord's Supper.

Official Text

A Formula of Agreement

Between the

Evangelical Lutheran Church in America, the Presbyterian Church (U.S.A.), the Reformed Church in America, and the United Church of Christ

On Entering Into Full Communion On the Basis of *A Common Calling*

Approved by the 209th General Assembly (1997)
and declared made by the 210th General Assembly (1998).

A FORMULA OF AGREEMENT

Between the

Evangelical Lutheran Church in America, the Presbyterian Church (U.S.A.), the Reformed Church in America, and the United Church of Christ On Entering into Full Communion On the Basis of *A Common Calling*

Preface

In 1997 four churches of Reformation heritage will act on an ecumenical proposal of historic importance. The timing reflects a doctrinal consensus which has been developing over the past thirty-two years coupled with an increasing urgency for the church to proclaim a gospel of unity in contemporary society. In light of identified doctrinal consensus, desiring to bear visible witness to the unity of the Church, and hearing the call to engage together in God's mission, it is recommended:

That the Evangelical Lutheran Church in America, the Presbyterian Church (U.S.A.), the Reformed Church in America, and the United Church of Christ declare on the basis of *A Common Calling* and their adoption of this *A Formula of Agreement* that they are in full communion with one another. Thus, each church is entering into or affirming full communion with three other churches.

The term "full communion" is understood here to specifically mean that the four churches:

- recognize each other as churches in which the gospel is rightly preached and the sacraments rightly administered according to the Word of God;

- withdraw any historic condemnation by one side or the other as inappropriate for the life and faith of our churches today;

- continue to recognize each other's Baptism and authorize and encourage the sharing of the Lord's Supper among their members;

- recognize each others' various ministries and make provision for the orderly exchange of ordained ministers of Word and Sacrament;

- establish appropriate channels of consultation and decision-making within the existing structures of the churches;

- commit themselves to an ongoing process of theological dialogue in order to clarify further the common understanding of the faith and foster its common expression in evangelism, witness, and service;

- pledge themselves to living together under the Gospel in such a way that the principle of mutual affirmation and admonition becomes the basis of a trusting relationship in which respect and love for the other will have a chance to grow.

This document assumes the doctrinal consensus articulated in *A Common Calling: The Witness of Our Reformation Churches in North America Today*, and is to be viewed in concert with that document. The purpose of *A Formula of Agreement* is to elucidate the complementarity of affirmation and admonition as the basic principle of entering into full communion and the implications of that action as described in *A Common Calling*.

A Common Calling, the report of the Lutheran-Reformed Committee for Theological Conversations (1988–1992) continued a process begun in 1962.[1] Within that report was the "unanimous recommendation that the Evangelical Lutheran Church in America, the Presbyterian Church (U.S.A.), the Reformed Church in America, and the United Church of Christ declare that they are in full communion with one another" (*A Common Calling*, pp. 66–67). There followed a series of seven recommendations under which full communion would be implemented as developed with the study from the theological conversations (*A Common Calling*, p. 67). As a result, the call for full communion has been presented to the four respective church bodies. The vote on a declaration of full communion will take place at the respective churchwide assemblies in 1977.

Mutual Affirmation and Admonition

A concept identified as early as the first Lutheran-Reformed Dialogue became pivotal for the understanding of the theological conversations. Participants in the Dialogue discovered that "efforts to guard against possible distortions of truth have resulted in varying emphases in related doctrines which are not in themselves contradictory and in fact are complementary. . .") *Marburg Revisited*, Preface). Participants in the theological conversations rediscovered and considered the implications of this insight and saw it as a foundation for the recommendation for full communion among the four churches. This breakthrough concept, a complementarity of mutual affirmation and mutual admonition, points toward new ways of relating traditions of

---

[1]For a summary of the history of Lutheran-Reformed Dialogue in North America, see *A Common Calling*, pp. 10–11. The results of the first round of dialogue, 1962–1966, were published in *Marburg Revisited* (Augsburg, 1966). The second round of dialogue took place in 1972–1974. Its brief report was published in *An Invitation to Action* (Fortress, 1983), pp. 54-60. The third series began in 1981 and concluded in 1983, and was published in the book, *An Invitation to Action*. Following this third dialogue a fourth round of "Theological Conversations" was held from 1988 to 1992, resulting in the report, *A Common Calling: The Witness of Our Reformation Churches in North America Today* (Augsburg, 1993). In addition, the North American participants in the Lutheran-Reformed Dialogue have drawn on the theological work found in the *Leuenberg Agreement*, a Statement of Concord between Reformation churches in Europe in 1973, published in *An Invitation to Action*, pp. 61–73, as well as the Report of the International Joint Commission of the Lutheran World Federation and the World Alliance of Reformed Churches, 1985–1988, *Toward Church Fellowship* (LWF and WARC, 1989).

Reformation churches that heretofore have not been able to reconcile their diverse witnesses to the saving grace of God that is bestowed in Jesus Christ, the Lord of the Church.

This concept provides a basis for acknowledging three essential facets of the Lutheran-Reformed relationship: (1) that each of the churches grounds its life in authentic New Testament traditions of Christ; (2) that the core traditions of these churches belong together within the one, holy, catholic, and apostolic Church; and (3) that the historic give-and-take between these churches has resulted in fundamental mutual criticisms that cannot be glossed over, but need to be understood "as diverse witnesses to the one Gospel that we confess in common" (*A Common Calling*, p. 66). A working awareness emerged, which cast in a new light contemporary perspectives on the sixteenth century debates.

The theological diversity within our common confession provides both the complementarity needed for a full and adequate witness to the gospel (mutual affirmation) and the corrective reminder that every theological approach is a partial and incomplete witness to the Gospel (mutual admonition) (*A Common Calling*, page 66).

The working principle of "mutual affirmation and admonition" allows for the affirmation of agreement while at the same time allowing a process of mutual edification and correction in areas where there is not total agreement. Each tradition brings its "corrective witness" to the other while fostering continuing theological reflection and dialogue to further clarify the unity of faith they share and seek. The principle of "mutual affirmation and admonition" views remaining differences as diverse witnesses to the one Gospel confessed in common. Whereas conventional modes of thought have hidden the bases of unity behind statements of differences, the new concept insists that, while remaining differences must be acknowledged, even to the extent of their irreconcilability, it is the inherent unity in Christ that is determinative. Thus, the remaining differences are not church-dividing.

The concept of mutual affirmation and admonition translates into significant outcomes, both of which inform the relationships of these four churches with one another. The principle of complementarity and its accompanying mode of interpretation make it clear that in entering into full church communion these churches:

- do not consider their own traditional confessional and ecclesiological character to be compromised in the least;

- fully recognize the validity and necessity of the confessional and ecclesiological character of the partner churches;

- intend to allow significant differences to be honestly articulated within the relationship of full communion;

- allow for articulated differences to be opportunities for mutual growth of churchly fullness within each of the partner churches and within the relationship of full communion itself.

A Fundamental Doctrinal Consensus

Members of the theological conversations were charged with determining whether the essential conditions for full communion have been met. They borrowed language of the Lutheran confessions: "For the true unity of the church it is enough to agree (*satis est consentire*) concerning the teaching of the Gospel and the administration of the sacraments" (*Augsburg Confession*, Article 7). The theological consensus that is the basis for the current proposal for full communion includes justification, the sacraments, ministry, and church and world. Continuing areas of diversity, no longer to be seen as "church-dividing," were dealt with by the theological conversations under the headings: The Condemnations, the Presence of Christ, and God's Will to Save.

On Justification, participants in the first dialogue agreed "that each tradition has sought to preserve the wholeness of the Gospel as including forgiveness of sins and renewal of life" (*Marburg Revisited*, p. 152). Members of the third dialogue, in their Joint Statement on Justification, said "both Lutheran and Reformed churches are. . .rooted in, live by, proclaim, and confess the Gospel of the saving act of God in Jesus Christ" (*An Invitation to Action*, p. 9). They went on to say that "both. . .traditions confess this Gospel in the language of justification by grace through faith alone," and concluded that "there are no substantive matters concerning justification that divide us" (*An Invitation to Action*, pp. 9–10).

Lutherans and Reformed agree that in Baptism, Jesus Christ receives human beings, fallen prey to sin and death, into his fellowship of salvation so that they may become new creatures. This is experienced as a call into Christ's community, to a new life of faith, to daily repentance, and to discipleship (cf. *Leuenberg Agreement*, III.2.a.). The central doctrine of the presence of Christ in the Lord's Supper received attention in each dialogue and in the theological conversations. The summary statement in *Marburg Revisited*, reflecting agreement, asserts:

> During the Reformation both Reformed and Lutheran Churches exhibited an evangelical intention when they understood the Lord's Supper in the light of the saving act of God in Christ. Despite this common intention, different terms and concepts were employed which. . .led to mutual misunderstanding and misrepresentation. Properly interpreted, the differing terms and concepts were often complementary rather than contradictory (*Marburg Revisited*, pp. 103–4).

The third dialogue concluded that, while neither Lutheran nor Reformed profess to explain <u>how</u> Christ is present and received in the Supper, both churches affirm that, "Christ himself <u>is</u> the host at his table. . . and that Christ himself <u>is</u> fully present and received in the Supper" [emphasis added] (*An Invitation to Action*, p. 14). This doctrinal consensus became the foundation for work done by the theological conversations.

The theme of ministry was considered only by the third dialogue. Agreeing that there are no substantive matters which should divide Lutherans and Reformed, the dialogue affirmed that:

Ministry in our heritage derives from and points to Christ who alone is sufficient to save. Centered in the proclamation of the word and the administration of the sacraments, it is built on the affirmation that the benefits of Christ are known only through faith, grace, and Scripture (*An Invitation to Action*, p. 24).

The dialogue went on to speak of the responsibility of all the baptized to participate in Christ's servant ministry, pointed to God's use of "the ordained ministers as instruments to mediate grace through the preaching of the Word and the administration of the sacraments," and asserted the need for proper oversight to "ensure that the word is truly preached and sacraments rightly administered" (*An Invitation to Action*, pp, 26, 28, 31).

The first dialogue considered the theme of church and world a very important inquiry. The dialogue examined differences, noted the need of correctives, and pointed to the essentially changed world in which the church lives today. Agreeing that "there is a common evangelical basis for Christian ethics in the theology of the Reformers," (*Marburg Revisited*, p. 177), the dialogue went on to rehearse the differing "accents" of Calvin and Luther on the relation of church and world, Law and Gospel, the "two kingdoms," and the sovereignty of Christ. The dialogue found that "differing formulations of the relation between Law and Gospel were prompted by a common concern to combat the errors of legalism on the one hand and antinomianism on the other." While differences remain regarding the role of God's Law in the Christian life, the dialogue did "not regard this as a divisive issue" (*Marburg Revisited*, p. 177). Furthermore, in light of the radically changed world of the twentieth century, it was deemed inappropriate to defend or correct positions and choices taken in the sixteenth century, making them determinative for Lutheran-Reformed witness today. Thus, the theological conversations, in a section on "Declaring God's Justice and Mercy," identified Reformed and Lutheran "emphases" as "complementary and stimulating" differences, posing a challenge to the pastoral service and witness of the churches. "The ongoing debate about 'justification and justice' is fundamentally an occasion for hearing the Word of God and doing it. Our traditions need each other in order to discern God's gracious promises and obey God's commands" (*A Common Calling*, p. 61).

Differing Emphases

The Condemnations:

The condemnations of the Reformation era were an attempt to preserve and protect the Word of God; therefore, they are to be taken seriously. Because of the contemporary ecclesial situation today, however, it is necessary to question whether such condemnations should continue to divide the churches. The concept of mutual affirmation and mutual admonition of *A Common Calling* offers a way of overcoming condemnation language while allowing for different emphases with a common understanding of the primacy of the Gospel of Jesus Christ and the gift of the sacraments. *A Common Calling* refers with approval to the *Leuenberg Agreement* where, as a consequence of doctrinal agreement, it is stated that the "condemnations expressed in the confessional documents no longer apply to the contemporary doctrinal position of the assenting churches" (*Leuenberg Agreement*, IV.32.b). The theological conversations stated:

We have become convinced that the task today is not to mark the point of separation and exclusion but to find a common language which will allow our partners to be heard in their honest concern for the truth of the Gospel, to be taken seriously, and to be integrated into the identity of our own ecumenical community of faith (*A Common Calling*, p. 40).

A major focus of the condemnations was the issue of the presence of Christ in the Lord's Supper. Lutheran and Reformed Christians need to be assured that in their common understanding of the sacraments, the Word of God is not compromised; therefore, they insist on consensus among their churches on certain aspects of doctrine concerning the Lord's Supper. In that regard Lutheran and Reformed Christians, recalling the issues addressed by the conversations, agree that:

> In the Lord's Supper the risen Jesus Christ imparts himself in his body and blood, given for all, through his word of promise with bread and wine. He thus gives himself unreservedly to all who receive the bread and wine; faith receives the Lord's Supper for salvation, unfaith for judgment (*Leuenberg Agreement*, III.1.18).

> We cannot separate communion with Jesus Christ in his body and blood from the act of eating and drinking. To be concerned about the manner of Christ's presence in the Lord's Supper in abstraction from this act is to run the risk of obscuring the meaning of the Lord's Supper (*Leuenberg Agreement*, III.1.19).

The Presence of Christ:

The third dialogue urged the churches toward a deeper appreciation of the sacramental mystery based on consensus already achieved:

> Appreciating what we Reformed and Lutheran Christians already hold in common concerning the Lord's Supper, we nevertheless affirm that both of our communions need to keep on growing into an ever-deeper realization of the fullness and richness of the eucharistic mystery (*An Invitation to Action*, p. 14).

The members of the theological conversations acknowledged that it has not been possible to reconcile the confessional formulations from the sixteenth century with a "common language . . . which could do justice to all the insights, convictions, and concerns of our ancestors in the faith" (*A Common Calling*, p. 49). However, the theological conversations recognized these enduring differences as acceptable diversities with regard to the Lord's Supper. Continuing in the tradition of the third dialogue, they respected the different perspectives and convictions from which their ancestors professed their faith, affirming that those differences are not church-dividing, but are complementary. Both sides can say together that "the Reformation heritage in the matter of the Lord's Supper draws from the same roots and envisages the same goal: to call the people of God to the table at which Christ himself is present to give himself for us under the word of forgiveness, empowerment, and promise." Lutheran and Reformed Christians agree that:

In the Lord's Supper the risen Christ imparts himself in body and blood, given up for all, through his word of promise with bread and wine. He thereby grants us forgiveness of sins and sets us free for a new life of faith. He enables us to experience anew that we are members of his body. He strengthens us for service to all people. (The official text reads, *"Er starkt uns zum Dienst an den Menschen,"* which may be translated "to all human beings") (*Leuenberg, Agreement*, II.2.15).

When we celebrate the Lord's Supper we proclaim the death of Christ through which God has reconciled the world with himself. We proclaim the presence of the risen Lord in our midst. Rejoicing that the Lord has come to us, we await his future coming in glory (*Leuenberg Agreement*, II.2.16).

With a complementarity and theological consensus found in the Lord's Supper, it is recognized that there are implications for sacramental practices as well, which represent the heritage of these Reformation churches.

As churches of the Reformation, we share many important features in our respective practices of Holy Communion. Over the centuries of our separation, however, there have developed characteristic differences in practice, and these still tend to make us uncomfortable at each other's celebration of the Supper. These differences can be discerned in several areas, for example, in liturgical style and liturgical details, in our verbal interpretations of our practices, in the emotional patterns involved in our experience of the Lord's Supper, and in the implications we find in the Lord's Supper for the life and mission of the church and of its individual members. . . We affirm our conviction, however, that these differences should be recognized as acceptable diversities within one Christian faith. Both of our communions, we maintain, need to grow in appreciation of our diverse eucharistic traditions, finding mutual enrichment in them. At the same time both need to grow toward a further deepening of our common experience and expression of the mystery of our Lord's Supper (*An Invitation to Action*, pp. 16–17).

God's Will to Save:

Lutherans and Reformed claim the saving power of God's grace as the center of their faith and life. They believe that salvation depends on God's grace alone and not on human cooperation. In spite of this common belief, the doctrine of predestination has been one of the issues separating the two traditions. Although Lutherans and Reformed have different emphases in the way they live out their belief in the sovereignty of God's love, they agree that "God's unconditional will to save must be preached against all cultural optimism or pessimism" (*A Common Calling*, p. 54). It is noted that "a common language that transcends the polemics of the past and witnesses to the common predestination faith of Lutheran and Reformed Churches has emerged already in theological writings and official or unofficial statements in our churches" (*A Common Calling*, page 55). Rather than insisting on doctrinal uniformity, the two traditions are willing to acknowledge that they have been borne out of controversy, and their present identities, theological and ecclesial, have been shaped by those arguments. To demand more than fundamental doctrinal consensus on those areas that have been church-dividing would be tantamount to denying the faith of those Christians with whom we have shared a common journey toward wholeness in Jesus Christ. An even greater tragedy would occur were we, through our divisiveness, to deprive the world of a common witness to the saving grace of Jesus Christ that has been so freely given to us.

The Binding and Effective
Commitment to Full Communion

In the formal adoption at the highest level of this *A Formula of Agreement*, based on *A Common Calling*, the churches acknowledge that they are undertaking an act of strong mutual commitment. They are making pledges and promises to each other. The churches recognize that full commitment to each other involve serious intention, awareness, and dedication. They are binding themselves to far more than merely a formal action; they are entering into a relationship with gifts and changes for all.

The churches know these stated intentions will challenge their self-understandings, their ways of living and acting, their structures, and even their general ecclesial ethos. The churches commit themselves to keep this legitimate concern of their capacity to enter into full communion at the heart of their new relation.

The churches declare, under the guidance of the triune God, that they are fully committed to *A Formula of Agreement*, and are capable of being, and remaining, pledged to the above-described mutual affirmations in faith and doctrine, to joint decision-making, and to exercising and accepting mutual admonition and correction. *A Formula of Agreement* responds to the ecumenical conviction that "there is no turning back, either from the goal of visible unity or from the single ecumenical movement that unites concern of the unity of the Church and concern for engagement in the struggles of the world" ("On the Way to Fuller Koinonia: The Message of the Fifth World Conference on Faith and Order," 1983). And, as St. Paul reminds us all, "The one who calls you is faithful, and he will do this," (1 Thessalonians 5:24, NRSV).[2]

---

[2]**The Evangelical Lutheran Church in America:**
To enter into full communion with these churches [Presbyterian Church (U.S.A.), Reformed Church in America, United Church of Christ], an affirmative two-thirds vote of the 1997 Churchwide Assembly, the highest legislative authority in the ELCA, will be required. Subsequently in the appropriate manner other changes in the constitution and bylaws would be made to conform with this binding decision by an assembly to enter into full communion.

The constitution and bylaws of the Evangelical Lutheran Church in America (ELCA) do not speak specifically of this church entering into full communion with non-Lutheran churches. The closest analogy, in view of the seriousness of the matter, would appear to be an amendment of the ELCA's constitution or bylaws. The constitution provides a process of such amendment (Chapter 22). In both cases a two-thirds vote of members present and voting is required.

The Presbyterian Church (U.S.A.):
Upon an affirmative vote of the General Assembly of the Presbyterian Church (U.S.A.), the declaration of full communion will be effected throughout the church in accordance with the Presbyterian *Book of Order* and this *Formula of Agreement*. This means a majority vote of the General Assembly, a majority vote in the presbyteries, and a majority vote of the presbyteries.

The Presbyterian Church (U.S.A.) orders its life as an institution with a constitution, government, officers, finances, and administrative rules. These are instruments of mission, not ends in themselves. Different orders have served the Gospel, and none can claim exclusive validity. A presbyterian polity recognizes the responsibility of all members for ministry and maintains the organic relation of all congregations in the church. It seeks to protect the church from every exploitation by ecclesiastical or secular power ambition. Every church order must be open to such reformation as may be required to make it a more effective instrument of the mission of reconciliation. ("Confession of 1967," *Book of Confessions*, p. 40).

The Presbyterian Church (U.S.A.) shall be governed by representative bodies composed of presbyters, both elders and ministers of the Word and Sacrament. These governing bodies shall be called session, presbytery, synod, and the General Assembly (*Book of Order*, G-9.0100).

All governing bodies of the Church are united by nature of the Church and share with one another responsibilities, rights, and powers as provided in this Constitution. The governing bodies are separate and independent, but have such mutual relations that the act of one of them is the act of the whole Church performed by it through the appropriate governing body. The jurisdiction of each governing body is limited by the express provisions of the Constitution, with the acts of each subject to review by the next higher governing body. (G-9.0103).

The Reformed Church in America:

Upon an affirmative vote by the General Synod of the Reformed Church in America (RCA), the declaration of full communion will be effected throughout the church, and the Commission on Christian Unity will, in accordance with the responsibilities granted by the *Book of Church Order*, proceed to initiate and supervise the effecting of the intention of full communion as described in the *Formula of Agreement*.

The Commission on Christian Unity has advised the General Synod and the church of the forthcoming vote for full communion in 1997. The Commission will put before the General Synod the *Formula of Agreement* and any and all correlative recommendations toward effecting the Reformed Church in America declaring itself to be in full communion with the Evangelical Lutheran Church in America, the Presbyterian Church (U.S.A.), and the United Church of Christ.

The Constitution of the RCA gives responsibility for ecumenical relations to the General Synod (BCO, Chapter 1, Part IV, Article 2, Section 5). To be faithful to the ecumenical calling, the General Synod empowers its Commission on Christian Unity to initiate and supervise action relating to correspondence and cooperative relationship with the highest judicatories or assemblies of other Christian denominations and the engaging in interchurch conversations "in all matters pertaining to the extension of the Kingdom of God."

The Constitution of the RCA gives responsibility to the Commission on Christian Unity for informing "the church of current ecumenical developments and advising the church concerning its ecumenical participation and relationships" (BCO, Chapter 3, Part I, Article 5, Section 3).

Granted its authority by the General Synod, the Commission on Christian Unity has appointed RCA dialogue and conversation partners since 1962 to the present. It has received all reports and, where action was required, has presented recommendations(s) to the General Synod for vote and implementation in the church.

The United Church of Christ:

The United Church of Christ (UCC) will act on the recommendation that it enter into full communion with the Evangelical Lutheran Church in America, the Presbyterian Church (U.S.A.), and the Reformed Church in America, by vote of the General Synod in 1997. This vote is binding on the General Synod and is received by local churches, associations, and conferences for implementation in accordance with the convenantal polity outlined in paragraphs 14, 15, and 16 of the Constitution of the United Church of Christ.

The UCC is "composed of Local Churches, Associations, Conferences, and the General Synod." The Constitution and Bylaws of the United Church of Christ lodge responsibility for ecumenical life with the General Synod with its chief executive officer, the President of the United Church of Christ. Article VII of the Constitution grants to the General Synod certain powers. Included among these are the power:

- to determine the relationship of the UCC with ecumenical organizations, world confessional bodies, and other interdenominational agencies (Article VII, par. 45h).

• to encourage conversation with other communions and when appropriate to authorize and guide negotiations with them looking toward formal union, (VII, 45i).

In polity of the UCC, the powers of the General Synod can never, to use a phrase from the Constitution, "invade the autonomy of Conferences, Associations, or Local Churches," The autonomy of the Local Church is "inherent and modifiable only by its own action" (IV, 15). However, it is important to note that this autonomy is understood in the context of "mutual Christian concern and in dedication to Jesus Christ, the Head of the Church," (IV, 14). This Christological and convenantal understanding of autonomy is clearly expressed in the Constitutional paragraphs which immediately proceed and follow the discussion of Local Church autonomy:

The Local Churches of the UCC have, in fellowship, a God-given responsibility for that Church, its labors and its extension, even as the UCC has, in fellowship, a God-given responsibility for the well-being and needs and aspirations of its Local Churches. In mutual Christian concern and in dedication to Jesus Christ, the Head of the Church, the one and the many share in common Christian experience and responsibility (IV, 14).

Actions by, or decision or advice emanating from, the General Synod, a Conference, or an Association, should be held in the highest regard by every Local Church (IV, 16).

About the Presbyterian Church (U.S.A.) Seal

The seal of the Presbyterian Church (U.S.A.) is a symbolic statement of the church's heritage, identity, and mission in contemporary form. Its power depends on both its simplicity and complexity, as well as its traditional and enduring qualities.

The seal is designed with a simplicity that enables the viewer to retain the image in the mind's eye. The clean, carefully measured lines and shapes can be readily recognized as a distinctive symbol, even when it is reduced in size. At the same time, the complexity of the seal stimulates the imagination and suggests several levels of meaning. The symbolic and visual qualities remind the Presbyterian Church (U.S.A.) of its identity and call to be the servant of Jesus Christ.

The basic symbols in the seal are the cross, Scripture, the dove, and flames. The dominant structural and theological element in the design is the **cross**—the universal and most ecumenical symbol of the Christian church. The cross represents the incarnate love of God in Jesus Christ, and his passion and resurrection. Because of its association with Presbyterian history, the Celtic cross was chosen as a model for this contemporary rendering of the ancient symbol.

In experimenting with the basic lines and shapes of the cross, the contour of a **book** began to emerge in the horizontal section, and the two center lines of the cross became the representation of an open book. This integration of the horizontal dimensions of the cross with the book motif highlights the emphasis that the Reformed tradition has placed on the role of Scripture as a means of knowing God's word.

The slightly flared shape of the Celtic cross also makes possible the transforming of the uppermost section into the shape of a descending **dove**. As a symbol of the Holy Spirit, the dove is intimately tied to the representation of the Bible, affirming the role of the Spirit in both inspiring and interpreting Scripture in the life of the church. The dove also symbolizes Christ's baptism by John and the peace and wholeness that his death and resurrection bring to a broken world.

Beneath the image of the book is the suggestion of a lectern or **pulpit**, which captures the important role of preaching in the history of Presbyterian worship.

Integrated into the lower part of the design are **flames** that form an implied triangle, a traditional symbol of the Trinity. The flames themselves convey a double meaning: a symbol of revelation in the Old Testament when God spoke to Moses from the burning bush, and a suggestion of the beginning of the Christian church when Christ manifested himself to his apostles at Pentecost and charged them to be messengers of the good news of God's love.

The **triangle** also suggests the nature of Presbyterian government, with its concern for balance and order, dividing authority between ministers of the Word and laypersons and between different governing bodies. This understanding of the church was based in part on an important idea in Reformed theology, the covenant, which God establishes with people to affirm God's enduring love and to call us to faith and obedience to Jesus Christ.

Looking more closely at some of the visual components of the design, viewers may discover elements that seem to fuse with some of the more obvious theological symbols. In the shape of the descending dove, for example, one might also discern in the body of the bird, the form of a fish, an early Christian sign for Christ, recalling his ministry to those who hunger. For some, the overall design evokes the calligraphy of Hebrew and Greek manuscripts. Others have seen a baptismal font or a communion chalice (cup).

In 1 Corinthians, Paul described the church as a body with many members, illustrating the pluralism of the church and the many gifts that God gives to its members. So also the seal's individual parts, when taken together, form an encompasing visual and symbolic unity, while not exhausting the richness of possible interpretations.

For more information about the seal design, order the book *Sealed in Christ* by John Mulder, PPC # 18091004, Cost $4.95. To order call: 800-227-2872

About the Use of the Presbyterian Church (U.S.A.) Seal

The seal of the Presbyterian Church (U.S.A.) is a registered trademark, registered in the United States Patent and Trademark Office on the principal register. In addition, the seal is registered with the United Stated Copyright office. The seal is comprised of the symbol, the basic components of which are cross, Scripture, a descending dove at the upper part of the cross, and flames on either side of the lower part of the cross, and the name of the denomination, Presbyterian Church (U.S.A.), encircles the symbol.

The seal was approved by the 197th General Assembly (1985). Each congregation and governing body may use the seal without receiving prior permission. Congregations and governing bodies many not license use of the seal to anyone else. All other organizations, groups, and members must receive prior written permission to use the seal from the Office of the General Assembly; 100 Witherspoon Street; Louisville, Kentucky 40202.

While every use of the seal may not provide an opportunity to display the statutory notice (the cirlce "R", ®) and use of the statutory notice is not mandatory, it is good practice, when practicable, to give public notice of the trademark registration by using one of the following:

- *The letter R enclosed in a circle:* ®
- *Reg. U.S. Pat. & Tm. Off.*
- *Registered in the U.S. Patent and Trademark Office*

So, while it is not practical to display the statutory notice on a stained glass window or church sign, it is possible to note it on the reverse of a piece of jewelry or other inconspicuous place.

Trademark protection may be lost through improper use, abandonment, and dilution. To minimize this risk, the symbol should always be used in its entire and original form.

As is the case with the notice of trademark registration, copyright notice is not mandatory, but whenever possible, it is desirable to include some notice of the copyright on the inside cover of publications displaying the seal. The following language is suggested: "The cross and flames seal is the exclusive property of the Presbyterian Church (U.S.A.) and is registered in the U.S. Copyright Office. This seal may not be used or reproduced without the prior written permission of the Office of the General Assembly of the Presbyterian Church (U.S.A.); 100 Witherspoon Street; Louisville, Kentucky 40202."

In addition, any suspected unauthorized use should be promptly brought to the attention of the Legal Services Office or the Office of the General Assembly by forwarding the name and address of the user as well as a sample of their use of the seal.

Any products marketed in wholesale or retail settings must be specifically licensed by the Office of the General Assembly. An application for use must be filed and a fee must be paid for each design. A sample of the product should be sent to the Office of the General Assembly so approval may be based on the finished product.

For more information or a license to use the seal, contact:

Office of the General Assembly
Attn: Janet M. De Vries
100 Witherspoon Street
Louisville, Kentucky 40202
502.569.5438

OTHER RESOURCES IN CHURCH LAW AND POLICY

Available from Presbyterian Distribution Services (PDS)
1-800-524-2612:

The Book of Confessions—OGA-99-017 (print) $7.50. The church confesses its faith when it bears a present witness to God's grace in Jesus Christ. Available Fall 1999

Annotated Book of Order—OGA-99-013 (print) $15.00. The text of the B/O with notes to actions of the General Assembly and the Permanent Judicial Commission; a guide to find authoritative interpretations. September 1999

Companion to the Constitution—500242 $9.00. A readable manual for elders and pastors; summarizes the *Book of Order* for the session.

Catalogue of Theological Statements of the Presbyterian Church (U.S.A.) 7042096300 $9.95. Summaries of all theological statements from 1935 through 1996.

Presbyterian Social Witness Policy Compilation, 1946–1998—68-600-99-001 $15.00 (subject to increase) produced by Advisory Committee on Social Witness Policy.

The Making of the Book of Order; Blood on Every Page, by Bill Chapman—097450 $19.95. Historical accounts of the major events in the development of governance and mission organization.

Available from Nancy Hamilton, General Assembly Council, 502-569-5507; email NHAMILTO@ctr.pcusa.org

Mission Policy Checklist—A guide to current mission policies, position statements, strategies, guidelines and actions of the Presbyterian Church (U.S.A.) 1973 1999. No charge.